POLICY AND POLITICS

POLICY
AND POLITICS

Essays in honour of
NORMAN CHESTER
Warden of Nuffield College 1954–1978

Edited by
DAVID BUTLER and A. H. HALSEY
Fellows of Nuffield College

Editorial matter and selection © David Butler and A. H. Halsey 1978

Chapter 1 © A. H. Halsey 1978 Chapter 2 © David Butler 1978
Chapter 3 © Lord Northfield (Donald Chapman) 1978 Chapter 4 ©
F. M. G. Willson 1978 Chapter 5 © Geoffrey Marshall 1978
Chapter 6 © George Jones 1978 Chapter 7 © L. J. Sharpe 1978
Chapter 8 © Uwe Kitzinger 1978 Chapter 9 © Nevil Johnson 1978
Chapter 10 © Aubrey Silberston 1978 Chapter 11 © M. FG. Scott
1978 Chapter 12 © Sir Donald MacDougall 1978 Chapter 13 ©
Lord McCarthy (William McCarthy) 1978

First published 1978 by
THE MACMILLAN PRESS LTD
London and Basingstoke
Associated companies in Delhi
Dublin Hong Kong Johannesburg Lagos
Melbourne New York Singapore Tokyo

Printed in Great Britain by
The Bowering Press Ltd,
Plymouth and London

British Library Cataloguing in Publication Data

Policy and politics

1. Great Britain—Politics and government—1945- —Addresses,
essays, lectures
I. Butler, David, b. 1924 II. Halsey, Albert Henry III. Chester,
Sir Norman
320.9'41'085   JN231

ISBN 0-333-23561-4

Contents

1 Norman Chester and Nuffield College

A. H. HALSEY

Norman Chester retires in 1978 from the Wardenship of Nuffield College, Oxford – a post he has held since 1954. He was not the first Warden: the College was founded in 1937. But it is no disrespect to his predecessors, Sir Harold Butler, Sir Henry Clay, and Alexander Loveday, to say that he has been the major force in the establishment of a unique institution. Over the thirty-two years of his service to the College – he was an official Fellow from 1946 to 1954 – he became a familiar and formidable Oxford figure. Yet to understand the man and his work it is essential to begin with his Lancastrian origins. He was born the son of a factory worker in Chorlton-cum-Hardy, learned to speak as Lancastrians do and retained a style and a mode of speech which marked him off from the typical Oxford Head of House by its short vowels, hard consonants and frequent recourse to homely metaphor.

English notables can be caricatured as having one or the other of two very different biographies. The first is sent to Eton, goes up to Oxford, finds his way into politics or the Civil Service, is called to service in the Imperial domain in both war and peace and is, in short, portrayed as having led a life of inevitable and impersonal success. The second follows the more difficult path from what used to be called provincial obscurity by the scholarship ladder to professional achievement and public recognition. He typically emerges as a striving individual out of the solidarity of 'the working-class movement'. His education is owed to obscure bookshops in northern industrial towns and he finds his way to the top. If there be only two categories, then Norman Chester belongs to the second.

At all events, nothing could be more contrasted than the early biography of Norman Chester and that of Lord Halifax, who laid the foundation stone of the College building three years after Norman Chester took up a fellowship following war service in the Economic Section of the War Cabinet Secretariat. Norman Chester left school at fourteen to work in the Treasurer's Department of the City Council of Manchester and worked in the evenings towards an external degree of the University until he won a scholarship in local government studies and was given a post as research assistant in the Economics Research Division of his local university. The combined Town and Gown experience, and the civic assumptions and outlook involved, remained part of Norman Chester's character and directed his intellectual interests. He was a city councillor and alderman in Oxford for many years and moved as easily in the parlour of the Mayor or the reception rooms behind the stand of Oxford United Football Club as he did in the senior common room of his college or the committees of his university.

His intellectual outlook was faithfully fashioned by the civic traditions of Manchester – a university which was conspicuously successful in the earlier part of this century in striking a balance between cosmopolitan scholarship and realistic practical concern with its immediate industrial environment through the application of natural and social science to its problems. During and after the war, Norman Chester made his way into what Edward Shils has called the metropolitan triangle or the Oxford/Cambridge/London axis. Yet his successful journey was made with no fundamental modification of his Mancunian conception of the role of academic institutions in society.

Nuffield College, it seems to me, bears the indelible stamp of that conception. To be sure, it is also very much an Oxford college, firmly linked to the ancient traditions of commensality and close domestic relations between dons and students which are so distinctive of that tradition. But Norman Chester intended, and quickly effected, a fundamental modification of the older tradition. He made Nuffield a different place from any of the other thirty-odd collegiate societies which had been previously formed in Oxford down the centuries. The idea and the short history of Nuffield College deserves a review in its own right. The point here is to underline the influence and the achievement of Norman Chester in relation to it.

One element which ought not to go unremarked is the affinity between Norman Chester and the founder, Lord Nuffield. These two men had a common view of the place of the academy in a practical world. There had been a coolness between the founder and his foundation before Norman Chester became Warden. But it is hard to think of anyone who could have represented better the academic interests of the college in its Oxford context in the period when the architect's drawings were being turned into a working institution. His sympathetic appreciation of Lord Nuffield's desire for an intellectual centre which would have clear relevance to the practical issues of industry and public affairs turned disappointment into satisfaction in the last years of the founder's life. This particularly happy coincidence of personality had the important practical implication that the College became the residual legatee in Lord Nuffield's will; and thus a rapprochement of the 1950s, by contributing to the College finances in the 1960s, helped to meet the threat to a small but independent centre of support for the social sciences in the financially harsher climate of the 1970s.

While the establishment of happy relations with the founder was only one of Norman Chester's achievements as Warden, the fitting of Nuffield into Oxford and the development of a graduate research college in that milieu was an even more difficult and subtle task in which he was equally successful. It was no easy task. Not only was this new foundation to be the first graduate college but it also set out to admit women on equal terms with men, to concentrate on the social sciences and to offer privileged residential facilities to students thought of as scholars rather than commoners. To have such a strange creature accepted into the community of Oxford colleges would have tested the ingenuity of any Warden. Norman Chester accepted the challenge with sturdy Mancunian resolve.

OXFORD GRADUATE STUDIES

Traditional Oxford had no collegiate organisation for graduates in the arts and social studies. Organised graduate work in the science laboratories was, of course, familiar from the end of the nineteenth century and medical students also had their distinctive arrangements. Though All Souls had existed in its peculiar eccentricity for some centuries, there was no college before Nuffield, either in Oxford or in any other British university, which was organised expressly for the purpose of teaching and supervising the research of graduate students.

When the idea of Nuffield College was conceived, just before the war, the total number of post-graduate students in the arts and social sciences was only 378 and the official records do not tell us how this small group was subdivided between faculties and subjects. However, less than one in five were reading for second degrees in social studies and there must, therefore, have been about 70 of them all told. They were scattered about the colleges and attached to Oxford primarily through their personal relationship to their supervisor, who would not necessarily be a member of the same college. It is against this background that the distinctive character of the new college is seen.

By 1964/5, when the Franks Commission was set up to examine the anatomy of collegiate Oxford, graduates numbered more than a quarter of the students in ten colleges, notably Balliol, Jesus, Merton

and New College. By 1976 the number of post-graduate students in
Oxford as a whole was 2849, of whom 1886 were in the arts and social
studies. In the meantime, the new colleges of St Antony's, Linacre,
Wolfson and St Cross had followed Nuffield. All Souls had resisted
strong pressure to become a graduate college in the Nuffield sense.
Other colleges, like Balliol, had organised strong middle common
rooms. In effect, then, Norman Chester lived through and pioneered
the incorporation of the graduate student into collegiate life. Nuffield
College anticipated, to an extent as remarkable as it has been unremarked, the main principle for the future development of Oxford as
the Franks Commission eventually put it forward in 1966.

THE FRANKS COMMISSION

Following on the expansive vistas for higher education which opened
with the Robbins Report in 1963, it was inevitable that some form or
another of self-examination would be undertaken in Oxford. A Royal
Commission was avoided and an internal committee (which was
suggested by Norman Chester) was the instrument of self-appraisal.
When Lord Franks and his colleagues reported in 1966[1] they followed
a firm line, planning a future in which new developments were to be
incorporated into the collegiate traditions of the past. Oxford, the
Commissioners insisted, was an ancient university, and still, perhaps, *the*
collegiate university. It drew its senior and junior members nationally
and internationally, selected its students carefully and offered a rich
education within the dense intellectual network of small interlocking
residential communities. The university was still rich in material and
social resources, it was autonomous and governed by a democracy of
its own academic members and, in short, was still the symbol of
academe throughout the world.

Nevertheless, new conditions required reappraisal of Oxford life.
New academic subjects and new methods of scientific research had
called for new buildings, new equipment and new organisations. New
vocationalisms and new professions, including especially those which
constitute the academic succession itself, had led to the development of
graduate studies and hence to the appearance of the unfamiliar
graduate student. The inherently centrifugal tendencies of modern
teaching and research, which had elsewhere produced the 'multi-
versity', were beginning to threaten the capacities of colleges to
maintain their high teaching standards and their attractive careers for
the college tutor. And, perhaps above all, the emergence of the state
as the single serious patron of universities had led to the incorporation

of Oxford into the 'system of higher education' in which it had now to define and justify its place.

The Franks Commission therefore set out a programme for Oxford in which new developments would be made to fit into or revolve around a modernised and federated college system. They recognised all the new threats to the viability of collegiate organisation and attempted to produce solutions which would make Oxford safe for commensality. The graduate student was to be incorporated and be tutored by dons in his college; the university was to complement the federated colleges; there was to be redistribution of income from the richer to the poorer colleges; and at the same time the university was to have a more streamlined administration and government which could explain itself more quickly and more clearly to the UGC and the outside world by better statistical services. These measures were aimed to ensure the continuing reality of the collegiate ideal in which teaching is linked harmoniously to research and administration gives unobtrusive direction to both.

The Commissioners envisaged Oxford as a medium-sized university growing in the 1970s and 1980s to accommodate 13,000 students, including 3000 to 4000 graduates.[2] Lord Franks and his colleagues had noticed that the expansion of Harvard and other leading American universities had involved the creation of large graduate schools and research centres, more or less separated from undergraduate schools. But in rejecting this strategy of expansion they correctly anticipated college opinion in Oxford. 'Our reasons', Lord Franks told Congregation in 1966, 'were that we thought, first, that if they came into being in Oxford, undergraduate education would almost certainly be devalued. Secondly, it leads to a division in the academic staff between those who do research and teach graduates and those who teach undergraduates. We believe that this would be a bad thing in that society of equals to which Oxford aspires.' It was feared that the development of post-graduate schools would drive the colleges into a secondary place in Oxford but since it was their purpose to preserve the life, the enterprise, the initiative, and the responsibility of the colleges, they therefore turned away from separate great graduate schools. Though they did not say so, they were in effect advocating the collegiate innovation which had emerged from Lord Nuffield's foundation thirty years before.

The question was how increased numbers were to be fitted into the colleges. For their part, the Commissioners did not baulk at the prospect of creating one or two new colleges, recognising that 'in the collegiate university those who are not fully brought into college life inevitably suffer'. It is, however, debatable how far graduate students should be integrated into a fully collegiate organisation. Many would argue that the teaching and research of graduates, who must be specialised and may be married, is best organised through departments. The doubters, who presented evidence to the Commissioners in open hearings, included the students themselves as represented by the Student Council,[3] the economists as represented by their sub-faculty,[4] and some scientists who would similarly transfer teaching responsibilities from college to university even in the case of undergraduates.

The nub of this problem was, and still is, to ensure a proper distribution of students and staff between colleges. The difficulties here are most acute in the case of graduates, but they also affect the undergraduates in so far as the need to concentrate specialist dons for specialist graduates is combined with the aim of involving all dons in both undergraduate and graduate teaching so as to avoid the American experience of steady devaluation of the former as the latter expands. To incorporate the graduate fully into the intellectual and the social life of the colleges was a novel, large and complicated task. The Commissioners did not exaggerate when they said that

> if post-graduate training is to be brought into the system of college education and made part of the balance of life of the fellow-lecturer, the consequence will be a fundamental change in the nature of Oxford, and the magnitude of this change should not be underestimated.[5]

The advantage of the traditional undergraduate college is that it brings together a comprehensive range of scholarship among the dons, who then pass on a wide cultivation to their students through the close personal contacts of college residence and the tutorial system. Intimacy plus breadth necessitate small numbers of dons in any particular subject. But, as the boundaries of knowledge widen, conversation at lengthening high tables narrows. Nevertheless, for the undergraduate, or at least for the arts undergraduate, the educational advantages remain immense.

However, the traditional college had hitherto made no serious attempt to teach graduates and, with a few recent exceptions, very inadequate efforts to offer them social amenities. If college teaching was now to be offered to graduates at least one of the arguments for the traditional college had to be abandoned. One logical solution was to forsake breadth of studies and specialise. Nuffield College is a highly successful venture along these lines. The concentration on the social sciences gives it unity; there is genuine academic discussion among colleagues and comprehensive teaching for students which is clearly related to the research interests of the dons. Every student has a college supervisor in addition to his university supervisor and frequent contact with senior members of the college is 'built in' to the domestic arrangements by a shared junior common room and a simple rule of taking the next available seat in the dining hall.

THE NUFFIELD SOLUTION AND ITS PROBLEMS

Nuffield College, then, is the outstanding example of a successful adaptation of graduate studies to the collegiate ideal which Oxford represents in the world of learning. To make this assertion is to applaud Norman Chester's major achievement, to recognise the possibility of successful innovation within the framework of a tradition of centuries, and to celebrate a civilised conception of the way in which established scholars can be effectively related to those who aspire to succeed them. At the same time, however, it is not to deny that the Nuffield solution raises its own particular problems.

Nuffield College developed as an adaptive variant of the college principle. In doing so it, of necessity, had to abandon that element of the collegiate conception which assumed that a college was a microcosm of the *universitas*. Though it is arguable that some breadth of conversation may have been lost, there was clearly a compensating gain in the concentration of a limited range of intellectual preoccupations. On balance, this would seem to be a realistic adaptation to the modern world of specialist scholarship. The charge of narrowness in the intellectual milieu of the college is not, in my view, to be taken very seriously. If it is true that the lowest common denominator of conversation between specialists is chat about the weather then, in the case of Nuffield, the denominator is a search for the meaning of the words between the lines of this morning's newspaper. I have lost count of the number of visitors to the college who have remarked on the superior interest of Nuffield conversation even when characterised in this dismissive manner. In reality, of course, the college does not live constantly at its lowest common denominator and frequently deploys the theories and interpretations collectively possessed by its economists, modern historians, political scientists and sociologists to illuminate the public issues of the day.

At the same time it must be recognised that the reputation of the college as one with close links to Westminster, Whitehall, Transport House and the CBI has been bought at some cost. Critics from within as well as from without the college point to the dangers of undue preoccupation with worldly interests and especially with definitions of problems in the social sciences which are set by politicians and administrators. Admittedly, practical problems deserve academic attention and public service helps to justify the support which universities seek from society. But the effective application of the social sciences also requires freedom for academic social scientists to define problems in the theoretical terms of their own disciplines. A subtle bargain has always to be made between the universities and the 'powers'. Moreover, and ironically, the idea of the visiting fellowship for leading politicians, trade unionists and business men, which is a conspicuous feature of Nuffield, is probably one of the least successful in practice.[6]

Nuffield students have gone on to fill teaching places in many universities at home and overseas and, over the past generation, the number who have been elected to fellowships in other Oxford colleges is such that, whatever the institutional boundaries, there is a strong network of intellectual and social connection between social scientists in the colleges, of which Nuffield is the hub. Nevertheless the Nuffield studentship is less enjoyed than it might be expected to be on the conventional definition of it – that is, as a much sought-after prize of two or three years' induction into the academic succession for those who have demonstrated unusual academic talent. Perhaps the conventional definition has to be questioned. To be marked as a high-flyer is not wholly comfortable and to follow an academic career was always a norm rather than a rigid rule. In recent years departing students have had to go to more diverse destinations; and the intrinsic loneliness of the doctoral journey is surely exacerbated when the assurance that the road leads to the Senior Common Room is attenuated. And if students go to a widening range of careers it may be asked what this implies for a notion of teaching which, having assumed the norm of academic succession, defines junior members as integrated into the college through the research interests of the seniors.

The idea of a research college as Nuffield has developed it, apart from being unique in Oxford, is tied to a special period of university expansion, especially in the social studies. The future may be very different and, if so, the college will have to move if it is to stay the same. It will have to think hard, for example, about its tradition of providing for a student body in such a way as to contribute crucially to the highest standards at the point of transition from *statu pupillari* to established social scientist.

A more serious problem was that, as the social sciences developed rapidly in Britain and overseas in the period after the Second World War, the college had to face the dilemma of either pursuing a policy of incorporation of all of Oxford social studies which would have made it too large, or to work out ways in which it could have selective relations with them. The college took the latter course. Quite apart from size, there would in any case have been strong resistance from other colleges to any attempt on the part of Norman Chester and his colleagues to monopolise graduate social studies. The other colleges would thereby have been confined to undergraduate teaching with all that this implies for the research and career interests of their senior members on the social studies side.

The charge inevitably followed that the college had created an elite institution for the minority of graduate students in the social studies, leaving the majority in less favoured circumstances elsewhere in Oxford. Certainly, the selective rather than the comprehensive course meant that Nuffield had to work out a set of delicate relations to the faculty, its sub-faculties and to the social studies graduate body in Oxford as a whole. The spirit in which it pursued this course, under Norman Chester's guidance, was one of pragmatic innovation and leadership.

An example of innovative leadership is that of research services to those social scientists who use survey and quantitative methods of analysis of data. With respect to these methods, the social sciences are in an intermediate position between the sciences and the arts. It is not possible sensibly to assimilate social studies to either traditional arts scholarship which is located in the library and the study, or to modern science which is located in the laboratory. At the same time, there was no faculty organisation, despite the existence of the Institute of Economics and Statistics, offering facilities for dons in the social studies or their research students who wished to use these methods in order to tackle their chosen problems. Accordingly, what Chester's Nuffield did was to start a small computing and research services unit within the college on its own resources, primarily having the needs of its own dons and students in mind but also extending these facilities to other Oxford scholars outside Nuffield. The end of the story is now in sight. Nuffield pioneered what has turned out to be an extremely valuable and indeed necessary technical base for social studies scholarship, and when the faculty centre finally comes into being in 1978 this Nuffield initiative will be put on a faculty-wide basis.

Another example is Nuffield College library, which is an immensely valuable resource for research and study in the social sciences. Here again, the policy pursued by the college has been one of maintaining and improving the library but at the same time not restricting it to members of the college. It is in fact very widely used by senior members of the Faculty of Social Studies as a whole and by the many social scientists who visit Oxford every year.

A similar policy of building up resources, focusing them on the college but encouraging their use by other Oxford members of the Faculty of Social Studies, has been followed with respect to graduate seminars. Similar remarks can be made about the association of University appointees who are attached to other colleges. Nuffield has had to strike a nice balance. On the one hand, it makes no secret of the fact that it would prefer the Gladstone Professorship of Government and Administration to be transferred from All Souls to Nuffield. On the other, it has drawn the line far short of any aspiration to incorporate all such university posts. Many Oxford social scientists are quondam in relation to Nuffield and others have been offered permanent or temporary associateship in one form or another. The details might be open to criticism but the general policy, given the historical and numerical circumstances, is both realistic and generous. Moreover, it must be added that the Warden of Nuffield, as well as his collegiate fellows, has consistently played an active part in the development of the work of the Faculty of Social Studies. Norman Chester has been a central figure in the Social Studies Board and in the work of admitting graduate students to the University to read second degrees in politics. He has been a firm supporter of the development of faculty facilities in general and the Faculty Centre in particular. In addition to enthusiastic devotion to the building up of a highly successful research college in the social studies, he has laboured long and devotedly in the interests of Oxford social studies as a whole.

His labours, however, have by no means been confined to Oxford. He has been assiduous in linking the college by regular visits to and from the Ecole de Science Politique in Paris. He was one of the founders of the British Political Studies Association in 1950 and he was the first British President of the International Political Science Association. For many years he was the editor of *Public Administration*. And he has been an active public figure in politics and administration in the wider world, taking especially strong interest in building research, water, the organisation of association football, the police, and, above all, local government affairs in Oxford and the country as a whole.

NORMAN CHESTER'S WRITINGS

To record these considerable achievements is, however, to say virtually nothing of Norman Chester's steady cultivation over a long period of his chosen field of scholarship. This book ends with a bibliography, prepared by Miss Christine Kennedy, the college librarian, which indicates a remarkable diversity of intellectual interests. These aspects of his working life, at once more private than his Wardenship in the sense of personal labour and more public in the sense of contributing to political science writing and debate beyond the college and Oxford, are appreciated in the essays which follow. Here it is appropriate only to remark their range. Written by thirteen authors who are connected with Nuffield, or have been in the past, they demonstrate how far Norman Chester's writing and tutelage continues to influence those who have been associated with him.

His range, as the essays illustrate, runs the whole gamut of the political process in modern Britain. David Butler writes about electoral procedure and thus reminds us of both an established feature of the empirical study of politics at Nuffield and the encouragement he has had from Norman Chester from his earliest days as a student of the college. Lord Northfield discusses the reform of the House of Lords and so calls our attention to Norman Chester's sustained interest in Parliamentary procedure. Glenn Willson has contributed a discussion of the organisation of the ministries, which also reflects Norman Chester's interest in the workings of the executive.

These essays on central government are followed by one from Geoffrey Marshall on police accountability and then by two papers on aspects of local government and its relation to Whitehall and Westminster. Jim Sharpe's discussion of the reform of local government and George Jones's survey of the debate over its financing together raise issues on which Norman Chester has occupied a central position as a historian and critic since before the Second World War.

At this point the focus shifts towards another of Norman Chester's lifelong interests – the economic organisation of society. Uwe Kitzinger has taken a topic related to Norman Chester's fostering of the Oxford Management Centre. Donald MacDougall's reminiscences of central economic management recall Norman Chester's wartime service in the Cabinet Secretariat and provide a background to the papers by Nevil Johnson on the public corporation and by Aubrey Silberston and Maurice Scott on the nationalised industries – a field of study in which Norman Chester is an acknowledged authority. Finally, a contemporary preoccupation in central economic management is taken up by Lord McCarthy in an essay on the recent history of incomes policy.

The authors offer these essays in glad and respectful salute to a productive and authoritative scholar, a valued colleague and a remarkable Head of House.

NOTES AND REFERENCES

1 *University of Oxford: Report of Commission of Inquiry* [Franks Report], 2 vols (Oxford University Press, 1966). The evidence was published separately by OUP in 14 Parts, 1964–5.
2 The total number of students by 1975/76 was 11,547, of whom 2849 were graduates.
3 Franks Report, *Written Evidence*, Part III, p. 77.
4 Ibid., p. 70.
5 Franks Report, para. 256.

6   These fellowships are valued by both residents and visitors. But most visiting fellows come seldom and many feel at a loss as to how to be of greater service to the college.

2 Modifying Electoral Arrangements

DAVID BUTLER

The making of public policy should involve a tough-minded assessment of the *status quo* and an equally informed look at the likely consequences of any proposed change. At their best Royal Commissions, civil servants, Ministers and MPs can do this very well. But they often falter. This chapter explores one area where no one seems to deserve very high marks, even though there have been no disasters.[1]

The British electoral system has worked smoothly enough in this century. It has absorbed successive expansions of the franchise and minor administrative changes without serious difficulty. It has, with its rough justice, produced strong single-party governments whose democratic legitimacy has not been challenged. Yet a detailed study of the way politicians have modified electoral arrangements, or attempted to modify them, does not provide a very reassuring example of the British system of government in operation.

The government's official advisers have tended to live in a rather closed world, shunning outside consultation, while Cabinet and Parliament have tried intermittently to hide behind the uncertain device of a Speaker's Conference. But, although Speaker's Conferences seem to have become established parts of the Constitution, their record is not very impressive either in achieving consensus on controversial matters or in seeing their recommendations translated into law. The House of Commons has never been at its best in debates on electoral matters and governments have been wayward; unilateral and arbitrary behaviour has alternated with bipartisanship.

Before almost every big change in this century there has been a Speaker's Conference, an all-party committee of MPs meeting under the august and neutral chairmanship of the Speaker and designed to achieve consensus, to take decisions about the rules of the game outside party politics. As Mr Churchill wrote to Speaker Clifton Brown in 1944,

I am reluctant to add to your already heavy burdens . . . but it is most important that the issues before the Conference, affecting as they do the interests of all the political parties, should be considered in as impartial a spirit as possible and the Government are sure that the best method of realising this object is by following the precedent of 1916 and asking you to preside.[2]

The first Conference, under Speaker Lowther, took place in the coalition circumstances of 1917. It managed to reach and legitimise an inter-party compromise on allowing women to vote,[3] but its unanimous advocacy of proportional representation was not accepted by Parliament. (The House of Commons opted for the Alternative Vote, which was rejected by the House of Lords.) And even the terms of the agreement on votes for women became the subject of bitter controversy over the next decade, as the members of the Conference argued whether there had been a deal that rendered any further attempt to equalise the franchise a breach of faith.[4]

In the 1924 election Mr Baldwin promised to refer the question of equalisation to 'a Conference of all the political parties'. The pledge was reiterated in 1925 and early in 1927 inter-party negotiations over a Conference took place; it may be that they came to nothing because Ramsay MacDonald suspected a trap but it also seems clear that the Speaker made difficulties. Mr Baldwin reported 'as party controversy had been renewed since 1918, he [the Speaker] felt that, in order to preserve the impartial position of the Chair, he would prefer not to preside at such a Conference'.[5] Since the 1928 Equal Franchise Act was short and simple and received overwhelming parliamentary support (the majority was 387 to 10 on the Second Reading) there was perhaps little reason for having a Conference on that one issue.[6]

In 1929, when Liberals were seeking electoral reform as a price of their support for the MacDonald Government, Speaker Fitzroy and his predecessor Speaker Whitley both refused to preside over a Speaker's Conference because they were 'too busy', though the reason may equally have been the one given in 1928 – a distaste for involving the office in a partisan conflict. In the end Lord Ullswater (Speaker Lowther of the 1917 Conference) chaired an unsatisfactory gathering which, on straight party votes (eight Labour and five Liberals against eight Conservatives), advocated the alternative vote. Lord Ullswater reported to the Prime Minister as he wound up the Conference:

The main purpose of our Conference had failed us as no agreement had been reached or was likely to be reached. The Conference could only at the best submit to you [the PM] a few resolutions carried on party lines. This would not fulfil the purpose which was in view when the Conference was appointed.[7]

In the wartime and coalition situation of 1943 Speaker Clifton Brown found no difficulty in presiding over a new Conference which, with substantial unanimity, agreed on a number of minor amendments to electoral law. But, as with the 1917 Conference, the inter-party understandings, easily reached in wartime, became a subject of controversy a few years later. The Labour Government's abolition of the business vote and of the University seats, under the Representation of the People Bill of 1948, was bitterly attacked as a breach of faith. Whether in fact there were binding understandings in 1917 or 1944, and if so for how long they were binding, is not clear,[8] but the fact that there was such confusion, even with these relatively successful Speaker's Conferences, is a poor advertisement for them.

In 1966–8 Speaker King presided over yet another Conference. Its most notable proposal was the lowering of the age of voting from 21 to 20. But when the Government put through the Representation of the People Act of 1969, they reduced the age to 18.[9] They also ignored one majority recommendation (the banning of opinion polls in the 72 hours before an election) and they unilaterally introduced two changes which had been explicitly rejected by the Speaker's Conference (the extension of voting hours from 9 p.m. to 10 p.m. and the inclusion of party labels on the ballot paper).

In 1972–4 Speaker Lloyd presided over yet another Conference which dealt mainly with technicalities about service voting and the compilation of registers by computer. No Government legislation followed except for a 30 per cent increase in permitted election expenses, enacted through all its stages by Parliament on the day of its abrupt dissolution, 7 February 1974.[10]

In March 1974, when the Conservatives were seeking terms on which to involve the Liberals in a coalition, Mr Heath offered to refer the question of proportional representation to a Speaker's Conference. And in March 1977, when Labour was seeking to conciliate minor parties, Mr Callaghan made a similar proposal to the Ulster Unionists over the number of Northern Ireland MPs.[11] In all the speeches and discussions in recent years, politicians have tended to make it a constitutional axiom that a Speaker's Conference must precede any electoral change. In the White Paper on *Direct Elections to the European Assembly* the proposal for giving the franchise to UK citizens resident overseas was dismissed thus: 'The Government do not consider that this important extension, which would have obvious relevance to the franchise for Westminster, should be made without prior consideration by a Speaker's Conference.'[12]

It is hard to see the virtue of Speaker's Conferences. They have been large bodies, composed of backbench MPs (apart from a few Peers and Shadow Ministers). They have always met in secret and they have

COMPOSITION OF SPEAKER'S CONFERENCES

Year	Con.	Lab.	Lib.	Other	Total
1917	11 + 3*	10 + 2*	3	3	32
1929–30	7 + 1*	7 + 1*	4 + 1*	–	21
1944	17 + 1*	8 + 1*	1 + 1*	3	32
1966–8	13/11	15/17	1	–	29
1972–4	15	13	1	–	29

* Peers

seldom taken much evidence.[13] They have not been good investigative bodies, producing reports that command intellectual respect. Nor has their membership been weighty enough or selective enough to produce inter-party deals, agreements between Government and Opposition of the sort that could take any argument over electoral rules outside the party battle. In 1943–4, though not in 1917, the Speaker's Conference recommendations were implemented almost in full.[14] But outside wartime, the achievement of consensus has been limited. The 1930 Ullswater Conference saw the entrenchment of party lines. The 1966 Conference report bore only limited relation to the 1969 Act and the 1972 Conference achieved nothing of substance.

If one looks back at the Committees dealing with electoral matters, the record of the Vivian (1942), Oliver (1946) and Carr (1947) Committees on electoral law and machinery is much more impressive. These Home Office bodies, composed in varying degree of MPs, Home Office officials, Town Clerks, and party officials, produced sensible, well-researched reports, each of which was fully implemented. Their remits were limited but the expertise of the members was much greater than in Speaker's Conferences and they worked quickly and smoothly and presented clear advice to the Government and Parliament.

There is no evidence that Speakers have welcomed the task of presiding over these bodies. Lord Ullswater does, it is true, offer in his memoirs a rather bland description of the first and most successful one but his two immediate successors refused to be involved in 1929.[15] Lord Selwyn-Lloyd, the only other Speaker to write at length about presiding over such a body, is decidedly critical.[16]

The Conference over which I presided had twenty-nine other members. We met or tried to meet once a week. The average attendance was about half. A move to allow the Deputy Speaker to stand in for me from time to time was narrowly defeated.

I found it a very time-consuming and cumbersome operation. We were too large a body to consider some of the more detailed matters put to us. It was difficult to assemble the necessary evidence.

. . . I was glad that no attempt was made to set up another conference while I was Speaker. I think that there is advantage occasionally in a body presided over by the Speaker with his 'aloof impartiality'. But its methods of working need re-examination.

. . . If the Government with the agreement of the Opposition indicate their wish that the Speaker should preside over a conference to consider certain electoral matters, the Speaker should then act as follows. He should choose three or four experienced Members to examine with him the particular topics designated, and to decide what papers upon them would be required by way of evidence, and what witnesses should be asked to prepare oral evidence. When that has been done, and the papers received, a conference with a larger membership, but not exceeding twenty, should be convened, and the material already assembled put before it. Of course other papers could be called for and other witnesses summoned as proved necessary. I believe that this method would save a lot of time, both for the Speaker and for the members of the conference.

The electoral system, both in its broad working and in its detailed rules, is too important politically for party leaders to devolve decisions about it to others. The Government, either unilaterally or after consultation with other parties, is going to use its parliamentary authority to get its own way. It is not going to feel bound by agreements made at a lower level in a Speaker's Conference: deals on such matters can only be made between the Front Benches. But any government must want the facts and the alternatives clarified – and that can be done much better by a departmental committee of experts (including MPs and party officials) than by an unwieldy group of MPs in a Speaker's Conference.

One special snag about Speaker's Conferences lies in their title, in the very fact that they are chaired by the Speaker. The Speaker's presence is, of course, supposed to guarantee a neutral and harmonious discussion. The Speakership, as developed at Westminster, is one of the proudest achievements of parliamentary government. One politician after another has shown himself capable of abjuring all partisanship and exercising a quasi-judicial role, enshrining in himself the traditional majesty of Parliament. But Speakers are at best 'ordinary men with extraordinary qualities'; moreover their normal role is to chair the House of Commons, the forum in which MPs are at their most partisan and unharmonious: for a Speaker to preside over a smaller body is hardly likely to produce reflexes of unity and moderation. Indeed the Speaker's very neutrality, and the habits which are necessary to its preservation, reduce the likelihood that he will be an active and interventionist chairman even though such a figure is often needed to get the best results from a committee dealing with a controversial subject. The Speaker's skills focus more on the preservation of order than on the promotion of compromise.

None the less, MPs and governments do repeatedly turn to the Speaker as a refuge from the consequences of their own partisan, controversial instincts. Speaker's Conferences are only one of the areas where Ministers and MPs have tried to give legitimacy to their decisions by invoking the neutral aura of the Speaker's office.

The Speaker has been the nominal Chairman of the Boundary Commissions. This began in 1917–18; and in 1942 the Vivian Committee, which recommended the establishment of permanent boundary commissions, also asked that the Speaker should be their Chairman to ensure

> that no considerations of Parliamentary importance had been disregarded. We suggest, moreover, that the function of maintaining the equal representative status of Members of the House of Commons approaches so nearly to a vital domestic concern of the House itself that there is a special propriety in placing the machinery of a permanent Commission under the presiding genius of the Speaker.
>
> We appreciate the heavy burdens already sustained by a Speaker of the House of Commons; but it would seem unnecessary that he should occupy the Chair of the Commission except on special occasions or when, in his opinion, the business to be transacted required this course.[17]

Since then in three general revisions of boundaries (a fourth is now under way) and in some minor adjustments, the Speaker has presided over the Boundary Commissions. But it is not clear what function he performs. As Speaker Morrison said in 1954:

> The House will realise that, as Chairman of the Commission, I cannot, myself, take part in all the individual decisions to which the Boundary Commissioners come. I am the only Member of Parliament on the Commission, and it would, I think, be improper for me to intervene so as to influence a decision by those independent gentlemen which might affect the constituency of another Member of this House.[18]

Indeed his chairmanship inhibited parliamentary discussion of boundary matters. MPs wanting to be critical found themselves in danger of being ruled out of order. The Speaker warned:

> So far as my own part in the Commission is concerned, I must remind the House of the ancient and salutary rule, that any criticism, implied or expressed, of the Chair should be put down in the form of a Motion.[19]

As a senior Conservative MP, Ralph Assheton, remarked:

> I am sorry . . . that Mr. Speaker is the nominal Chairman of the Commission. I find that a rather embarrassing thing. If . . . legislation is introduced to deal with this problem of the work of the Boundary Commission, I suggest that it might be less awkward if the nominal Chairman is someone other than Mr. Speaker, because we all know that his heavy duties make it impossible for him to give detailed consideration to these questions.[20]

The Speaker's role is only one of a number of confusions about boundary drawing, where Parliament having laid down ambiguous instructions to the Commissioners was faced with embarrassing results about which it could do nothing.

In December 1954 some Labour MPs, feeling that the boundary revision was disadvantageous, sought (via some Labour-controlled Borough Councils) to enjoin the Home Secretary not to present to the Queen the Statutory Orders that gave effect to the changes, and on 17 December 1954 Mr Justice Roxburgh granted an interim injunction. Three days later the Court of Appeal annulled the injunction – to the general relief. For the Courts to deny a Minister access to the Queen to implement a resolution of the House would constitute a fundamental threat to the sovereignty of parliament. But the basis for the action lay in the confusion of the Boundary Commission's instructions: were they to allocate English seats on the basis of an electoral quota based on the U.K. electorate or on the English electorate? The rules as laid for the Boundary Commissioners by Parliament in the Redistribution of Seats Act 1944 were flatly contradictory – and no one in Parliament or the Home Office had noticed the ambiguities. The Redistribution of Seats Act 1958 solved the legal confusion, at the expense of enshrining permanently the under-representation for England which helped to bedevil the devolution debates of 1977.

Indeed Parliament, too, does not come well out of the story of electoral legislation. The debates on the subject were never of high quality. Occasionally there were good, earthy speeches about the difficulties that candidates or party workers faced from anomalous regulations or arbitrary boundary changes. But eloquence was on the whole reserved for partisan charges, for allegations of broken faith or suggestions that the law was being altered for party advantage.

The most rigorous arguments always tended to be not so much about the merits of the proposals at issue as about the propriety of putting them forward. The consequences of electoral change became submerged in disputes over political ethics and parliamentary manners, as anyone who glances at the relevant columns of Hansard for 1931 or 1948 will see.

In the nineteenth century Parliament reserved to itself, as a matter of privilege, jurisdiction over controverted elections: it proved a poor judge over matters affecting its own members. Collusive withdrawal of petitions and arguments on the lines 'there but for the grace of God go I' led to increasing despair at the capacity of MPs to deal evenhandedly with electoral corruption. Election petitions were transferred from the Commons to the Courts in 1870 and within a few years a body of case law was built up and enforced. In less than a generation the country changed from having a remarkably corrupt to having a remarkably honest electoral system.[21]

It would be wrong to press too far the analogy between questions of malfeasance that are essentially justiciable and questions of administration and structure – rules of the game – that are essentially political. Yet, as with electoral corruption, so with other electoral questions, Parliament and governments have been too introverted, regarding the problem as a private matter to be settled internally, and not on the whole a subject for open discussion drawing on expertise from this country and from abroad.

NOTES AND REFERENCES
1   This chapter treads over ground that I first tackled in *The Electoral System in Britain* (2nd ed., Oxford, 1963) and the definition of the subject was directly due to a conversation with Norman Chester in 1949. It also draws on themes in an article, 'The Redistribution of Seats', commissioned by Norman Chester for *Public Administration* 33, 2 (Summer 1955).
2   Cmnd 6534 (1943).
3   The minimum age of 30, linked with a local government qualification, was specifically designed to keep the number of women voters below the number of men.
4   Even during the 1918 debates there was disagreement on what the Conference had agreed about plural voting within a multi-member borough.
5   *HC Deb.* 215, c. 1471.
6   But the failure to hold a conference was the issue before an extraordinarily fraught Cabinet, held on 12 April 1928. In an almost unique annexe to

the Cabinet minutes, sealed and 'to be opened only by the Secretary to the Cabinet', the Chancellor of the Exchequer (Winston Churchill) insisted on recording his total dissent from the Cabinet's decision.

7 Cmnd 3636 (1930).

8 See D. E. Butler, *The Electoral System in Britain*, pp. 21–3, 115–22. From the available evidence, it does not seem that, on either occasion, there were specific agreements. Yet at least one Labour participant in the 1943–4 Conference admitted to a guilty conscience about what was done in 1948.

9 This went against an explicit vote of 22 to 3 in the Speaker's Conference. But the Government had an excuse. In 1967 the Latey Commission had recommended the lowering of the legal age of majority from 21 to 18.

10 See D. E. Butler and D. Kavanagh, *The British General Election of February 1974* (Macmillan, 1974) pp. 67, 239–40. There was also a Private Member's Bill two years later: a Conservative MP piloted through an Act to amend the law on the registration of service voters, exactly on lines agreed by the Speaker's Conference in 1973.

11 See *The Economist*, 5 Feb 1977, for a well-argued attack on such a use of a Speaker's Conference.

12 Cmnd 6768 (Apr 1977) para. 32. However, almost every aspect of European elections could have relevance to the Westminster electoral system. Why the franchise should be singled out as uniquely requiring a Speaker's Conference is not clear.

13 For example, the 1967 proposal to ban pre-election opinion polls was made without seeking the views of any pollster, any journalist or any academic student of elections. The 1972–4 Commission was the first to publish transcripts of evidence or to allow the public to attend sessions where witnesses appeared; they had agreed to this initiative by Dick Leonard, MP, while rejecting his suggestion that their deliberations too should be in public.

14 But even in 1944 the Cabinet did reject a proposal for standardised polling hours and a modification of the conditions for the forfeiture of deposit. Moreover on 17 January 1945 Labour MPs, by 41 to 16, defied the Whips over the deal on the business vote – and nine out of the loyal 16 were not free, being either in the Government or members of the Speaker's Conference.

15 *A Speaker's Commentaries* (London, 1925) vol. II, pp. 196–205.

16 Lord Selwyn-Lloyd, *Mr. Speaker, Sir* (London, 1976) pp. 116–17, 166–7.

17 Cmnd 6408 (1942) paras 104–5.

18 *HC Deb*. 535, c. 1920.

19 Ibid.

20 Ibid., c. 2125.

21 See C. O'Leary, *The Elimination of Corrupt Practices in Britain, 1868–1911* (Oxford, 1960).

3 Reforming Procedure in the Lords

LORD NORTHFIELD

I

The constitutional role of the House of Lords, already changing in the nineteenth century, has been sharply reshaped in the first part of the twentieth. The Lords are proud of their ability to adapt and survive, and it is therefore slightly curious that they have not consciously paused to take the measure of this change in role and to modify rules of procedure and methods of working to make them more suitable to the new period. By and large, procedures in the all-important area of public Bills remain the same in form as half a century ago. They parallel those in the Commons, as if the Chamber were still exercising co-equal legislative power rather than, as is now the case, seeking to influence a more powerful Commons; and when the Government proposed, in 1976, a special Select Committee on Practice and Procedure, similar to one in the Commons, the Leader of Conservative Peers agreed to it only grudgingly.

The measures and events that have altered the position of the Lords are plain enough. In the early 1900s, a Prime Minister and half his Cabinet could be hereditary peers, even though the supremacy of the Commons was tacitly accepted. Within ten years, by rejecting the Liberal Finance Bill of 1909 and provoking the Parliament Act of 1911, the Lords found themselves with only a two-year delaying power over ordinary Bills and no authority over financial and budgetary measures. After 1945, faced with an overwhelmingly Labour Commons, Lord Salisbury kept his hundreds of Conservative peers in check with his 'doctrine of the mandate'. If Commons measures had been in an election manifesto of the governing party, then it was not for the Lords to seek to delay, but only to try to revise and amend. Confrontation over iron and steel nationalisation led to the 1949 Parliament Act, reducing the delaying power to about one year; and attendance on an average day declined to about one hundred.

In 1958, the introduction of life peers and women began to give the Chamber a new lease of life; and a daily expenses allowance has also helped. In the mid-1970s a busier House would have two or three hundred peers present on average days. The House remains dominated by about 400 peers (mainly hereditary) taking the Conservative whip; and they face about 150 Labour peers, mostly life peers, about 40 Liberals and about 180 'crossbenchers' who take no party whip. It is this irrational and anachronistic composition that denies legitimacy to the Lords and secures the superior role of the Commons. In general the Lords have not until very recently tried to make far-reaching changes in Government Bills and have not attempted to insist on amendments which, when sent to the Commons, have then been rejected there. Despite the influx of life peers, who now number nearly three hundred, administrations commonly have only two or three peers in the Cabinet and about fifteen other and junior Ministers in a government of over one hundred in all.

The House now thinks of itself as a 'revising chamber' seeking influence rather than power on the basis of the experience – often expert and indeed eminent, reflecting diverse groups in society – of the recruits that have arrived as life peers. Lord Windlesham, a former Conservative Leader of the House, is among those who have described the new role:[1]

> The way the House of Lords has developed since the mid-1950s has been typical of the way in which the British Constitution has evolved . . . In any well-tuned parliamentary system there is a need and a place for a third element besides efficient government and the operation of representative democracy. This third element is the bringing to bear of informed or expert public opinion . . . It is now one of the principal roles of the Lords to provide a forum in which informed public opinion can take shape and be made known. The Upper House also provides a means and an opportunity to bring this body of expert opinion to bear on the problems of the day, either through the medium of the government or through other channels that are open . . . It should leave to the Commons the main business of forming and upholding administrations, of probing abuses, of voting taxes, and of reaching the main political decisions in accordance with what are regarded as the wishes of the people expressed through their elected representatives. Nor should the Lords ape the ways of the Commons either procedurally or in style of debate. In seeking to formulate public opinion and influence the political climate the Upper House has a distinctive parliamentary role.

II

The Lords will no doubt subscribe to this elegant statement of the new place of the Second Chamber. As will be suggested shortly, they have not, however, taken to heart Lord Windlesham's point that procedures should suit the changed role and should not ape those of the Commons. Before coming to that matter it is perhaps appropriate to clear from the way the question of whether changes in procedure for a House constituted at present would be needed if the membership and also the powers of the Lords were reformed. Procedure, powers and composition are of course linked in some degree; and lethargy about procedural reform may stem from the feeling that composition should be changed first.

In 1977, reform of the Lords is again an issue, as it has been at intervals since 1910. In 1968 parliamentary agreement was nearly reached on a reform that would have reflected the revising role. The leadership of the three parties had agreed on a scheme[2] for voting and non-voting peers, all nominated in carefully calculated numbers that would have given the Government of the day a small majority over Opposition parties, but not an absolute majority in the whole House. The balance would be held by crossbench peers. Powers, though altered, were to remain roughly the same, partly because it was agreed – even by Labour – that a House with powers any further reduced would hardly attract attendance. Other existing peers would be allowed to attend and speak, but not vote.

The 1968 proposals were approved by a large majority in the Lords, but foundered when opposition from the Left (which, led by Mr Michael Foot, MP, thought that the House would become too credible and might pit its authority against the Commons) and from the Right (led by Mr Enoch Powell, MP, but including others who objected to the power of patronage involved in a system of nominated peers) made it impossible to find a Commons majority for a timetable motion that alone could have stopped the interminable debates in Committee and got the Bill through.

After this failure, the issue lay quiet for some years, and many thought that the House might simply wither away by becoming increasingly lacking in legitimacy. Events since 1974, when a minority Labour Government came to power, have reopened matters in more acutely divided form.

The National Executive Committee of the Labour Party, now acknowledged to be dominated by the Left – but in this case probably reflecting wider views in the party – has become irritated by apparent departures from the Lords' normal revising role. In the 1975/76 session, major pieces of Government legislation, including the Aircraft and Shipbuilding Industries Bill, the Rent (Agriculture) Bill, the Education Bill (to enforce comprehensive secondary education), the Dock Work Regulation Bill and, to a lesser extent, the Health Services Bill (to phase out pay-beds), were heavily amended by large majorities of Conservative and other peers and, in some cases, were returned to the Commons in quite different form. In virtually all cases, the Bills had been in the election manifesto, but the Conservative Lords took the view that their duty to revise applied particularly when the Government had no overall majority in the Commons and was merely profiting from the inability of the other parties to combine against major issues, and when the Government had been elected by less than 40 per cent of those who voted at the election. The fact that the peers did not attempt, except in one or two cases, to insist on their amendments, did not calm the anger of Labour MPs, who had to spend weary nights voting down the Lords amendments and who had finally to accept defeat on one major change, cutting ship-repairing from the bill to nationalise the shipbuilding industry. Another significant change was made to the Dock Work Bill.

Cries about 'obstruction of democratic government' have been raised and the National Executive, on the basis of a 1977 Party Conference resolution, will attempt to include abolition of the Lords in the future election policies of the Labour Party. Whether such a fundamental change would be made by a victorious Labour Government is open to doubt. Moderates in the Labour Party acknowledge the need for a Chamber able, for example, to override a Commons that tried to prolong its life, able to prevent a slide from democracy. Others accept a short delaying power as sometimes helpful to democracy; and a significant number are concerned at having to find means and the time to do the final revising work if the Lords were abolished.

In this connection, the evidence given by Mr Michael Foot, MP, to the Commons special Select Committee on Procedure in December 1976 may be significant.[3] He went so far as to say (with the experience now of being in government and, indeed, Leader of the House) that because of the speed with which a lot of legislation has to pass through, there is need for calm scrutiny after it has left the Commons. For that purpose he suggested a revising chamber – 'not a second chamber but a revising body' – which would look at Bills and return them 'a month or so later, having taken into account all that has been said, and having taken into account the amendments that have been offered, and all the rest'. He justified this proposed limited role by suggesting that many of the amendments that at present come back from the Lords have not come from wisdom in the peers but have been inspired and drafted by the government departments after further thought. The limited contribution of peers was reinforced by a letter to *The Times* by a parliamentary draftsman:[4] 99 per cent of Lords amendments, he said, are such later work by officials. That may be an exaggeration, but it backs Mr Foot's essential point.

While Labour is moving in one direction away from the 1968 agreed reform, the Conservatives have moved in the other. They in turn have been irritated by the spectacle of a Labour Government that is in a minority in the Commons and yet has been able for nearly three years to carry contentious legislation almost as if it were a majority. In broadcast lectures, Lord Hailsham has talked of an elected dictatorship practised by the Commons in the absence of a Bill of Rights. The *Times* newspaper, in a leader of November 1976, has joined in with regrets that 'with its present composition the House lacks the authority to set its judgement against that of the Commons with any frequency'. And it concludes that: 'A reformed chamber would therefore need to be primarily or even wholly elected.' As an example of a form of election it mentions the minority report from the Kilbrandon Commission on the Constitution of Lord Crowther-Hunt and Mr Alan Peacock,[5] suggesting indirect regional election to supplement a House that would have nominated and possibly hereditary members.

Finally, Lord Carrington, Leader of the Conservatives in the Lords, has abandoned support for the 1968 proposals in favour of an elected chamber:[6]

> It could happen in the future that a government of an extreme character is elected on a minority vote, a government dedicated irreversibly to changing society in a way clearly contrary to the wishes of most of the electors. There are in the British Constitution no safeguards to prevent a bare majority in the House of Commons achieving that purpose in a very short time . . . The best safeguard is a Second Chamber with more power, with authority and with a composition that is politically credible.

Lord Carrington agrees that 'ultimately the will of the House of Commons must prevail' but he wants sufficient delaying power in the Lords to enable 'the people of this country to make their views felt'. It might be a House elected regionally on a system of proportional representation, and with powers which the Lords possessed after the 1911 Act.

Once again it is perhaps fair to suggest that a victorious Conservative Party might not try to get through such an extreme change. There would be attempts to get all-party agreement; and even in its absence, some form of compromise might emerge as the final plan put to Parliament.

Whatever the future may hold in this matter of reform of composition and powers, it is reasonable to suggest from views described above that the more likely forms of a new second chamber would leave it basically as a revising body, striving to influence a Commons admitted to be superior – and with or without powers of delay, or partial legitimacy through an elected element, to give final backing and authority in extreme cases of conflict with the Commons. Any changes in procedure that could improve the revising function and the influence of the present Chamber should not, therefore, be held up or pushed aside by some over-simple assertion that procedure cannot be considered in advance of composition and powers.

III

Given, then, that the House of Lords is expected to be mainly a revising chamber, seeking to influence the Commons in various ways, what is wrong with present procedure? The 1968 White Paper listed six main activities as the function of the Lords: revision of Bills brought from the Commons and initiation of less controversial and Private Members' Bills; study of subordinate legislation; scrutiny of activities of the executive; provision of a forum for debate on matters of public interest; and scrutiny of private legislation.

The first two duties are carried out by the House's procedure on public Bills. As has been mentioned already, it has changed little, if at all, from the days when the Chamber was striving to remain co-equal with the Commons in legislative power. Bills are given a formal First Reading without debate; a full debate follows on the principles of the Bill at Second Reading; nearly all Bills are then committed to a Committee of the Whole House, where clauses are studied one by one, with formal moving of amendments and debate on them; a Report Stage normally follows, for further amendments and thoughts; and finally comes the Third Reading, sometimes abbreviated, and the old motion 'That the Bill do now pass'. Unlike procedure in the Commons, amendments can be taken at Third Reading stage. The Bill then returns to the Commons (or passes to the Commons when it starts its life in the Lords). Amendments, or reasons for disagreeing with amendments, arrive from the Commons later, and are debated.

Just how this works in practice can be seen by taking a typical bill in the 1975/76 session. The Race Relations Bill, chosen because it was not highly controversial in the party sense and because it might be expected to provide full play for expert debate, is a reasonable example to take.

Eighteen peers spoke in a five-hour Second Reading debate in July.

B

The Committee stage took place in late September and early October. It occupied about 24½ hours of debate in the full Chamber, equivalent to, say, five sitting days; and because of congestion of business, the work went late into the night on two occasions. A few further hours followed on amendments moved at Report stage and on Third Reading, some of them to meet points raised earlier, and the Bill was then passed and sent back to the Commons with the proposed amendments. In all, over one hundred amendments were discussed, and fifty were sent to the Commons. Of the latter, about ten were both substantial and controversial and were carried in the Lords by use of the Conservative majority. They were resisted by the Commons in 9½ hours of debate; and the Lords then accepted the Commons' refusals in 2½ hours, after which the Bill passed into law in November. Some twenty peers spoke in a regular fashion during these later stages, and another dozen made an occasional intervention.

There is no doubt that a good deal of this work was effective. Amendments made in response to probing by the peers improved the Bill, although many changes were the Government's own further thoughts following reflection on debates in the Commons. On the other hand, the work might have been much more productive if it had been done in a different way.

In the first place, it was surely a waste of time for the full Chamber to be occupied for the equivalent of five or more sitting days for the activities of thirty peers discussing relatively technical and legal issues at Committee stage. Such work could have been done, and done more quickly, in a small Committee off the Floor of the House, where – in the atmosphere of a Select Committee – informal interchange could have got through quite speedily the probing and questioning about meaning and intentions. Moreover, if the Commons were to be influenced, the controversial issues in the Bill were eminently suitable for discussion, again in a Select Committee, with outside witnesses who could offer new and expert evidence.

There was, for example, an attempt to delete Clause 25, extending the range of clubs or associations covered by the law against discrimination. There are strong arguments for and against such a clause, and as to whether it is really enforceable. Outside evidence from the Club and Institute Union and other affected interests would have greatly enlightened the debate and might well have altered or fortified the Lords' decision. Opposition peers wished to delete Clause 65, which gives an aggrieved person the rather novel right to put questions to the respondent in order to help get at the reasons for the less favourable treatment which he thinks may constitute racial discrimination. Evidence on how parallel provisions in the Sex Discrimination Act are working, and on how workers in the race relations field regard the need for the complainant to have such a right, would all have been helpful and relevant – and could have influenced the Committee's proceedings. The debate which actually took place consisted simply of a dialogue between Lord Hailsham and the Minister, followed by a vote.

Again, trade unions and the TUC might well have provided forceful evidence about a disputed amendment concerning whether a shop-steward should be liable if a complaint were to be made that he discriminated in failing to resolve a grievance brought to him by one of his members; and if the Lords had nevertheless remained un-convinced by the Government's case on this point, the alleged weakness in the case and the evidence would have been on the record. Finally, there was heated debate about the Bill's proposal to delete the element of intention to stir up racial hatred from the offence of incitement to hatred. This is a deep and complicated issue, with wide-ranging effects on free speech and newspaper reporting. The Guild of Newspaper Editors, the Race Relations Board and others all feel strongly one way or the other, and their views should have been sought, recorded and assessed.

Other examples could be given equally well among the handful of issues that, in the end, divided the Lords and Commons and were the substantial revisions that the Lords voted upon. In almost all cases, less formal debating and more informal discussion and taking of evidence – as is appropriate to a Chamber less concerned with adversary politics and aiming to carry out dispassionate revision – might well have had important results. Any amendments finally made would, first, have been backed by the record of supporting evidence, much of it fresh to the Commons and, indeed, never taken in Commons procedure. Other amendments might, second, never have stood up to expert evidence or might have been significantly modified by it. The dialogue with the Commons on the amendments would have been greatly improved, perhaps transformed.

The established procedure on public Bills (which definition includes Bills introduced by private Members) contrasts oddly with elaborate procedure which the Lords have developed since 1974 to deal with draft legislation arising from membership of the European Economic Community. Legislation is made by the Council (i.e. the Ministers of member states) on the basis of proposals of the EEC Commission, although the latter also has certain powers to make minor law. The Lords sensed that it was important to begin scrutinising such proposals, commenting on those of medium importance, and directing the attention of the full House to major drafts, so that Government policy in the Council could be influenced.

A Select Committee in the European Communities was therefore established in the Lords (after the Commons had rejected the idea of a joint committee) and its work has reached considerable proportions. It works through a main Committee of 23 members and seven specialist sub-committees (roughly corresponding to the parallel committees of the European Parliament, which also monitor the Commission's work). Some 80 peers take part in this work. In 1975/76 they held 165 meetings, took public evidence on 82 occasions, and produced over 50 reports either for the information of the House or to guide the House in full debate on major issues.[7] Part-time specialist advisers are employed as needed. Terms of reference are wide, enabling sub-committees to enquire into important proposals (e.g. the Tindemans Report on European Union) that may not necessarily involve immediate Community legislation. Witnesses may include Ministers.

The Committee, in a memorandum prepared for the Select Committee on Practice and Procedure,[8] commented on the disparity between scrutiny of domestic statutory instruments – rarely receiving much attention from Parliament – and the amount of time and effort being given to similar measures coming from Brussels. They also highlighted the need to discuss domestic legislation at the similar pre-legislative stage, for example when it arrives in the form of White or Green Papers. This would enable Parliament 'to concentrate on policy at a stage when it is in practice most possible to influence it'.

While acknowledging the importance of the Floor of the House for Committee and Report stages of public Bills, the European Communities Committee suggested that the committee system, for both EEC and domestic legislation, should be developed and the 'whole workload and effectiveness of the House should be examined together. . . . The present discrepancies between procedures and the time given in Committee to EEC legislation and to domestic legislation or international affairs, should be carefully examined.'

A small beginning may come from the modest proposals made by the Select Committee on Practice and Procedure. In its First Report of 1977[9] it suggested a new set of Select Committees, perhaps two or three to start with, based on convenient policy areas, and mainly dealing with Bills. Such committees would follow progress of Bills through the Commons, noting time taken and issues discussed or neglected, would take evidence on particular issues in the Bill, and thus prepare a report to guide the House on matters needing particular attention in the Lords. Later, after Second Reading in the Lords, the same Committee would take the Committee stage of the Bill, hearing new evidence if need be, paying attention to matters identified as important, and also reserving more contentious issues, if appropriate, for decision by the full House at Report stage. Such committees, it advocated, might also study Green and White Papers (as well as statutory instruments) so that a small start could be made on pre-legislative influence.

It is early to say whether this will lead to a great change in the Lords' revising work. The report does not amount to the thorough examination of the House's workload that the European Committee called for. Government and Opposition leaders were suspicious of the Report's proposals when they were debated on 5 July 1977, and only one committee, on an experimental basis, was offered for the session 1977/8. A more direct and conscious approach to legislative procedure would suggest a full set of committees, perhaps seven or eight, sitting regularly through the session as in other foreign legislatures, and building up a group of specialists able to check the work of the executive as well as to deal with draft laws. White Papers and Green Papers, statutory instruments, policy statements, EEC proposals (increasingly intertwined with domestic issues), reports by specialist advisers on important topics, draft Bills, ideas for Bills to be pressed on the Government or to be introduced by individual peers or even the Committee itself – all these would form part of the work in the early part of the session, partly through sub-committees, while the House is awaiting the session's load of Bills coming up from the Commons. Such Committees would then take the Committee stage of Bills within their area, as described earlier, would call further evidence if needed, and would prepare reports to back amendments that are to be pressed on the Commons. These varied activities would doubtless throw up suggestions for topics that the House could fruitfully debate in its role as a 'forum for debate on matters of public interest'. In short, such committees would enable the House more systematically to approach five of the six main activities (the sixth – private legislation – being a matter quite apart and not dealt with here) that the 1968 White Paper listed as functions of the Second Chamber. The pattern is familiar enough: other legislatures have adopted it, even some (like Canada and the Australian Senate) based on the Westminster model.

At least one further change in present practice may be needed to accompany changes of this scale and nature. So far, and unlike the Commons, the Lords have refused to put into the hands of the Chair any power to select amendments for debate and to refuse to call others. The rather suspect reason given is that, it is said, the House does not have the equivalent of a Speaker (the Lord Chancellor is a presiding officer without power, and the House is itself master of Order) and so cannot entrust such an important power to anyone with his authority and impartiality. In fact, however, the power to select in Committee is, in the Commons, entrusted both to the Deputy Speaker and to ordinary Members who, from the panel of Committee chairmen, preside over Standing Committees. Moreover, the principles on which selection is made are set out in Erskine May, the House of Commons reference book on procedure, and could easily be adapted. The

Chairman of Committees of the Lords is already regarded with respect and is expected to act, in his general duties, quite as impartially as the Deputy Speaker, and could well be entrusted with the duty of such selection. It would probably be needed on some bills not simply so as to restrain the tendency to table unnecessary amendments (sometimes to delay a Bill and congest business) but also to prevent the Report stage – when Select Committees are taking the Committee stage – from being a re-run in the full House of amendments disposed of in Committee.

Objections to the general proposals can be anticipated. How, it will be asked, can the party balance (whatever it is) be secured in Committees restricted to a few peers? It is possibly of no great concern, since the Committee will be acting, in the main, in a non-party-political manner; politically controversial amendments can be reserved for Report stage. Indeed, the procedure itself will be sometimes unsuitable for fiercely contested Bills, and it will always be open to the House to suspend the sending to such a Select Committee and to take the Committee stage of such Bills on the Floor of the House, as now. This is not unfamiliar practice in the House of Commons.

Others may question whether a Committee can do both investigatory work – taking evidence, discussing White Papers, etc. – and also become a full debating body when formal amendments may be moved at Committee stage. The answer is that other legislatures manage this problem easily enough: it is simply the case that the UK Parliament is not very familiar with such a double role in Committee work. What, it may be asked, is to be the position of peers who are not on a Committee but wish to take part, from particular interest or knowledge, in the Committee stage of a Bill? This should be no problem for several reasons. Members can easily be added to a Committee, exactly as Ministers will need to be added, for a Committee stage; peers can, in any case, attend and speak at such Committees under existing Standing Orders; and if the power to vote is a concern, then that will always remain at Report stage, for the Chair will almost always call an amendment – even if it has been discussed in some form in Committee – if it attracts the names of the leading Front Bench spokesmen.

It may be asked how the House can draw the attention of the Commons to the supporting reasons and evidence uncovered in the case of particular amendments. At present the Commons do give perfunctory reasons, in a formal document, when rejecting Lords' amendments. There would seem every reason why, on the basis of this precedent, the Lords should, when necessary, accompany their suggested amendments with a message of explanation, indeed an argued case. This would be a logical way to conduct a revising role.

A very real fear may be that not enough peers will be found to man such Committees on a year-round basis. This could indeed be difficult. On the other hand, the number that have volunteered to work in the European Communities' sub-committees, and have attended the scores of meetings, has been a surprise. If they are merged into the new system, that will provide a good start. Further than that, if the House does not have the manpower to do its work properly, then it should make clear the need for more working peers.

How much independence of judgement and dispassionate revising work can we expect? The claim should not be pitched too high. Most obviously, all will depend on composition; but the present House gives some clues. The British parliamentary system, in contrast to most in Western Europe, focuses sharply the conflict between left and right and is an arena for continuous confrontation. The simple two-party system and the absence up to now of coalitions have highlighted Labour's challenge to the economic *status quo*. This division and the confrontation are bound to affect the upper House in some degree.

When a left-wing Government is pressing public ownership measures, for example, speeches and committee work reflect the party conflict, and if the Government, from whatever cause, is weak, then that shows in votes on crucial amendments, with 'crossbenchers' joining in on the side of the right. But several factors combine, when the issue or the general situation is less acute, to make the scrutiny less adversarial. A deep instinct for public service and genuine pride in moderation motivate hereditary peers and life peers, particularly those who have mellowed after years in the Commons. There is widespread respect for the genuine expert, the academic, the trade unionist or industrialist, who has not spent a lifetime in the arena. Above all, there is a sense of independence from constituents or party machine looking 'over the shoulder'. Inside many peers a streak of independence tries con- tinuously to break out. In the end, this strengthens impartial study of issues on less important parts of highly controversial Bills and cross- party voting on details of other legislation. It is here that experts and argument reign and influence the vote; and the experience will be reinforced if more Bills are taken away from the glare of the Chamber, where confrontation is provoked, and are studied instead in the relaxed atmosphere of a Select Committee. This is, in fact, all of a piece with the reputation of the Lords for being in the van on social matters – for example on Bills about sexual freedom or abortion, and tackling issues which tend to scare the Commons because of public pressure.

The tradition of public service is strong and suggests there will be people willing to do this less glamorous revising work in a Second Chamber, and do it well; and governments do respect much of the tempering of the political output of the Commons. But there should be doubts whether the esteemed qualities of the present Second Chamber would endure in a House very differently recruited, particularly as the relatively disinterested – who do a great deal to enhance the effectiveness of revising work – would not stand for election. An elected revising chamber may indeed be a contradiction in terms in the British context.

The House of Lords would be a different place, of course, with a thoroughgoing committee system of the kind described here. Facing up to the challenge of organising the Lords to become a true revising Chamber would be hard for many who revere the existing institution, and serve it with distinction. But any Second Chamber with reformed membership can be expected to seek a systematic way of working, and it might be as well to run in the changes in advance. If the composition is not reformed, it is at least questionable whether the Lords will attract attendance from new peers who sense that the changes in role, established for all to see, remain unmatched with changes in procedure and working methods.

NOTES AND REFERENCES

1   'Politics in Practice' (Jonathan Cape, 1975) pp. 140–2.
2   *House of Lords Reform*, Cmnd 3799 (HMSO, 1968).
3   *House of Commons Select Committee on Procedure 1976/77*: Minutes of Evidence, 20 Dec 1976 (HMSO).
4   *The Times*, 18 Nov 1976.
5   *Report of the Royal Commission on the Constitution 1969/73*, Cmnd 5460/1 (HMSO, 1973) vol. II, Memorandum of Dissent.
6   'Reforming the Second Chamber', *Illustrated London News*, Mar 1977.
7   *Select Committee on the European Communities: Special Report, Session 1976/77* (HMSO, 25 Jan 1977).
8   Minutes of Evidence. *First Report from the House of Lords Select Committee on Practice and Procedure* (HMSO, 1977), Minutes of Evidence.
9   Ibid.

4 Coping with Administrative Growth: Super-Departments and the Ministerial Cadre, 1957–1977

F. M. G. WILLSON

One of the very few unarguable propositions about British central government throughout the first three-quarters of the twentieth century is that, despite some contraction for short periods after both World Wars, the work which it has undertaken and the number of people it has employed to do that work have grown, albeit at varying speeds, but with an apparently relentless and inexorable certainty.[1] The most popular (or unpopular) explanations of this phenomenon tend to relate wholly or mainly to the inevitable progress of collectivist political, social and economic thinking, and to the alleged insatiability of the appetites of politicians and civil servants for more power. Neither explanation can be ignored, though a better hearing is bound to be given to the former than to the latter. But, in truth, the growth of central administration also reflects, to a very large degree, many more mundane factors, such as the increase in population, the greater complexity of technology, and the transfer of responsibility in a number of crucial areas not from private to public bodies, but from local authorities and other public services to departments in Whitehall. Moreover, once a decision has been made to introduce or extend a particular service to the community, the full impact is often if not always delayed or concealed, because the early effects may be minimal and the incremental pressure over years and even decades may pass almost unrealised until, under the stress of a 'crisis' and the probe of an inquiry, a 'new administrative colossus' is 'discovered'. Rather similarly, the adjustments made to the administrative structure so that it can cope with an almost continuous if irregular increase in workload are often either unrecognised as genuinely new departures when they are introduced, or are claimed to be significant innovations which, as it turns out, do not live up to what they were expected to achieve. This essay looks at administrative growth over twenty years and at two particular aspects (and their interrelationship) of the structural attempts to adjust to its demands. One was the introduction of extremely large departments: the other was bound up with the expanding complexity of the corps of Ministers – the more and more frequent appearance of the 'intermediate' Minister.

The mid and late 1950s, in retrospect, seem clearly destined to be regarded as watershed years in many aspects of national life, and certainly deserve to be so regarded in the context of central administration. For a short spell there seemed to be an end to the almost continuous series of changes in departmental boundaries which had taken place ever since before the outbreak of war in 1939. And that main, though in some respects inadequate, measure of governmental activity, the size of the Civil Service, reached a post-war low in 1960. For the first part of his premiership, immediately following the Suez affair, Harold Macmillan presided over a nation which may have been somewhat chastened by international misadventure, but which was becoming apparently more prosperous. It was a period which, in many senses and without too much strain upon the imagination, can be characterised as marking the real end of the Second World War and its protracted aftermath. The second half of Mr Macmillan's tenure of 10 Downing Street ushered in a relatively new era of administrative growth and structural change – an era which, in turn, may well have reached its climax a decade later.

This is a study of some of the arrangements made to that area of government which is unequivocally within the direct responsibility of Ministers: it is not a study of the whole of what might be called 'governmental' activity of an administrative kind. The latter concept would properly include the duties of local authorities and the enormous area of work done by institutions for which nobody has yet devised a wholly acceptable collective name, but which range across our national life from the control of betting to the production of coal, from the development of water resources to the encouragement of arts and crafts. Here we are concerned only with the load on the central, and unequivocally ministerial, departmental structure, a structure manned by civil servants properly so called. In that context, with a very few exceptions which are relatively insignificant in number, a civil servant is

a servant of the Crown (not being the holder of a political or judicial office) who usually is paid wholly and directly out of money voted by Parliament and who works in a civil capacity in a department of government.

Within this definition, the Civil Service covers members of the Home Civil and Diplomatic Services, but not the Northern Ireland Civil Service.

But despite the apparent clarity of the above definition, the cold statistics of the Civil Service have to be used with care. In the years from 1957 the biggest changes of status, in manpower terms, took place at the Post Office. Until October 1969 the Post Office was an orthodox government department, headed by a Minister, the Postmaster General, whose huge staff were all civil servants. Until 1965 about three-quarters of them were classified as 'non-industrials' while the remaining quarter were 'industrials'. In 1965 all but a few hundred of those previously classified as 'industrial' became 'non-industrial'. Four years later, when the Post Office became a public corporation, all its staff from then onwards ceased to be civil servants. About 15,000 of the former establishment remained civil servants, however, some in the new and short-lived Ministry of Posts and Telecommunications (its separate identity was lost in 1974), but the majority in the new Department of National Savings which took over the banking services of the 'old' Post Office.

It is tempting to compare like with like over our period by taking no cognisance of the Post Office at all. But in terms of the size of the organisation which Ministers had to control, it is essential to include the postal workers up to October 1969. In another context, that of employment services, the detailed figures look somewhat odd because of the creation of the Manpower Services Commission as a statutory body. During 1974 the Commission took over 18,000 staff from the Ministry of Employment, and they lost their Civil Service status; but at the beginning of 1976 they were transferred back into the Civil Service. On a smaller scale, one can mention the transfer in April 1973 into the Civil Service of 5400 staff of the Atomic Weapons Research Establishment who became members of the Ministry of Defence instead of belonging, as previously, to the non-Civil Service Atomic Energy Authority. And over several years there has been a considerable transfer into the Civil Service of previously locally employed officers who have been brought within the fold of the Courts Service under the direct control of the Lord Chancellor. Neither transfers into the Civil Service nor growth within its own establishment, however, have come near balancing the loss of 400,000 to the 'new' Post Office.

The table on p. 38, read in conjunction with the two previous paragraphs, reveals several clear trends. First, the total Civil Service was 25 per cent smaller in 1976 than it was in 1957: non-industrial numbers have gone down by 10 per cent, and industrial employees have dropped dramatically by 70 per cent. But this macro picture is misleading, except in so far as it indicates the enormous reduction caused

NUMBERS EMPLOYED IN THE CIVIL SERVICE IN SELECTED YEARS, 1957–76

	NON-INDUSTRIAL					INDUSTRIAL					TOTALS		
Year	Defence	Civil excl. Post Office	Post Office	Total Civil	Total	Defence	Civil excl. Post Office	Post Office	Total Civil	Total	Defence	Civil	All Civil Service
1957	133·7	251·5	252·3	503·8	637·5	289·6	43·5	85·2	128·7	418·3	423·3	632·5	1,055·8
1960	131·1	250·5	254·6	505·1	636·2	236·5	38·2	83·6	121·8	358·3	367·6	626·9	994·5
1965	133·5	286·0	383·8	669·8	803·3	182·7	53·1	·4	53·5	236·2	316·2	723·3	1,039·5
1971	129·8	369·9	—	369·9	499·7	154·2	49·0	—	49·0	203·2	284·0	418·9	702·9
1976	131·0	433·8	—	433·8	564·8	137·2	43·1	—	43·1	180·3	268·2	476·9	745·1

NOTES

1 Defence includes Ministry of Defence, Admiralty, War Office, Air Ministry, Ministry of Supply (to 1959), Ministry of Aviation (1959–67), Ministry of Technology (1967–71), Ministry of Aviation Supply (1971). This means that until 1963 the figures for Defence are somewhat too large, because the supply departments had some civil functions, though those functions did not occupy more than a minority of their civil servants. However, in April 1963 most of the works services of the three Service Departments were transferred to the Ministry of Public Building and Works, which was merged in 1970 into the Department of the Environment. This transfer removed well over 20,000 civil servants from the Defence category. The much smaller numbers of 'non-Defence' civil servants in the supply departments between 1963 and 1971 would compensate to a small extent for the loss of the works people, but since 1971 there is no such offset. In the absence of a detailed breakdown of works staff, it is necessary to draw attention to the sizeable understatement of total Defence staff since 1963 and particularly since 1971. The same factors explain the large increase in the 1965 and later figures for Industrials in civil work: without the Defence building work done by the Department of the Environment the number of truly 'civil' Non-Industrials would probably not have exceeded about 20,000 in 1976.

2 The 1965 figures are for 1 April: all the others are for 1 January.

3 Most of the figures are taken directly from Civil Service statistics: a few have been calculated from the relevant published figures available.

by the change of constitutional status of the Post Office. Secondly, the number of industrial civil servants employed in defence administration has dropped by about half, though the number of non-industrials in that area has hardly changed at all. Third, the number of industrials employed by all civil departments other than the Post Office has apparently remained about the same; but, as the footnote to the table explains, this conceals a considerable reduction in the civil context. All this clears the way for the fourth and most significant point: the non-industrial Civil Service in civil departments other than the Post Office increased from about 250,000 in the late fifties to about 434,000 in 1976 – by some 80 per cent. That enormous growth reflects an approximate doubling of staff in three major areas – social services, tax collection, and the oversight of economic affairs; an even larger proportionate increase in law, order and justice, and 'Home Affairs', including the decentralised administrations in Scotland and Wales; and a 50 per cent rise in the staffs dealing with external relations.

With these developments – and especially the fourth point – in mind we can examine broadly what happened to the departmental structure during the last two decades, and look particularly at the experience of introducing very large units.

Given the rate of growth and the experience of earlier periods, it would be more than surprising if such a stretch of twenty years could pass without there being a considerable amount of change in the allocation of functions and the number of departments and Ministers. There certainly has been such change since 1957, but one particular pheno-menon which caused much publicity and debate was the appearance of very large units which have often been referred to as 'giant' or 'super' departments. In order to put this experience into a proper perspective, it is as well to consider exactly which departments fitted the new unofficial nomenclature, and, equally important, why some did not belong in that category. First, however, let us look briefly at the general character of structural change since the Civil Service began to grow again at the end of the fifties.

The diagram overleaf shows the impressive overall reduction in the number of ministerial departments ten to twelve years after the new growth began, despite the appearance in the sixties of new departments like the Ministry of Technology, the Civil Service Department and the Welsh Office, and the short-lived Department of Economic Affairs and Ministry of Land and Natural Resources. When the Labour Govern-ment went out of office in 1970 there were 19 major departments as compared with 24 at the beginning of 1960 and 25 in 1965–6. But the reduction was given a further impetus by Edward Heath, and by mid-1971 the number was down to 15. One has to go back before 1914

MAJOR DEPARTMENTS 1961–76

1961 1962 1963 1964 1965 1966 1967 1968 1969 1970 1971 1972 1973 1974 1975 1976

Economic Affairs
Treasury   Treasury
                                                                                            Civil Service
Technical Co-operation   Overseas Development
Foreign   Foreign and Commonwealth
Colonial
Commonwealth Relations   Commonwealth
Central Africa
Admiralty
War
Air
Defence   Defence
Aviation   Aviation Supply
Technology   Energy
Power   Trade
Trade   Trade and Industry

                                                            Industry

                            Posts and Telecommunications

Post Office   Prices and Consumer Protection
                                                                                Agriculture, Fisheries, Food
Agriculture, Fisheries, Food   Employment
Labour   Lord Chancellor
Lord Chancellor   Home
Home   Scottish
Scottish   Welsh
                                                                                Northern Ireland

Science   Education and Science
Education
Health   Social Security   Health and Social Security

Pensions and National Insurance

Works   Public Building and Works
Transport and Civil Aviation   Transport
Housing and Local Government   Environment
               Land and Natural Resources

to find so small a number, and it is interesting to compare the departmental concentration achieved in the early seventies with the much quoted Haldane formula for the division of work contained in the *Report of the Committee on the Machinery of Government* in 1918.[2] What we might call the years of departmental amalgamation were the years 1964–71: the reduction in the number of units was a bipartisan affair, beginning and ending with a Conservative Government in office.

Another glance at the diagram will reveal that the reduction in the number of departments began and ended with the area of defence – a pacemaker here as in earlier administrative developments of the twentieth century. The culmination of a very long movement towards a comprehensive departmental arrangement for defence came in April 1964, when the Admiralty, War Office, and Air Ministry were merged into the Ministry of Defence. In May 1971 the last military supply functions provided by a separate and partly civil department, the Ministry of Aviation Supply, were transferred to the Ministry of Defence, making the whole defence function departmentally self-contained, except for building work, which the old Service departments lost in 1963 to the Ministry of Public Building and Works, now part of the Department of the Environment. It was the Labour Government of 1964–70 which carried through the inevitable post-imperial combination of the Foreign, Commonwealth and Colonial Offices, completed in 1968; and the Conservatives merged the Ministry of Overseas Development into the new Foreign and Commonwealth Office in October 1970. In the general area of social services, the Department of Education and Science has since 1964 been charged with functions previously administered by the Lord President as Minister for Science and by the Treasury in the context of the universities and most of the provision for the arts: the Ministries of Health and of Social Security were brought together in 1968: and it was Mr Heath's Government which finalised, late in 1970, a move which probably would have been made by a continuing Labour Administration, to forge the Department of the Environment out of the previously separate Ministries of Housing and Local Government, of Transport and Civil Aviation, and of Public Building and Works. Lastly, by a series of mergers from 1967 onwards, four economic departments – the Board of Trade and the Ministries of Aviation (in 1970–1 the Ministry of Aviation Supply), Technology and Power were combined to form the Ministry of Trade and Industry.

Of all these concentrations of administrative function, those in the areas of defence and of education and science have gone apparently unchallenged; that in the field of external affairs has held up, except for the detachment of Overseas Development in an arrangement whereby the Minister is in charge of a separate department and yet remains part of the Foreign and Commonwealth Office team under the direction of the Secretary of State;[3] that represented by the Department of Health and Social Security is unchanged structurally but, as we shall see, its continuance may be at some risk; and those which took the forms of the Department of Trade and Industry and the Department of the Environment have been severely diluted, the more so in the former than in the latter case. Trade and Industry began to break up while the Conservatives were still in power, in January 1974, when the Department of Energy was established; and the break-up was completed as soon as Labour succeeded to power in March 1974, when Harold Wilson divided the remainder of the department into three parts – the Departments of Trade, of Industry, and of Prices and Consumer Protection. At the same time the Ministry of Posts and Telecommunications – the last remnant of the 'old' Post Office – was abolished and its functions distributed between the Department of Industry and the Home Office. The Department of the Environment suffered the loss of a sizeable part of its jurisdiction in September 1976, when the Department of Transport was set up. By the end of 1976, therefore, mainly as a result of reversals in two areas, there were twenty major departments.[4]

Three departments stand out from this period of development as undisputed 'giants': the Ministry of Defence, with a quarter of a million staff and about 120 officials of Under-Secretary rank and above: the Department of Trade and Industry which, at its high point had over 26,000 staff and over a hundred top-level officers; and the Department of the Environment, with approximately 75,000 staff and over ninety high-level civil servants at its peak. But it is sometimes suggested that there are two other 'giants' – the Foreign and Commonwealth Office, which has a mere 12,500 staff but not far short of 200 top-level officers; and the cluster of departments answering to the Chancellor of the Exchequer, of which the Treasury and the two Revenue Boards are obviously the most important – that cluster produces well over 100,000 staff and ninety-odd seniors.[5] The question to face, therefore, is whether there are reasonable doubts as to what constitutes a 'giant' or 'super' department and, in the light of any such doubts, which of the five departments listed qualify. In discussing this, it is necessary to consider a topic hitherto not mentioned – the 'double-banking' of Cabinet Ministers at some departments.[6]

The pros and cons of 'super' departments were discussed, with the weight behind him of personal experience as a Permanent Secretary who helped to launch such a department, by the late Sir Richard Clarke, and it is unnecessary to repeat his arguments here except in summary.[7] Sir Richard was a supporter of the idea of very big units, and based his case as much or more on the broad policy, ministerial and constitutional advantages which he saw accruing from having such departments than on the less 'political' administrative aspects, though he did see considerable advantages in those as well. He was relatively unworried by 'sheer numbers of staff and public expenditure', and felt that from a staffing point of view the numbers of the most senior officers was perhaps as good a measure of effective size as any – and, again, as much or more in the context of the extent of parliamentary interest in the subject-matter of a department's work than in the internal technicalities of its operation. But when it came to the political leadership of a department, Sir Richard Clarke took an uncompromising line. He claimed that

> The 'giant' department is constitutionally just like any other department, but much bigger. It is likely to have at least another Minister, in addition to its head, of status equivalent to that of a Minister in charge of a department not represented in the Cabinet. . . . There have been many cases of having two Cabinet Ministers in one department. . . . But this is inconsistent with the idea of a small Cabinet; and it is difficult to justify the concept of a 'giant' department with more work of national and political importance to the Cabinet than its Minister can comprehend and handle. The same argument refutes the idea of allowing the No. 2 Minister to attend the Cabinet for particular business. If the Cabinet business cannot be handled effectively by the one Cabinet Minister, the department is too big.[8]

If this judgement is applied strictly, then the Department of Trade and Industry was only a legitimate 'giant' in Clarke's sense between October 1970 and November 1972; the Department of the Environment between October 1970 and March 1974; and the Department of Health and Social Security from its origins in October 1968 until September 1976. It may well be significant that neither the Department of Trade and Industry nor the Department of the Environment survived for long as 'super' departments after experiencing 'double-banking'. If their precedents are followed, then the 'double-banked' Department of Health and Social Security may be a candidate for early dissolution.

Strict application of the one-Cabinet-Minister idea would rule out both the Treasury and the Foreign and Commonwealth Office as super departments for a considerable part of the period between 1957 and 1977. But in any event there are other doubts about their inclusion. 'Double-banking' is rather 'old hat' at both departments. There has tended to be ministerial duality in foreign affairs because, with the exception of Baldwin, most Prime Ministers have wanted to be involved deeply in foreign affairs and one or two have tried to be, in effect, their own Foreign Secretaries. But aside from that, particular problems of international diplomacy have made it quite common to have a senior member of the Government with a special brief in the area of foreign affairs alongside the Foreign Secretary, though in no sense in charge of the Foreign Office. Perhaps the main doubt about the advisability of thinking of the Foreign and Commonwealth Office in 'super' terms, however, is connected with the size of the team of senior officials. That team is very large indeed, if the whole Diplomatic Service, wherever based, is included; but if one looks only at the Whitehall headquarters, then the senior team is relatively modest by comparison with the big domestic departments which had or still have claims on the title 'giant'.

As for the Treasury, we find ourselves dealing with a plurality of departments rather than a single entity comparable in form to, for instance, the Department of the Environment. Again, as with the Foreign and Commonwealth Office, 'double-banking' can be misleading. The Prime Minister is First Lord of the Treasury and has always been intimately mixed up in that complicated area nowadays covered by the Treasury, its numerous associated departments, the Civil Service Department and the Cabinet Office, and has of political necessity been heavily involved in all those attempts to cope, organisationally, with the demands of economic affairs and the struggles to find appropriate mechanisms of control and planning for the national economy. The Prime Minister and the Chancellor of the Exchequer are locked into a sometimes nightmarish duality, and round them and the collection of big and small departments which fall into their purview have danced with increasing intensity a bevy of Ministers, departmental and non-departmental, more and less senior, in and outside the Cabinet. The whole central complex of the Treasury and its associated but organisationally separate departments, together with those like the Civil Service Department for which the Prime Minister is directly responsible, employ between them a total group of civil servants and a complement of seniors both large enough to make the complex comparable in sheer size to a 'unitary' giant department. But the very lack of unity makes it difficult to accept the complex as being in the same category as, for instance, the old Department of Trade and Industry. And it is inconceivable that this maelstrom of political and administrative activity at the highest levels could possibly be dealt with by less than two Cabinet Ministers, however the departmental jurisdictions were arranged. Indeed, in our period there have often been three or four Cabinet Ministers involved. For a variety of reasons, therefore, the 'Treasury complex' is hardly a candidate for the title of 'super' department.

Thus we are left with only four departments in the 'super' category. If the very large size of total staff, the largeness of the top echelon of civil servants, the requirement of having only one Cabinet Minister, and an organisational structure essentially unitary in character are accepted as the main criteria governing inclusion, then we have only one 'giant' department in April 1977 – the Ministry of Defence. We had three others – Trade and Industry, and Environment, both of which have been subdivided, though in differing degrees; and Health and Social Security, which retains its original size but, since September 1976, has had two Cabinet Ministers. It will be some time before any balanced analysis and explanation can be given of how and why at least two of these big units had so short a life in their largest form. To suggest that the Department of Trade and Industry lasted only $2\frac{1}{2}$ years in its 'super' state, and then was split within three months into four separate departments because of weaknesses in its basic 'administrative' structure, could be tendentious and naive. Ministerial jurisdictions are in the Prime Minister's gift, and may be altered for political and personal reasons relating, for example, to the size and balance of Cabinet membership, or for any of half-a-dozen reasons which might have little or no connection with administrative structure. The likelihood that the big Departments of Trade and Industry and of the Environment were divided up without reference to their operational administrative effectiveness certainly cannot be confirmed or denied yet. But it is not unreasonable to wonder, in the context of administrative structure, why those two departments 'fell apart', while the Ministry of Defence remains and flourishes as a 'giant', and while the Department of Health and Social Security at least retains its 'super' size. And it is at least conceivable that the answer lies not in any technical aspect of 'bigness', but in the relation of great size to the state of political opinion towards the work entrusted to the units concerned.

If there is a 'law' for giant departments, it might run like this. In the British parliamentary, Cabinet, system, no ministerial department can survive as a separate administrative unit if its area of responsibility is so wide and attracts so much public controversy and parliamentary attention as to make its representation in the Cabinet by one Minister impracticable. Which could be translated as meaning that in the period since 1964 national defence policy and administration has been relatively uncontroversial, whereas trade and industry, environmental and welfare matters have been too politically complex to allow of their administration being successfully channelled through single Cabinet Ministers at the head of huge departments, on more than a temporary basis. Political sensitivity has come up against and pushed aside notions of the desirability of more compact Cabinets and large, tidy, administrative packages. Like the attempts to produce two-tiered ministerial systems through the use of 'Overlords' a decade earlier, the notions of 'giant' departments and 'double-banking' have been tried and, in their essentials, rejected in all but the field of defence and, with many very special reservations, in the unique areas of the Treasury and of external affairs. But despite a considerable degree of rejection of the idea, the era of the unitary, domestic, 'super' units – DTI, DOE, DHSS – can be seen as one of interesting and useful experimentation which has left the central administration more compact, its fewer departments bigger and, overall, its functional boundaries more clearly defined.

While all the attempts to meet the demands of growth by creating 'super' departments and 'double-banking' Cabinet Ministers have been going on with mixed and, overall, not too happy results, there has been a steady and separate development within the total cadre of Ministers which might be described as a more modest but more successful long-term contribution to coping with bigness – the consolidation of the intermediate Minister. This story is best seen in the context of the size and the internal division of the total Ministry. So far as overall size is concerned, the sixties witnessed the most recent stepping upwards. From the 1870s to the First World War the inclusive figure was between 55 and 60 Ministers; in the inter-war years it was between 60 and 70; from 1945 until the end of the fifties the ministerial teams each numbered about 80, but grew to 90 by the end of the Conservative regime in 1964. Since then, with the exception of the first two years of Mr Heath's Administration, the Government has jumped to around 110 members.[9] During our twenty years, the Government, rather like the central departments, has become both larger and somewhat more 'tidy', and this is perhaps best explained by reviewing very briefly the categories into which Ministers fall.

The biggest and most significant division within the Government is between those members who form the Cabinet and all the rest. But within the Cabinet we can distinguish three groups. First, those usually called non-departmental, in the sense that the extent to which they have responsibilities for the operation of 'line' departments is either nil or very limited – the Prime Minister, the Lord President, the Lord Privy Seal and any others who may be appointed with special tasks outside and/or across the normal Whitehall administrative structures. Second, and most numerous, the heads of 'line' departments with whom must be included nowadays the Lord Chancellor, whose administrative responsibilities have grown very considerably. And, thirdly, the 'second' Cabinet Ministers at 'double-banked' departments. The Cabinet has hardly grown at all, but since 1957 it has certainly become more departmentally inclusive.

The other easily explained group within the Ministry is that including all the Whips and those Household Officers in the House of Lords who combine whipping with some duties of departmental representation. That group has become half as big again as it was in Mr Macmillan's Government, no doubt reflecting in part both the closeness of the political struggle and the additional complexities of an ever-widening governmental involvement. Nor need much space be given to the Law Officers, who have remained unchanged, and to the traditional juniors in the administrative departments, the Parliamentary Secretaries, except to point out that the latter have increased only slightly in number, going up from 29 in the early months of Mr Macmillan's premiership to as many as 36 under Mr Wilson and down again to 34 at the end of 1976.

It is in the remaining categories that the most significant changes have occurred. Ever since the later part of the nineteenth century there have been Ministers at the heads of departments who have been excluded from the Cabinet, but the numbers were tiny until after 1945, wartime experience apart. After 1945 they were quite numerous, but broadly speaking there has been a steady decline in this group from the high peak of the Attlee years. In 1957, though, there were still no less than eight heads of departments outside the Cabinet, and nine in 1963. The up-grading of the Ministry of Defence in 1964 and the accompanying disappearance of the three Service Ministers introduced a decade in which the numbers dropped down, as departments were merged, to nil in 1975. In the spring of 1977 only one Minister falls into this category – the Minister for Overseas Development – and that post is part of the team answerable to the Secretary of State for Foreign and Commonwealth Affairs.

There have never been many Ministers outside the Cabinet without regular departmental duties, but since the late fifties such a Minister has been particularly rare. This, and the near disappearance of departmental heads outside the Cabinet discussed in the previous paragraph, throws into clearer relief the remarkable growth of what is being called, in this essay, the category of 'intermediate Ministers'.

A Minister outside the Cabinet who, whatever his title, is in fact attached to a department, who regards the head of such department as his chief, and whose standing is at some intermediate level between that of his chief, on the one hand, and that of the junior Ministers – the Parliamentary Secretaries – on the other hand, is for our purposes an intermediate Minister. Such Ministers were never numerous before the Second World War: the three clearest examples were the Financial Secretary to the Treasury (whose role had for more than half a century been regarded with special respect on account of its integral importance and also because tradition indicated that a man who was made

Financial Secretary was firmly on the ladder leading to the Cabinet) and the Secretaries for Mines and for Overseas Trade, each of whom presided over sub-departments of the Board of Trade. All these received somewhat higher salaries than Parliamentary Secretaries. Since 1945, and more especially since 1957, however, a much more numerous intermediate fraternity has been developed. Most members of it have been or are now called Ministers of State, but some have had quite specific titles peculiar to particular departments, such as Ministers of Defence (after 1964), Chief and Economic Secretaries to the Treasury, Minister of Planning and Local Government, Minister for Aerospace, and so on. Moreover, on several occasions holders of the Paymaster-Generalship, of the Chancellorship of the Duchy of Lancaster, and of the post of Minister without Portfolio have been allotted to departments in this sort of intermediate position. It is not surprising that there developed a variety of salaries payable to Ministers in this class, but since 1972 uniformity has been established.[10]

The extent of growth of these intermediate posts has been dramatic. From only two or three in the Attlee Administration, there came to be seven in 1957, fifteen by the end of the Conservative Government in 1964, and a peak of 28 in 1975, dropping only to 26 in early 1977. Much the greatest part of all the growth of the cadre of 'administrative' Ministers in the last twenty years can be attributed to the build-up of this intermediate tier. It is a pointer to the future career patterns of senior Ministers that two-thirds of the members of the Cabinet in April 1977 had served spells in intermediate posts.

When Mr Macmillan formed his Administration at the beginning of 1957, it was possible to describe the shape of that Administration as fairly typical of the post-1945 era. The Cabinet did not include ten senior Ministers, most being heads of departments and one or two being non-departmental. Every department had a Parliamentary Secretary (to have two was not unknown but can fairly be said to have been unusual): there was a mere handful of what are called here 'intermediate' Ministers, and they were concentrated in only five departments. The range in the size of departments was, as always, very considerable but, excluding the Post Office and the Defence departments and their political heads, twenty senior Ministers (Cabinet members plus heads of departments outside the Cabinet) presided over the efforts of 296,000 civil servants. Two decades later the position is markedly different. In the spring of 1977 Mr Callaghan leads a Cabinet from which only one (quasi) departmental head is excluded. All but two or three small departments have either one, two or even three intermediate Ministers and, except in two special cases, every department has from one to four Parliamentary Secretaries. Excepting defence (the Post Office having disappeared from the scene), twenty-four senior Ministers have authority over 476,000 civil servants.

In the course of adapting to growth, an apparently acceptable – and therefore successful – constitutional innovation, the intermediate Minister, has been consolidated. Almost all departments have grown larger, some of them much larger; but except in the case of defence there are obviously some special problems revolving round the relationship of administrative structure and political objectives, which raise severe doubts as to the viability of such huge unitary departments as Trade and Industry, Environment, and Health and Social Security. And while the device of double-banking seems to be not unsuccessful in the special and rather plural areas of Treasury and 'central' jurisdiction, and in foreign affairs, its extension into big, unitary, domestic departments seems to underline the difficulties of preserving those departments, rather than to provide greater stability. If it is hard to envisage any massive reduction in the scope of central government and of its individual administrative units in the readily foreseeable future, it is equally hard to see any early abandonment or serious modification of the role of intermediate Ministers. But it is no easier to be confident that 'super', unitary, domestic departments and 'double-banking' at them will be more than two relatively short-lived contributions to the continuous search for optimal arrangement of the central administration.

NOTES AND REFERENCES

1   For a detailed study of its growth see D. N. Chester and F. M. G. Willson, *The Organisation of British Central Government, 1914–56* (Royal Institute of Public Administration, 1957); 2nd ed., *1914–64* (RIPA, 1968).

2   Cd 9230, 1918.

Haldane	*Heath*
1. Finance	Treasury
2. National Defence	Ministry of Defence
3. External Affairs	Foreign and Commonwealth Office
4. Research and Information	[No real equivalent]
5. Production (including Agriculture, Forestry, and Fisheries), Transport and Commerce	Department of Trade and Industry, Ministry of Agriculture, Fisheries and Food. [Forestry Commission] Transport within Department of the Environment
6. Employment	Department of Employment
7. Supplies	Within Ministry of Defence and Department of the Environment
8. Education	Department of Education and Science
9. Health	Department of Health and Social Security

50 *Policy and Politics*

	Haldane	Heath
10.	Justice	Lord Chancellor's Department and Home Office
	Plus	Civil Service Department
		Posts and Telecommunications
		Scotland, Wales and Northern Ireland

3 In March 1974 the newly separate Minister of Overseas Development was outside the Cabinet. In June 1975 the Secretary of State for Foreign and Commonwealth Affairs was given the additional title of Minister of Overseas Development: at the same time Mr Reg Prentice, while retaining his seat in the Cabinet, became a Minister of State in the Foreign and Commonwealth Office with the title of Minister for Overseas Development and with responsibility delegated by the Secretary of State to run the separate Department of Overseas Development. On Mr Prentice's resignation from the Government in December 1976 the post reverted to one held outside the Cabinet but still with the status of a Minister of State at the Foreign and Commonwealth Office and the same title and departmental jurisdiction.

4 The Northern Ireland Office, which was established early in 1972 as a result of the decision to dismantle the Stormont system, makes a comparison of total major departments a little unfair. Nineteen would be the more strictly comparable number to that of fifteen in 1971.

5 A very convenient source of numbers at 1 April 1973 is an appendix to the essay by Sir Richard Clarke on 'The Machinery of Government', in Wm. Thornhill (ed.), *The Modernization of British Government* (London, 1975).

6 An early and still highly relevant analysis of the phenomenon was contributed by D. N. Chester, 'Double Banking and Deputy Ministers', in *New Society*, 11 June 1964.

7 Sir Richard Clarke, *New Trends in Government*, Civil Service College Studies No. 1 (HMSO, 1971). See also the essay cited in note 5; an article on 'The Number and Size of Government Departments', in *Political Quarterly* 43, 2 (1972) pp. 169–86; Paul Draper, *Creation of the D.O.E.*, Civil Service Studies No. 4, HMSO (London, 1977); and A. Clark, 'Ministerial Supervision and the Size of the Department of the Environment', *Public Administration* 55, pp. 197–204 (Summer 1977).

8 *New Trends in Government*, pp. 1–2, 4.

9 For an examination of this growth, see the writer's article 'The Parliamentary Executive, 1868–1914, and after', in *Public Administration* 52, 3 (Autumn 1974) pp. 263–83.

10 Ministerial and Other Salaries Act 1972.

5 Police Accountability Revisited

GEOFFREY MARSHALL

Fifteen years after the Report of the Royal Commission on the Police seems an opportune occasion to review one of the central issues about the police role debated with some fervour between 1959 and 1964 and as yet unresolved. In what way and to whom should the police be accountable for their activities? The machinery of law enforcement, it is clear, presents special and confusing problems for any theory of democratic accountability. If we divide the functions of government into legislative, executive and judicial, how should we classify the police and especially the prosecutorial function? If it is an executive function those who exercise it ought in principle to be answerable to some elected body. But elected bodies are political bodies and our instincts suggest that partisan influences should be kept at a distance from law enforcement and that the decisions involved should be in some sense taken impartially. Could the function then be considered a judicial one? The judicial function certainly provides a model for impartial decision-making, since we do not suppose that judges should be answerable to elected representatives. But prosecuting is plainly not a judicial function and calling it a 'quasi-judicial function' is unhelpful since 'quasi' is simply a label for indecision. (When lawyers and administrators use the word 'quasi' it simply means 'not exactly' or 'after a fashion'.) So perhaps we are faced here with a function that is *sui generis*, or a fourth element in terms of the traditional political scientist's categorisation of governmental functions – one that calls both for a measure of accountability and a measure of independence. The dilemma was aptly described in the Hunt Report on the Police in Northern Ireland in 1969.[1] The Police Commissioner, it was said, 'should not be subjected to political pressures' but on the other hand there 'should be some body representative of the community as a whole to which he can be accountable'. The problem, it may be noted, is a general one that is not confined to any particular system of police organisation. It arises as between a national police force and a national legislature and executive as much as it raises an issue for a local or regional body with its police committee on the one hand and its police force on the other. The question can be posed, moreover, both as a legal question and as an issue of constitutional and administrative morality.

THE CONTROVERSY OF 1959–64

Surprisingly enough, no concerted debate on police accountability seems to have arisen before the late 1950s, although in the latter years of the nineteenth century control over police operations in London had raised the issue of the Metropolitan Commissioner's responsibility to the Home Secretary (as police authority for the metropolitan force). Outside London disagreements between county and borough police authorities and their chief officers had been rare. In 1959, however, a brief contest of wills in Nottingham brought to the surface two contrasting views about the independence of chief police officers *vis-à-vis* the county and borough police authorities. The issue in Nottingham turned upon a refusal by the Chief Constable to report to the Watch Committee on certain inquiries being made into the activities of council members and officers. The Town Clerk and Watch Committee considered the inquiries to have manifested a lack of impartiality on the Chief Constable's part and in view of his refusal to comply with their instructions suspended him from duty in exercise of their powers under the Municipal Corporations Act of 1882 – legislation which authorised watch committees to suspend or dismiss any constable whom they considered negligent or otherwise unfit for his duty. At this point the Home Secretary intervened and informed the Watch Committee that he did not consider the suspension justified and that in enforcing the criminal law a chief officer of police should not be subject to control or interference by the police authority. This was an explicit assertion by the Home Office of the view that a chief constable, like any constable, held an independent position as an officer of the Crown. The point had been successfully put by an earlier Home Secretary, Sir John Anderson. 'The policeman', he wrote, 'is nobody's servant . . . he executes a public office under the Law and it is the Law . . . which is the policeman's master.'[2] Legal support for this view was drawn from the absence of any master and servant relationship between police officers and police authorities. In 1930 in *Fisher* v. *Oldham Corporation*[3] it had been held that the Watch Committee could not be made liable for the wrongful actions of constables in carrying out their law enforcement duties as (to use the words of Mr Justice McCardie) 'servants of the state' and 'officers of the Crown or central power'.

The implications of this thesis did not commend themselves to the local authority associations, and when the Willink Commission began taking evidence in 1961 the Municipal Corporations Association and a number of other witnesses argued strongly that the supervisory powers of watch committees were not as narrow as had been implied; that the Oldham and Nottingham cases were in many ways special cases, and that they could not be used as foundations for a general theory of police independence in all matters of law enforcement. In 1960 the doubts of many who were involved in local government were voiced by the editor of *Public Administration*, Norman Chester.[4] Most people who spoke of law enforcement, he wrote, were thinking of particular cases, and no councillor or watch committee would claim to interfere in individual cases relating to the charging of offenders or would seek to instruct a chief constable not to enforce certain branches of the law; but since they had a duty to ensure that their area was efficiently policed might they not have a general concern with seeing that the law was adequately and properly enforced? Suppose that a chief constable were making no attempt to put down widespread public disorder, or the police were reacting in an over-violent way to political demonstrations, or were ignoring traffic offences, would the watch committee be helpless and could they not in such circumstances properly issue instructions to secure the proper enforcement of the law? Since the law itself gave no precise guidance as to general policies of enforcement what could it mean to say that the chief constable was 'answerable to the law alone'? If a chief constable were entirely independent, in what sense could police be said to be a local authority function?[5]

One other sceptic who gave evidence to the Commission was Professor E. C. S. Wade, editor of Dicey's *Law of the Constitution* and Downing Professor of the Laws of England at Cambridge University. Professor Wade suggested that the prosecuting discretion of a chief constable was not peculiar to him 'since anyone can normally start a prosecution on his own initiative and therefore there is nothing exceptional in a local police authority requiring the police to carry out this duty since each has an equal responsibility for it.'[6] The police authority, he added, could not be absolved from responsibility for enforcement of the law. The maintenance of public order was an executive function not requiring the freedom from interference attaching to judicial functions. In relation to some questions of law enforcement policy (such, conceivably, as the excessive use of force in maintaining order) it would not be *ultra vires* for the watch committee to issue instructions to the chief constable.

These views were not accepted by the police or by the Government in so far as they thought about the issue. The Royal Commission certainly thought about it, but what exactly their thoughts were never became clear. Two different questions arose and neither was clearly resolved by the Commission. First, what did statute and common law have to say, if anything, about the legal relationships of police and police authorities? Did it establish the independence of chief officers in all matters of law enforcement and the impropriety of all instructions even on matters of general policy? Secondly, what, irrespective of the legal position, ought sound administrative practice or constitutional morality to suggest as a proper relationship between police and an elected supervisory authority? Two further questions now need to be put. One is whether the 1964 police legislation that followed the Royal Commission, or any subsequent development, has changed the law. The other is whether anything has happened since 1964 that might affect views about sound or prudent administrative practice. In 1965 in a work entitled *Police and Government* the present writer, perhaps rashly, asserted that both the legal and political arguments for police independence were historically unsound and had been formulated in an exaggerated way. The conclusions that seemed appropriate at that time were set out as follows:

(1)   The legal independence of constables implies that supervisory bodies could not issue instructions that would amount to interferences with the course of justice or that would involve a chief officer who obeyed them in any breach of a duty clearly imposed upon him by statute or common law. An order to release an arrested felon (an example given in *Fisher* v. *Oldham*) or partisan interference in routine prosecution matters would obviously constitute illegal interference.

(2)   In matters of prosecution policy, whilst any intervention by a police committee would as a matter of strong convention and sound administrative practice normally be by way of advice, question or exhortation, no legal principle ruled out the possibility of an instruction framed in general terms (the position being in principle the same in the provinces as in the metropolitan relationship between the Home Secretary and the Metropolitan Police).

(3)   In matters other than prosecution, involving the disposition of police forces and law enforcement generally, an effective intervention by way of police authority directions was not unlawful and might in some cases be desirable if there were to be effective accountability for the exercise of executive discretion by the police.

But a question which cannot now be avoided is whether in 1977 all or any of these conclusions can still stand in the light of developments in the past decade. It may be advisable to approach the issue first from the standpoint of legal development and secondly from the standpoint of constitutional and administrative morality.

THE INDEPENDENCE OF CONSTABLES: THE LEGAL ISSUE

The argument about the misreading of *Fisher*'s case in assessing the degree of independence enjoyed by chief officers in the exercise of their constabulary functions need not be recapitulated in detail.[7] It amounted to saying that the thesis propounded in recent years on the basis of civil liability cases in England and in Commonwealth jurisdictions[8] was ill-founded and novel. The doctrine of constabulary independence in all law-enforcement matters was not, in fact, a well-established constitutional principle, but, on the contrary, one of which it is difficult to find any trace at all in the nineteenth and early twentieth centuries either in the metropolis or in the provinces. The metropolitan relationship is particularly significant since it has figured prominently in the only recent case about the exercise of police discretion, *R.* v. *Metropolitan Police Commissioner ex parte Blackburn*.[9] Though the exact chronology is unclear there had obviously been a change in the Home Office view of the Secretary of State's powers in relation to operational matters arising in the metropolitan area. In the nineteenth century there was never any doubt about the Home Secretary's right to issue instructions in matters of law enforcement. Home Secretaries such as Sir William Harcourt and Henry Matthews insisted upon and gave effect to the doctrine that it was for the Secretary of State to decide how far he should go in exercising his responsibility for what Matthews called the 'general policy of the police in the discharge of their duty'.[10] Many pertinent examples of intervention in police operations could be given. In 1880 the Home Secretary directed that no action should be taken to suppress advertisements for Irish lotteries. In 1881 Harcourt said that he had instructed that *agents provocateurs* were not to be used without his authority and in 1888 he insisted that whether public meetings were to be allowed or prohibited in the metropolis was 'a question of policy for the Home Secretary to decide'. In 1913 the Home Office told the Commissioner that proceedings were not to be instituted against whist drives except where there was evidence of serious gambling or profiteering.[11] In fact it could reasonably be concluded that 'the authority of the Home Secretary over the Metropolitan Police was regarded as unlimited, subject of course to the normal principle that public officers cannot be ordered to act unlawfully'.[12] No one supposed that any conflict arose between lawful instructions relating to law enforcement or prosecution policy and the original independent common law status of constables in the metropolis.

One fact is perhaps worth noting about the examples of intervention here cited, namely that they involved for the most part either public

order, or cases where the law was unclear or the morality of its enforcement a matter of dispute. Such cases are of course precisely those where
advocates of greater accountability might want to argue that the
exercise of discretion should be subject to challenge through some
mechanism of accountability. By the 1930s, however, the Home Office
seems to have begun to disclaim responsibility. Conceivably, they had
by then breathed in the spirit of *Fisher* v. *Oldham*. Possibly also they were
motivated by a desire to ward off Parliamentary questions directed to
the Home Secretary. When the Home Office came to give evidence to
the Willink Commission in 1960 they went as far as to say that the
Home Secretary 'could not be questioned . . . about the discharge by
individual police officers of the duties of law enforcement'. Any glance
at the index to *Hansard* would reveal that there is something amiss with
this statement. In fact the 1929 and 1963 Royal Commissions on Police
were both set up as the result of persistent parliamentary questioning
of Home Secretaries about the discharge by individual police officers
of their duties of law enforcement,[13] as also were the special inquiries
into actions undertaken by the Thurso Police in 1959,[14] the Sheffield
Police in 1963[15] and the Challenor case in the Metropolitan force in
1965.[16]

Outside the metropolitan area a parallel development took place. In
the nineteenth century, borough watch committees frequently treated
themselves as being competent to issue general instructions on matters
of policing. A good example is the action of the Liverpool Watch
Committee in 1890 which issued orders to the Head Constable, Sir
William Nott-Bower, 'to proceed against all brothels at present known
to the police without any undue delay and such proceedings shall be
by way of prosecution'. Sir William saw nothing improper in this. In
a public speech he remarked that the police 'were not responsible for
Policy or for Results. Policy was made for them, not by them.' The
police, he added, 'should be judged by the simple test of whether they
carried out their duties in a fair and honest manner in accordance with
the policy laid down for them by superior authority, which authority
alone must take the responsibility both for it and for its results'.[17] Can
it have been *Fisher's* case alone that brought about a change of heart
on the part of the police and the Home Office (though not on the part
of the local authority associations)? All that *Fisher's* case essentially
decided was that no action in tort for a constable's wrongful acts would
lie against anybody but him. Since no vicarious liability could be fixed
upon those who appointed him he could not be in a master-servant
relationship for civil liability purposes. Since there was almost a
complete absence of any decided cases directly bearing on the
constitutional status of the police, it may have been natural enough for
the decision in *Fisher's* case (to the effect that the police were not

'servants' for purposes of vicarious liability) to be picked out by textbook writers and others and given a wider significance than it deserved.

Since 1964 the police have in effect become for civil liability purposes 'servants' beyond a doubt since responsibility for their wrongful acts is now borne by the Chief Constable. S.48 of the 1964 Police Act provides that the chief officer of police for any police area

> shall be liable in respect of torts committed by constables under his direction and control in the performance or purported performance of their functions in like manner as a master is liable in respect of torts committed by his servants in the course of their employment.

The imposition of this 'servitude' upon constables as an incident of the law of tort is, however, as much or as little relevant to the constitutional status of constables as was its denial in *Fisher's* case. If *Fisher's* case had really been the foundation of the constable's autonomy then the Act of 1964 must have enslaved him again. In fact, neither the one nor the other helps to delimit the scope of the lawful orders or the degree of constitutional subordination to which constables are subject. It is clear, of course, that constables cannot be given orders to do what it would be unlawful for anyone to do or what would amount to an obstruction of the course of justice if done by them. A police constable is a person who, although not a Crown servant, holds an office under Her Majesty.[18] The oath that he takes on assuming the office is to serve in the office of constable without favour or affection, to cause the peace to be kept and to discharge all his duties according to law. What acts he may lawfully be required to do depends upon the statutes and regulations that govern police organisation and upon the powers conferred on police authorities and chief constables.

HAS THE LAW CHANGED?

Could it be argued that any change in the constitutional position was effected by the 1964 Police Act? The answer would seem to be that it left the law in this respect unchanged. The legislation was based, with some exceptions, on the recommendations of the Willink Commission. The Commission's report, though not a model of clarity, certainly suggests that they did not accept all the implications drawn by the Home Office and the police from the *Fisher* case. Indeed one section of the report is even given the title 'Subordination of Chief Constables to Democratic Supervision'. The supervision the Commission had in mind was related to what they called 'police policies in matters affecting the public interest' – the regulation for example of traffic, political demonstrations, strikes, processions and public order generally. The Commission argued that such policies, though involving the enforcement of the law, 'do not require the immunity from external influences that is generally thought necessary in regard to the enforcement of the law in particular cases'.[19] Various provisions were made in the 1964 Act to increase accountability to local police authorities and to the Home Secretary. Both were given formal powers to request reports from Chief Constables, but there was no obvious alteration in the police authorities' direct powers in the field of law enforcement as they existed before the Act. The Act provided that police forces should be under the direction and control of the chief officer, but since chief constables had always exercised the immediate operational direction and control of their forces these words do not seem intended to alter the pre-existing situation. It is noticeable that nothing was enacted directly about the *exclusive* control of the chief constable or the nature of his powers *vis-à-vis* the police authority. What really happened was that the Government avoided this direct issue, in view of the inherent difficulty of framing any precise prescription, and relied upon the Home Secretary's powers to act as a potential buffer and arbitrator between police authorities and chief constables.

Perhaps the most significant legal development touching on to the exercise of police powers since 1964 has been the decision of the Court of Appeal in *Ex parte Blackburn*.[20] The questions at issue here were whether the courts could control the exercise of police discretion in prosecuting and whether the police owed a duty to the public to enforce the law. Surprisingly, an affirmative answer was given to both questions. It was held that a policy instruction by the Metropolitan Police Commissioner not to enforce the provisions of the Betting and Gaming legislation could, had it not been withdrawn, have been controlled by the issue of *mandamus*. It was not asserted that a breach of the duty to enforce the law could be inferred from the mere existence of a policy of non-prosecution (as for example when prosecutions were not brought in relation to attempted suicide or juvenile sexual offences).[21] But some policies, it was suggested, would be improper (for example an instruction not to prosecute any person for stealing goods worth less than £100). In the course of the decision, however, both Lord Denning and Lord Justice Salmon made remarks about the status of the Metropolitan Police Commissioner *vis-à-vis* the Metropolitan Police authority, suggesting amongst other things that he was not subject to the orders of the Home Secretary. 'No minister of the Crown', Lord Denning remarked, 'can tell him that he must or must not keep observation on this place or that; or that he must or must not prosecute this man or that one, nor can any police authority tell him so.' Like every Chief Constable, 'he is not the servant of anyone save of the law itself. The responsibility for law enforcement lies on him. He is answerable to the law and to the law alone.'[22]

Can any weight be placed on these remarks? Both Salmon LJ and Lord Denning said clearly that it would be impermissible for the Secretary of State to issue any order to the police in respect of law enforcement.[23] But it was by no means clear on what this view was based except the insistence on the responsibility of the Commissioner to the law. This runs together questions about interferences in individual prosecution matters and questions about law enforcement policies and the deployment of forces generally. It is fairly plain that these categorical suggestions were merely repetitions of the orthodox and arguably mistaken inferences from *Fisher's* case. In any event the points were not in issue. It was unnecessary to decide what the relations of the Home Secretary and the Commissioner were or what the relations of chief constables to police authorities were. The question for decision was simply how far the admitted obligation to enforce the law was subject to judicial control. That in a proper case it would be was the *ratio decidendi* of the decision and it seems justifiable to treat the tangential views of Lord Denning and Lord Justice Salmon on the powers of police authorities and the Secretary of State as being *obiter*.

One other episode since 1964 deserves mention since it reinforces the traditional thesis that the initiation of prosecutions in England is in some sense an act of the private citizen. In 1974 a police constable (P.C. Joy) successfully pursued a private prosecution of a Member of Parliament which his superior officers were unwilling to authorise and in consequence of which it was reported that he might be made subject to disciplinary action. No action was taken, but it need not be the case that such action would necessarily have been legally improper. No one could have prevented Mr Joy as a private person from starting his prosecution. But it does not follow from that that his freedom so to act as a member of a disciplined force subject to a statutory scheme of organisation and regulation could not properly be curtailed by his superiors under powers given in the police legislation. So although Joy's case perhaps illustrates the wisdom of the English (as against the American and Scottish) system in not permitting the state to mono-polise the prosecution function, it adds nothing to the argument about the relative powers of constables and police authorities, especially in law-enforcement matters other than prosecution.

It seems fair to conclude that neither the 1964 Act nor any subse-quent development has changed the law on this subject or given the police any legal immunity from control which they did not enjoy before 1964. If that is so the legal argument for autonomy so frequently based upon *Fisher's* case remains as defective and unreliable as it always was.

c

Perhaps, however, that is not the most significant feature of the situation that now faces us.

ACCOUNTABILITY AND INDEPENDENCE IN PRACTICE

Frequently there is in the British system a difference between the law and the constitution. The law may say one thing, but the political and moral rules followed in practice may differ. Even if it is the case that the issuing of instructions by police committees in matters affecting law enforcement is not unlawful we still need to ask whether it would be a defensible or desirable administrative practice. And in asking that question in 1977 it may be necessary to take heed of some considerations that were not present twenty years earlier. In 1959 anyone who believed in the value of local control of administration and in democratic accountability could well believe in the need for greater control of police discretion. Situations could even be conceived where, in the interests of more effective or uniform or equitable law enforcement, even positive instructions might be justified. Few would have believed that instructions relating to the institution or withdrawal of particular prosecutions could ever be justified. But general policies related to prosecution and matters of public importance outside the field of prosecution affecting police operations and the disposal of police forces and resources could be conceived as potential areas in which police authorities might properly exercise influence and in the last resort exert control.

All such feelings are, however, contingent upon a number of assumptions about the processes of politics and administration at a particular time. One especially important unspoken premise is that the executive officers and elected persons through whom democratic control is exerted can be assumed to be by and large uncorrupt. But our experience in the last decade raises a serious question as to whether that pristine assumption can still be made. Nothing in British politics and administration is quite what it was in 1959 or ever will be. Suppose it to be the case that we cannot automatically assume that elected politicians will respect the rule of law, or reject bribes or refrain from exploiting their positions for self-interested or party-political, or even corrupt and unlawful, ends. Suppose that Watergates, Poulsons and Clay Crosses are not unique and unrepeatable phenomena. Nobody's faith in councillors or Congressmen or Members of Parliament can now be as firmly held as it was fifteen years ago.

What is the moral? Perhaps that democratic theory no longer gives a simple or straightforward answer here any more than it does in other fields. In many areas such as financial and economic regulation (including such issues as control of the money supply and health and safety requirements) there may be a tension between technical judgement and political preference or necessity. The long-run interests and rights of citizens may well be furthered by the construction of buttresses against some kinds of overt political pressures, even when exerted honestly and in the name of democratic majorities. The occasional frustration of such majority pressures may be required by the need to protect civil liberties and secure the impartial treatment of individuals. Bills of Rights are a standing acknowledgement of this. If therefore in the field of law enforcement we have to give a calculated and un-prejudiced answer in 1977 to the question whether civil liberties and impartial justice are more to be expected from chief constables than from elected politicians (whether on police committees or in the House of Commons or in ministerial departments) many liberal democrats would feel justified in placing more trust in the former than in the latter. If that is so then whether or not the theory of police independence as traditionally set out has any sound legal foundation (and it almost certainly has not) it may be possible to defend it as a constitutional and administrative convention.

Such a convention would suggest that direct orders, whether of a positive or negative kind, whether related to prosecution or other law-enforcement measures, and whether related to individual cases or to general policies, ought to be avoided by police authorities even when they involve what the Royal Commission called 'police policies in matters which vitally concern the public interest'.

TWO STYLES OF ACCOUNTABILITY

Where would such a formula leave the notion of police accountability and what would be its corollaries? Like all conventions it is of course vague at its edges. Questions can be asked, for example, about the borderline between the enforcement of law and order and the logistical issues involved in the management of police resources that are legitimate matters for political concern and financial control.

In the area of law enforcement itself the implication of independence from direct control is that accountability must take a different form. Other areas of British administration besides policing have shown a need for a form of accountability that differs from the familiar type of ministerial and political responsibility that might be dubbed the 'subordinate and obedient' mode in which the supervisor's responsibility is typically accompanied by administrative control and the ability to direct and veto. In contrast a style of accountability that might be called the 'explanatory and co-operative' mode has emerged

in some areas such as the relationships between independent commercial or regulatory bodies on one hand and Ministers and the House
of Commons on the other. Something like this style of accountability
to Parliament is written into the 1964 Police Act provisions for parliamentary questioning. The Home Secretary's responsibility to Parliament for policing throughout the country is one that rests not on an
ability to issue orders but on the capacity to require information,
answers and reasons that can then be analysed and debated in
Parliament and in the press.

The corollary of a conventional constabulary immunity from
mandatory instructions ought to be that explanatory accountability is
not confined within any particular bounds. There may be occasions on
which it should extend even in prosecution matters to particular cases
of prosecution or non-prosecution as well as general policies.

If we examine the central and local machinery that was set up in
1964 and subsequently modified by police reorganisation we cannot
conclude that it is ideally adapted to the exercise of explanatory
accountability. In some degree this is perhaps more the fault of elected
members than of the legislative machinery. The Police Act provisions
for requesting and debating reports from chief constables on the
policing of their areas have not been extensively used either in the
House of Commons or in local councils.[24] In the new district councils
to which many of the former cities and boroughs have been reduced
by local government reorganisation these powers cannot be used at all.
Nor does there appear to have been much significant debate at the
local level of either annual police estimates or of the decisions or
activities of police committees. This was a particular difficulty of the
combined police area where police committees were composed of
representatives drawn from a number of constituent councils.[25] It ought
in principle to be less difficult since 1974 with more police committees
drawn from a single elected body.[26] As to police committees it is
difficult to believe that in the past ten years they have been effective
instruments for carrying out the duties (for example those related to
complaints against the police) that were placed upon them by the 1964
Act.

The Police Act 1976 and the various regulations made under it have
now introduced into the machinery of police accountability a new
entity, the Police Complaints Board. Its purpose, however, is to provide
a mechanism for the independent review of existing disciplinary
procedures related to the activities of individual constables. Whether it
succeeds in this task or not, it is not a body which provides a forum for
complaints against collective activities or force policies of the kind that
were mentioned in the Royal Commission report as being subject to
potential challenge. It may be that a gap remains to be filled by some

body that would act in a manner analogous to that of the Press Council, the BBC Complaints Panel or the parliamentary and local government Complaints Commissioners. These provide a clear example of explanatory accountability in that without any power to bind or reverse executive decisions they provide an avenue for challenge, for the requiring of reasoned explanation and for advice and recommendation. The subjection of professional judgement and administrative discretion to this form of challenge and publicity is a relatively novel experiment in British administration, and it seems a mode of accountability well adapted to the area of law enforcement. When the Ombudsman system was introduced at the national level in 1967 there was a deliberate decision to exclude from it the operations of the independent public corporations, the Health Services, local government and the police. Almost all these omissions have now been made good but the police exception remains. The Police Complaints Panel as now constituted does not provide what is needed to round off the machinery of public accountability for executive action. Law-enforcement policy is made by the exercise of executive discretion but it requires a special style of accountability which our institutions have not as yet fully succeeded in providing.

NOTES AND REFERENCES
1 Cmnd 535 (1969).
2 'The Police', *Public Administration* 7 (1929) p. 192.
3 (1930) 2 KB 364.
4 *Public Administration* 38 (1960) pp. 11–15. For similar views see the Minutes of Evidence in the *Report of the Royal Commission on the Police*, Cmnd 1728 (1962), Days 11–12, pp. 630–1 and 668–72.
5 See *Public Administration* 38 (1960), 'The Independence of Chief Constables' by Bryan Keith-Lucas, p. 1; and 'Some Questions' by D. N. Chester, p. 11.
6 Cmnd 1728, Minutes of Evidence, Appendix 11, pp. 33–4. The right of private prosecution is of course a right exercised in England and Wales. Scotland, like the United States, gives a practical monopoly to what are in effect public or state prosecutors. How far this fact modifies the conclusions drawn in England and Wales about the position of the police perhaps requires more discussion than it has had. The rights of private prosecutors, including the police, are now circumscribed in England and Wales by a considerable number of statutes requiring leave to be given by the Attorney-General or the Director of Public Prosecutions. For a complete list of statutes containing such restrictions see *Hansard*, 14 Mar 1977. Cf. J. Ll. Edwards, *The Law Officers of the Crown* (1964) pp. 237–46 and 396–401; and Bernard M. Dickens, 'The Prosecuting Roles of the Attorney-General and Director of Public Prosecutions', *Public Law*, spring 1974, pp. 50–73.

7   See G. Marshall, *Police and Government* (1965) ch. 3, and 'Police Responsibility', *Public Administration* 38 (1960) pp. 213–26.
8   Other cases such as *A.G. for N.S. Wales* v. *Perpetual Trustee Co.* (1952) 85 CLR 237; (1955) AC 457 indicate that constables are not servants in that their employers cannot recover against third parties for loss of their 'services'. But 'servant', 'serve' and 'service' are many-coloured terms and it is hazardous to draw any direct implications about subjection to lawful superior orders from the use of these terms in different contexts. Compare for example the situations of civil servants, judges and soldiers, all of whom 'serve' the Crown in some sense, though not the same sense.
9   (1968) 2 QB 118.
10   330 *Parl. Deb.*, 3rd ser., col. 1174. See G. Marshall, *Police and Government*, ch. 2, pp. 29–32 and 53–4. Cf. Sir Frank Newsam, *The Home Office* (1925) p. 104.
11   See R. Plehwe, 'Police and Government: The Commissioner of Police for the Metropolis', *Public Law*, winter 1974, pp. 316–35.
12   Plehwe, p. 332.
13   For the episodes leading to the 1929 Commission see Cmnd 3147, 1928 (*Inquiry in regard to the Interrogation by the Police of Miss Savidge*).
14   *Report of the Tribunal appointed to Inquire into the Allegation of Assault on John Waters* (Cmnd 718, 1959).
15   *Sheffield Police Appeal Inquiry* (Cmnd 2176, 1963).
16   *Report of Inquiry by Mr A. E. James, QC* (Cmnd 2735, 1965).
17   Sir William Nott-Bower, *Fifty Two Years a Policeman* (1926) p. 145.
18   *Lewis* v. *Cattle* (1938) 2 KB 454, 457.
19   *Report of the Royal Commission on the Police*, para. 91.
20   *R.* v. *Metropolitan Police Commissioner, ex parte Blackburn* (1968) 2 QB 118. On the issues raised by Blackburn's case see D. G. T. Williams, 'The Police and Law Enforcement', *Criminal Law Review* 58 (July 1968) pp. 351–62; and 'Prosecution, Discretion and the Accountability of the Police' in *Crime, Criminology and Public Policy* (ed. Roger Hood, 1974).
21   For a number of similar examples and of the uses of prosecutionary discretion generally see *The Decision to Prosecute* (1972) by A. E. Wilcox (a former Chief Constable of Hertfordshire); also Glanville Williams, 'Discretion in Prosecution', *Criminal Law Review* 3 (1956) pp. 222–31.
22   (1968) 2 QB 118 at 135–6.
23   For Salmon LJ's view see (1968) 2 QB at 138.
24   There is no easily available information on the use made by local police authorities and councils of their police powers. In Oxford City Council, for example, between 1964 and 1974 only one request was made for a report from the Chief Constable under S.12 of the 1964 Police Act. This may not be untypical.
25   On the effects of amalgamation on police committees cf. G. Marshall, 'The Government of the Police since 1964', in J. C. Alderson and P. T. Stead, *The Police We Deserve* (1973) pp. 59–60.
26   Some police comment has detected signs of more significant party organisation and party caucussing on county police committees drawn from a single local authority. This has even served to commend regional

police forces. ('The prospect of regionalisation presents the service with the opportunity of getting rid of some of its present ills, not least the growing influence of local politics': *Police Review*, 7 Jan 1977). There may be the beginning here of a reversal of the traditional arguments against a national police force. In the past many have assumed that it was local police forces that preserved England from political interference in law enforcement.

6 Central–Local Government Relations: Grants, Local Responsibility and Minimum Standards

G. W. JONES

THE CHESTER-LAYFIELD VIEW

Norman Chester welcomed the Layfield Report on Local Government Finance[1] with enthusiasm. He called it 'far more than a first class study of local finance'. He wrote: 'It is a document of considerable constitutional importance, for it is primarily concerned with political accountability in the British system of government.' He found it 'refreshing' that the report had a unity, which was 'derived from its emphasis on finding a political and administrative system which will give a much clearer answer than the present one to the question – where does responsibility lie?' He noted that, 'very courageously', the report posed two alternative sets of arrangements – 'one based mainly on central and one based mainly on local responsibility. This means either adopting a financial system which frankly recognises a need for strong central direction, or taking positive steps to increase the ability of local authorities to manage local affairs.'[2] Norman Chester showed that he, like the majority of the Layfield Committee, favoured the choice of greater local responsibility.

What he did not mention, however, was that the basic approach of the Committee was in fact a vindication of the thesis he had propounded in his book *Central and Local Government*, published in 1951,[3] and repeated in his evidence to the Committee in 1975.[4] He had begun research for his book as early as 1935, when the American Social Science Research Council asked him to examine the English experience of Exchequer grants to local authorities. The work was interrupted by his service in the Economic Section of the War Cabinet Secretariat, and was resumed in 1946 after his appointment as a Fellow of Nuffield College. As his investigations progressed he realised that he could not limit the inquiry to financial arrangements. It had to encompass the whole of relations between central and local government, constitutional, political and administrative. Similarly, the Layfield Committee, with the task of reviewing 'the whole system of local government finance', soon became aware that it could not be restricted to a technical treatise about rates and grants. Like Norman Chester, it concluded that local government financial arrangements should reflect the chosen relationship between the Government and local authorities. The nature of this relationship had to be considered and agreed first, before the appropriate financial system could be devised. Layfield argued: 'No system of local government finance can be regarded as wholly satisfactory unless it supports, in an unambiguous way, the desired pattern of relations.'[5]

The key concern of Norman Chester and the Layfield Committee was to promote responsible government, and for both, taxation was the crucial element. Drawing inspiration from the report of the Haldane Committee on the Machinery of Government,[6] Norman Chester in his evidence to the Layfield Committee urged that 'one cannot separate the function of raising money from that of spending it'.[7] The argument behind this assertion was laid out in *Central and Local Government*. 'Taxation is distasteful, whereas public expenditure is usually attractive – a combination of both is required to secure the proper balance – the praise and political power which an elected body gets from spending money on social and other services has to be measured against the direct political harm which the elected body may suffer when taxes corresponding to the expenditure have to be levied.'[8] In Layfield's view, too, 'responsible government meant whoever is responsible for deciding to spend more or less money on providing a service is also responsible for deciding whether to raise more or less taxation'.[9]

On the foundation of this principle Norman Chester developed the argument that there is no case for large sums to be paid by way of grants to local authorities, since to do so would offend against the concentration of money spending and money raising in the same hands.[10] In his book he opposed the use of grants to provide 'a general source of revenue' for local government, and advocated that 'additional independent sources of revenue' be made available to local authorities.[11] Rates were insufficient, too narrow and inflexible, and because of their inadequacy grant had increased. In his evidence Norman Chester felt that a local property tax was a perfectly good tax, as long as it was not asked to do too much, but if it were to remain viable and not be brought into disrepute, it needed to be supplemented with other local taxes.[12]

The majority of the Layfield Committee argued that grant was a key element in central – local financial arrangements. A high level of grant was acceptable if the main responsibility for local government expenditure and its financing were to lie with the central government. In that situation local government did not require any additional sources of tax revenue: rates could remain as the sole local tax. But if the main responsibility for local government expenditure and its financing were to lie with local government, then the level of grant had to be reduced and the gap filled by local taxes. Layfield did not propose the abolition of local rates; the Committee accepted the case for a local property tax, but felt it had reached the limits of political acceptability. It recommended a local income tax to replace part of the grant and to supplement rates. The target was to reduce grant from 65·5 per cent at least to 50 per cent;[13] in fact, the Committee found that if the objective of grant were limited simply to equalisation, to compensate for disparities in resources and spending needs, then grant could fall to 40 per cent of local revenue.[14] So the Layfield solution was that local income tax would take up the financing of the 25·5 per cent of local expenditure previously filled by grant. Both Norman Chester and the Layfield Committee majority focused on grant, believing that it 'severs the direct link between spending and taxing upon which sound democratic finance must be based', and that 'a greater measure of financial independence is essential if Local Authorities are not to be treated as agents of the Departments'.[15]

GRANTS AND LOCAL RESPONSIBILITY: THE CRITICISM

The Chester-Layfield position has come under formidable attack. It is argued that grant is not such an important element in central–local relationships, that a high level of grant does not undermine local government responsibility and that the Layfield choice was extremist and unduly polarised. A middle way of shared responsibility, with central and local government in partnership, is said to be more realistic. Joint responsibility, it is asserted, is compatible with a high level of grant and without recourse to a new source of local revenue.[16]

Critics have sought to undermine the basic assumption of Layfield that there is a connection between grant and responsible local decision making. They claim that theoretically there is none at all. If there were no grants and local authorities had to finance their expenditure totally out of their own taxes, that would not necessarily guarantee local responsibility, because the Government could still issue a large number of policy directives that could severely constrain local authorities. On the other hand, even if local authorities were financed totally out of grants, and the grant was in the form of a block general grant, without strings attached, local authorities would be free to spend the money as they wished. The source of the finance, it is suggested, is irrelevant. What matters for a local authority is to possess the freedom to spend the money, and it can be responsible to its voters for the way that money is spent.

It is further argued that the bulk of central controls over local government have little or nothing to do with finance, but arise from the Government's concern for policies and the attainment of national uniform and equal standards of provision throughout the country. The observation is also made that local authorities at the moment depend on central grant to varying degrees, some receiving as much as 90 per cent and others as little as 30 per cent,[17] but there is no evidence that the former are more tightly controlled from the centre than the latter.

This scepticism about the linkage between grant and local responsibility is widely held. Francis Cripps and Wynne Godley of the Department of Applied Economics at Cambridge allege that the 'fatal confusion' in Layfield's argument is that which 'supposes local autonomy to derive uniquely from its power to raise local taxes, thereby ignoring the autonomy that derives from a grant that is not hypothecated'.[18] The Labour Government's devolution proposals for Wales and Scotland in the Scotland and Wales Bill of November 1976 intend to finance their Assemblies through a 100 per cent block grant, which is deemed compatible with discretion over deciding on the priorities of spending the money. At the Conservative Party conference of October 1976 in Brighton the local government spokesman, Keith Speed, said: 'We question the basic assumption that the more money a council raises the more independent it feels. The view we Conservatives have is that the real independence of local authorities is seen in the discretion local councils have in deciding how they spend their money.'[19] Some local authorities, commenting on Layfield, declare that all that is needed is higher grant for them to spend as they wish. Grants, to them, do not seem to erode local responsibility.

There is also the argument that the higher the percentage of grant the more effective can be local responsibility. This argument is based on the 'gearing effect'.[20] In theory, a high level of block grant should help to make the local electorate aware of the expenditure decisions of local authorities by magnifying their influence on the rates. If rates contribute only a small proportion of an authority's income, any marginal increases in expenditure will have a disproportionately large impact on rate levels. For instance, if an authority which expects to spend £100 million receives a fixed block grant of £50 million, the remaining £50 million has to be raised from the rates. If the authority subsequently decides to spend 1 per cent more – £101 million – the extra million has to come entirely from the rates, which to meet this expenditure have to be raised to £51 million – an increase of 2 per cent. By contrast, if the block grant had been £75 million with rates having to meet only £25 million, then a similar 1 per cent increase in total expenditure would increase the rates by £1 million on £25 million, or 4 per cent. In the latter example the ratepayer would be faced with a percentage increase twice as large as in the former although the same increased expenditure is involved in each. Thus with a higher level of grant, 'the sensitivity of rates to local decisions on marginal expenditure has actually been increased'.[21]

GRANTS AND LOCAL RESPONSIBILITY: A REBUTTAL

The Layfield position is that where grant is a preponderant and growing part of local revenue the Government will accept increasing responsibility and ensure that it is spent in accordance with national policies and priorities.[22] The grant, after all, represents money that central departments have fought hard to obtain against the Treasury and other departments with their rival programmes. Each department seeks to advance the particular service it looks after – education, housing, social services or roads. Civil servants and ministers, having fought hard for grant on behalf of their service, are not likely to relinquish their concern with the money once it is handed over to local authorities to spend. As custodians of the taxpayers' money and as defenders and promoters of particular services they wish to ensure that the grant is spent on their services, as they said it would be. Civil servants also wish to protect their Minister from criticism in Parliament about the poor performance or inadequacies of services. A high grant, therefore, pulls the central officials to involve themselves in local affairs. Central civil servants and Ministers, observing the high level of grant, feel that they should intervene in local government matters. Similarly local authority officials and councillors, recognising the high level of grant, feel that they have little justification for resisting departmental pressures. Thus the key decision-makers, both centrally and locally, think that grant has control implications and behave as if it had too.[23]

However, a high grant may be significant, less for setting up pressures that push the central government to intervene in local government affairs and to assume responsibility, but much more for making local authorities feel less responsible. Local government responsibility is undermined by a high level of grant, and especially if it rises each year, because the attention of a local authority is turned more to the centre than to its voters in the local community. The size of the grant is more important to a local council than the wishes of local citizens. Through the 'gearing effect' quite a small change in the grant at the centre, in the total, in the formula and in the actual distribution can have major consequences locally, producing for some authorities an unexpected windfall and for others a dramatic shortfall even if they had all decided on similar increases of expenditure in that year.[24] In this situation neither the public nor elected members can assess whether the level or rate of change in the burden of local tax was the result of decisions of the local authority, or of central government or of fortuitous changes in the grant. A high level of grant in practice does not enable local taxes to reflect local spending decisions.[25]

The flaws in the argument that a grant of whatever level, even 100 per cent, does not undermine local responsibility as long as the grant is unhypothecated are that it is based on a restricted concept of responsibility and that it totally ignores the political consequences of a high grant. Cripps and Godley assume that responsibility can be meaningful simply if it relates to the distribution of a given level of expenditure between services. They ignore the wider view of responsibility which emphasises the need to focus at one point a variety of political pressures, not only those concerned about spending between different services but also those concerned about the financing of that expenditure and about the level of the expenditure itself. The Cambridge economists interpret responsibility narrowly and fail to take into account the political implications of the financial arrangements they advocate. Both central government and local authorities are elected; they have political bases and behave politically. They will seek political advantage for themselves from a grant system. When grant is high local authorities will try to place responsibility on the centre, claiming that local problems cannot be tackled because grant is inadequate. When it is so dependent on a large grant, that is also unstable, a local authority is transformed from a body that takes its own decisions in response to local pressures to become itself a pressure group on the centre urging more grant. It seeks to make out that it is a special case with distinctive features that the existing grant settlement has not taken account of. In turn the centre will respond with inspection to check up if the special case is justified and if the need to spend is present. So the departments are pulled into the detailed affairs of local authorities by a high level of grant. Indeed, Cripps and Godley urge that grant should be distributed on the basis of norms of standardised expenditure set for each authority.

In much the same way it can be predicted that if the Government's proposals for devolution in Scotland and Wales are carried out, then each year the Scottish and Welsh Assemblies will assert that their problems are so great that they require more grant than has been allocated from London. They will be encouraged to bid high since they will not have to face their electorates with proposals to raise taxes. Thus there will be each year a confrontation between London and Wales and Scotland over the level of the grant and the departments in London will be sucked into Scottish and Welsh affairs to tell the Assemblies that items of expenditure are or are not justifiable.

It should also be noted that the protracted and complex negotiations between central and local government over grant will have to be conducted by civil servants and local officials. Democratically elected representatives will be on the sidelines and engaged only at a late stage of ratification. Thus influence will slip away from representatives to appointees, further eroding local responsibility.

The argument that there is no linkage between grant and local responsibility because local authorities who vary in their dependence on grant do not exhibit similar variations in control is easily answered. The attitude of the central government is set by the total grant level and it does not discriminate between individual local authorities. It will not be conscious of the amount of grant received by each authority, but its general view of local government as a whole is shaped by its consciousness of a broad overall grant percentage. A lower percentage would discourage its propensity to intervene. As Norman Chester told the Layfield Committee: 'The trouble is that a good deal of the fussy controls owe little or nothing directly to the grant system, but they are made more defensible by the increasingly high proportion of local expenditure paid for out of Exchequer grants.'[26]

Layfield's proposal of a grant percentage of only 40 per cent envisages grant as performing one function only: equalisation. The Committee criticised the existing arrangements for loading on to the grant too many objectives, and urged that it should not be used for promoting particular services, nor as an instrument of economic management, nor to relieve the burden on certain classes of ratepayers. And like Norman Chester it disapproved of grant being used as a source of general revenue for local government. The objective of grant, to Layfield, was to put all local authorities on an equal footing to provide the same level of service for the same tax rate. It would, therefore, compensate local authorities for low resources and for high needs to spend. This objective is achieved now with a grant of 40 per cent: the remaining 25·5 per cent was a straightforward general subsidy in aid of rates. In the Layfield Report this remainder was to be replaced by local income tax. If the Government wanted to promote certain services it should do so, not by tinkering with the grant, but by explicit statutory direction; and for macro-economic management it should not manipulate the grant and induce instability but specifically design new instruments for that task. Layfield was able only to indicate a new approach and direction and to present examples observed on visits abroad.[27]

With a lower level of grant and more sources of revenue available to local authorities there would be less need to calculate grant with precision. One of the disadvantages of a high level of grant is that, because of the 'gearing effect', it is important to produce an accurate grant and so avoid instability in the local authority. But the continual search for more precision, for newer and better means of distribution and for calculating and measuring needs, is itself destabilising. With a smaller grant that would not loom so large in the life of a local council the grant-setting process could be simpler and more broad-brush than at present. There would be less need for a large rate-support-grant industry and the many working parties that pore over the figures, indulge in complex statistical exercises and search through the ramifications of regression analysis for a meaningless objectivity that is later tampered with for political reasons with devices like 'damping' and 'clawback'. Indeed, the exercise of determining grant could be made more comprehensible; decisions could be reached earlier; and the formula set further in advance so as to provide more stability and certainty in which local authorities could take their decisions.

The Layfield argument is subtle. It is not saying that a reduction of grant and the introduction of a local income tax will automatically guarantee local responsibility. The report states clearly that it would not be worth the expense and upheaval of doing so unless there was also a change of political attitude. There has to be a political will to make local responsibility work.[28] As Norman Chester told the Committee: 'There can be no major change, however, in the character and intensity of control without a major change in public attitude'; and in his book he stressed the importance of 'the working spirit' of the formal, legal and administrative relationships between central government and local authorities; there has to be a clear belief in the value of local government.[29] With the Layfield proposals, if this belief materialised then the financial arrangements would be designed to support and buttress local government responsibility, and not to undermine it, as the high grant does at the moment. Financial structures and procedures generate and channel political pressures. As the Layfield Report says:

> While it is not possible to demonstrate a direct connection between the proportion of grant and the extent of government intervention, we are satisfied that the amount of grant and, more importantly, the fact that total grant was increasing to make development of services possible, powerfully reinforced the political pressures for government intervention.[30]

In society there are pressures for centralisation and standardisation, for achieving national uniform standards of service everywhere, but there are also other pressures for decentralisation, for devolution and public participation in order to vary services to meet local conditions and wishes. A high grant does not create the pressures for centralisation; it sustains them. Similarly, a low grant will not create the pressures for local responsibility, but it will sustain and not counteract them.

THE MIDDLE WAY OF MINIMUM STANDARDS

The second major criticism of the Layfield Report focuses on the choice it posed, which has been called too extreme. Far better than either the 'centralist' model of responsibility or the 'localist', it is suggested, is the 'middle way' between the two extremes, which would have fitted more practically what happens in reality and would have been more acceptable to the political parties, central departments and local authorities.

It should be noted that the terms 'centralist' and 'localist' do not appear in the report. They occur in Professor Alan Day's note of reservation, but he is careful to observe that the Layfield majority's choice is between two possible sets of financial structure, 'one relatively centralist and one relatively localist'.[31] Layfield did not propose a sharp 'dichotomisation' between virtually total central control and virtually total local autonomy – with on the one hand central government in charge of everything and on the other local authorities with customs barriers around them. Layfield's argument was that the confusion of responsibilities was at present too great and could be reduced. It recognised that there can never be absolute clarity of responsibility, but there could be less confusion. Its concern was about locating 'the main responsibility for local expenditure and taxation'.[32] In fact the Layfield choice is a middle way, since, as Norman Chester recognised, it offered to central and local government, even in the local responsibility model, much scope for negotiation.[33] This middle way is far more a genuine middle way than the approach that has been dubbed the middle way – the 'minimum standards' approach associated with Professor Alan Day and championed by a number of so-called practical men.

This approach is based on the assumption that the present confusion of responsibilities can be clarified with precision. The Government should be responsible for setting minimum national standards and for finding the money to finance them. If local authorities want to go beyond these minimum standards they should be free to do so, but they would have to finance their discretionary decisions out of their own local tax. How this superficially attractive idea would operate in practice needs to be examined, in order to assess, above all, if it is a genuine middle way.

A CRITIQUE OF MINIMUM STANDARDS

First, almost every statute dealing with a local service would have to be rewritten to set a minimum national standard. Statutory minimum standards now are rare: even the pupil-teacher ratio in the 'quota' was non-statutory, voluntary and in fact a maximum that omitted many categories of teachers. Most mandatory obligations laid on local authorities are vague and general, leaving scope for local discretion. The Committee found that most local expenditure was determined neither by central requirement nor by totally free local choice, but fell between the two and was the outcome of a complex mixture of pressures, such as advice and urging from government departments, inspection, circulars and letters, accumulated past practice, professional attitudes, political influences and the activities of various pressure groups both local and national, and competition and emulation amongst local authorities themselves.[34] From this mélange emerged not specific nationally determined standards but common standards that had evolved and were continually developing.

Suppose, however, that a commitment were made to write minimum standards into statutory form, what would be their nature? Most national standards now are 'input' standards, such as staff ratios, unit costs, and measurements of buildings like houses and schools and of sites like playing fields. Such standards, however, do not indicate if local management is effective, efficient or extravagant, and are in effect requirements that money should be spent irrespective of what is achieved. They are not standards of performance. For such 'output' standards to be devised objectives of the various services would have to be identified and agreed. This task would be immense for, despite the valiant efforts of corporate planners, there is not yet consensus on the objectives of teachers, social workers and policemen or on how to measure their performance. One can imagine the difficulties in obtaining 'output' standards for education, the biggest spender in local government. Should they be based on examination attainment, numbers of 'O' levels gained, or 'A' levels or university places won? And how would standards be enforced? If a local authority failed to reach the national minimum would commissioners be sent in – and to do what? When the practical difficulties are confronted the minimum standards solution looks a far from easy middle way.

There is another complication: minimum standards would have to be costed, since grant would depend on the cost of meeting the set standards. Thus, the scale of provision needed to achieve the minimum standards for each service and in each local authority would have to be costed. Since local authorities vary in their physical characteristics, social composition, resources and needs the calculations would be exceedingly complex, if not impossible, and there would be considerable controversy between central departments and local authorities about the costs of providing the standard, which might have to vary from area to area. Each authority will argue ingeniously that it is a special case, deserving distinct treatment and extra grant. Variations in the costs of attaining the standards might be the result of inefficiency or of conditions beyond the control of the local authority. The centre would in the end have to decide, and the decision would be disputed. It would also have to identify the dominant element that influenced the cost of attaining the standard for each service, which again would be a daunting and controversial operation.

The consequences of this middle-way approach will be an increase in central civil servants, situated in regional offices so that they can inspect local authorities to ensure they conform to the minimum, and can check their claims about the costs of the standards. If civil servants in regional outposts of central departments are increased, there will follow an increase in headquarters civil servants to process and coordinate the reports from the regional offices. Thus the minimum standards solution is highly centralist, leading to a great increase in civil servants and in their involvement in detail with the affairs of local authorities.

If the costs of the minimum standards were based on average costs, then they would be too high for some local authorities and too low for others. Average costs would be too crude an indicator, especially if the level of grant remained high, since, as we have seen, a high level of grant makes it important to obtain a precise calculation of grant in order to avoid instability and disruption in the local authority. In any case, it is hard to imagine that, even if 'minimum standards' have been identified, agreed and costed, they would remain low and stable, so as to allow a worthwhile measure of local discretion. Once the Government were recognised as responsible for minimum standards, it would be under constant pressure to raise the standards, from pressure groups, voluntary bodies, professional associations, political parties, MPs, civil servants and Ministers, all eager to develop, improve and expand services by raising standards. Even local authorities would be advocating higher standards so as to qualify for more grant. The pressures for higher standards and more expenditure would be concentrated on the Government, instead of being dispersed as at present to local authorities as well, and the Government would find great difficulty in resisting such powerful forces calling for more spending. No Minister could stand up in the House of Commons and defend even an input standard set below existing levels. As a result, therefore, of the minimum standards approach there would be a steady diminution of local authority discretion as the minimum standards were continually raised. The pressures for centralisation would have been reinforced.

Further, the minimum standards approach is wasteful. Concentrating the pressures to spend at the centre would make the role of the Treasury more difficult. It would face greatly increased pressures to spend and would not find that local authorities were its allies in seeking a wise use of resources. One advantage for the Treasury of the Layfield local responsibility model would be that local authorities, with a greatly increased local tax base, would be taking their decisions to spend more responsibly, since they would have to justify their expenditure proposals more vigorously to their local electorates. But under the minimum standards approach and in the central responsibility model local authorities would be mainly pressure groups wanting more spending.

Another wasteful aspect of minimum standards is that they hinder creative thought about policy. Working within the context of statutory minimum standards a local authority would not have to ponder deeply about a problem but simply follow the national standard: innovation would be inhibited. Such standards would be artificial and rigid, concentrating the attention of the local authority on certain formal and technical requirements and distracting it from analysis of consequences, side-effects, political implications and impact on the locality. The value of local government is that it enables public policies to be shaped to meet local needs, wishes and conditions, all of which vary. The national minimum standard would not take account of such diversity, nor could it respond flexibly and quickly to changes in local conditions, in the environment, in technology or in views and values. National minimum standards cannot adapt easily to the sudden and the unexpected, nor do they encourage pioneering to solve old problems or to tackle emerging new problems. If a service is just starting and is experimental, when forecasting demand and costs is difficult, national minimum standards are useless. At any one time there will be a range of views about what provision is appropriate, and the most effective way is more likely to emerge out of debate and local experiments than from the imposition of a national standard. Indeed the development of social policies has often begun with a venture by a local authority that was later copied more widely and disseminated through the network of pressure groups and professional and political organisations.

A fear is often expressed that if the Government failed to lay down national minimum standards, then some local authorities would allow their services to deteriorate and the citizen would be faced with an unacceptable variation of standards between local authorities. But even now there are few statutory national minimum standards and thus the unacceptable and intolerable variations should be apparent. However, there are in fact common standards that have developed and continue to develop from experiment and debate. All the pressures that produce these common standards would still exist, if the Layfield local responsibility model were chosen, so that one would not expect a great divergence of standards of provision. Local authorities and central government operate in 'the same atmosphere of public opinion',[35] responding to similar political pressures and views about the broad range of what is acceptable. Common standards would prevail, but they would have been adopted freely and not imposed from the centre, and would fit local wishes and conditions.

The minimum standards approach is highly centralist and under-mines the rationale for local government. The central government, focusing on particular services and functions, cannot assess the conse-quences of providing a range of services territorially at the local level. Local government provides a means whereby local citizens and their elected representatives can produce the mixture of priorities and services that most suit their wishes and conditions. The approach of minimum standards, however, concentrates attention on particular elements in particular services and fails to have regard to the territorial impact of the totality of services.

The statutory minimum standards solution is a bogus middle way.[36] It would involve a major upheaval of administrative practices and require a vastly increased Civil Service to identify the standards, to up-date them, to cost them, to inspect local authorities and to check on their claims. It would introduce new opportunities for dissension between central and local government. It would damage creativity in public policy-making. It would not be easy to implement and would be highly centralist.

There is another middle way that is seductive to so-called practical men. Their argument runs that in politics and administration nothing is either black or white. There has to be give and take between central and local government. Clear definitions of responsibility cannot be achieved. So the relationship should be recognised for what it is – a partnership. Joint responsibility and shared responsibility are the concepts underlying this approach. The Layfield Committee con-demned this view (Chapter 3). It is a perfect description of the present arrangements that have produced the recent crisis. If the roles of each participant in a partnership are not specified then the result is that no one is responsible. Each can shuffle responsibility on to the other. And behind the rhetoric of partnership there occurs a drift to centralisation as the Government encroaches on to the discretion of local authorities without explicitly admitting responsibility. This middle way is the muddle way. Far better, argues Layfield, to put the main responsibility clearly on the Government, or best of all on local government. There will still be some confusion whatever model is adopted, but it will not be significant since the main responsibility will have been clearly located.

Norman Chester wrote in 1951 that: 'The issues at stake are very important. It is not just a question of administrative detail. It is a question of constitutional importance almost as great as that raised by the relations between the Executive and Parliament.'[37] The Layfield Committee, too, recognised that devising a system of local government finance raises major constitutional and political issues, about the provision of public services, the relationships between central and local government and about the distribution of power in society. Many people, Ministers and civil servants, local officials and elected councillors, have been embarrassed because Layfield dealt with such fundamental topics. Their first response was to by-pass the tricky questions. After publication of the report the Government and local authorities through the Consultative Council established working parties to review what they saw as the issues raised by Layfield. The subjects tackled were audit, grants, rates, fees and charges, and alternative sources of local revenue. There was no working party on central–local relationships, on the Layfield package as a whole and on the basic issues of how to promote responsible government. The setting-up of the working parties indicated that the main issue of responsibility was to be ignored. When the Government published its decisions in May 1977 it rejected not only the Layfield call for a choice to be made between local and central government responsibility but also the 'minimum standards' approach, and stressed the notion of 'partnership'. In the following words it totally cast aside the Chester-Layfield line:

> Local authorities are already accountable to their electorates because they are responsible for the way in which local needs are met and priorities are ordered, and for the level of rate poundages. The fact that a substantial part of local authority services is financed by Government grants, as opposed to locally raised revenue, does not necessarily reduce local authorities' accountability. Most of the Exchequer support is a block grant, which is not ear-marked by the Government to any particular service, and local authorities are free to order their own spending priorities within the framework of legislation.[38]

Both Norman Chester and the Layfield Committee have demonstrated that local government finance is not a technical subject: it raises major questions about government in our society, which our governors seem unwilling to confront.

NOTES AND REFERENCES

1 *Local Government Finance*, Cmnd 6453 (HMSO, 1976).
2 D. N. Chester, 'The Layfield Report: Constitutional Implications', *Local Government Studies*, vol. 12, no. 4 (Oct 1976) pp. 65–9.
3 D. N. Chester, *Central and Local Government* (Macmillan, 1951).
4 Sir Norman Chester, Memorandum of Evidence to the Committee of Inquiry into Local Government Finance, Apr 1975.
5 Ibid., p. 64.
6 Cd. 9230 (1918) pp. 18–19.
7 Memorandum, para. 5.
8 P. 31.
9 Layfield Report, p. 50.
10 Memorandum, para. 15.
11 *Central and Local Government*, pp. 358, 280.
12 Memorandum, paras 25, 23.
13 In this chapter the grant percentage refers to the proportion of grant contributed to the total of grant and rates financing relevant expenditure, which is current expenditure on the rate fund account net of receipt of fees and charges. The variety of uses of percentages in discussions about local government finance is considered in A. Crispin, 'Local Government Finance: Assessing the Central Government's Contribution', *Public Administration*, spring 1976, pp. 45–61.
14 Layfield Report, p. 219.
15 *Central and Local Government*, pp. 30, 369.
16 Many of the criticisms were expressed in responses to lectures given by the author during 1976 when he championed the proposals of the Layfield Committee, of which he had been a member.
17 Layfield Report, p. 216.
18 F. Cripps and W. Godley, *Local Government Finance and its Reform* (Cambridge, Department of Applied Economics, 1976) p. 11.
19 Quoted in *Municipal Engineering*, 15 Oct 1976.
20 This concept is explained in the Layfield Report, p. 40, and in *The Future Shape of Local Government Finance*, Cmnd 4741 (HMSO, 1971) p. 10.
21 *The Future Shape of Local Government Finance*, para 110.
22 Layfield Report, pp. 265, 78.
23 Ibid., pp. 65–8, especially para. 7.
24 Ibid., pp. 30–1.
25 Ibid., pp. 40–1.
26 Memorandum, para. 32.
27 Layfield Report, pp. 248–51.
28 Ibid., pp. 79–81, 288.
29 Memorandum, para. 33; *Central and Local Government*, pp. 324, 341–2.
30 P. 66.
31 P. 302.

32   P. 298.
33   'The Layfield Report: Constitutional Implications', p. 69; see also *Central and Local Government*, pp. 325–6.
34   Layfield Report, pp. 61 and 403–5.
35   *Central and Local Government*, p. 93.
36   The Layfield Report examines the standards issue at pp. 60–2, 73–4, 106, 213, 220, 243 and 287. Another attack on national minimum standards is John Stewart, 'No "middle way"', *Municipal Journal*, 9 July 1976, pp. 795–7. I am indebted to Professor Stewart, a former Student of Nuffield College and colleague on the Layfield Committee, for some stimulating insights into local government finance and for help in the early stages of this chapter.
37   *Central and Local Government*, p. 371.
38   *Local Government Finance*, Cmnd 6813 (HMSO, 1977) pp. 10–11, para. 3.24.

7 'Reforming' the Grass Roots: An Alternative Analysis

L. J. SHARPE

Criticism of the structure of local government and proposals for
its reform have been a popular pastime for many years now. . . .
The impression is given that if only the area problem were solved,
by which is usually meant the creation of a number of larger units,
then everything would be well with local government. . . . There
is no evidence to show that this is the case. [Sir Norman Chester
(*Central and Local Government*, 1951)]

INTRODUCTION

Never perhaps in the modern era has a structural change in British
government become so unpopular so quickly as the Walker Local
Government Act of 1972. Apart from occasional defensive utterances
by Mr Walker himself, it is hard to find anyone to defend it.[1] So
widespread is this disapproval, even among Mr Walker's party
colleagues, that the unsuspecting observer might assume that the Act
was thought up and pushed through Parliament by Mr Walker single-
handed without benefit of debate or vote. For many the Act is seen as
the root of all the major problems that are thought to beset local
government, including overstaffing, overspending and overtaxing as
well as the actual malfunctioning of the new system itself.

Undoubtedly, some of these criticisms are unwarranted. In the first
place, it is too early to make a fair and considered assessment of some
aspects of the new system. Moreover, when set in its historical context,
the Walker Act is a distinct improvement on what might have been.
Nevertheless, even when we have stripped away the various scapegoat
roles that a bewildered and perhaps vengeful public have foisted on the
new system, and when we have made due allowance for the relative
newness of the new system, experience so far suggests that the central
core of the criticism that has descended on it still stands. This I take

to be that the deficiencies of the old order were substantially less than those of the new. Even in relation to the performance of these services, such as planning and transportation, which the new system was specifically designed to improve, there seems to have been a distinct decline. In short, the Walker Act seems to have been a gigantic and expensive error.

SOURCES OF PUBLIC DISSATISFACTION

How did such an error come about? The rest of this essay will be devoted to trying to answer that question. One explanation for its public unpopularity is simply that the public never wanted change anyway. They were certainly never consulted in terms of specific proposals. The Redcliffe-Maud Commission which preceded the Walker Act, however, did include a question on local government reorganisation in its Community Attitudes Survey and the response is instructive: 77 per cent of those interviewed either favoured no change (57 per cent) or did not know or care about change (20 per cent).[2] This seems to be the nearest the process of change that led up to the Walker Act got to public consultation. The assumption seems to have been that redesigning local government is not fundamentally different from re-designing any other part of the government apparatus, such as British Rail or the Department of Employment. This is not to say that either Mr Walker or the Redcliffe-Maud Commission were unaware of the virtues of local democracy, and the latter asserted: 'If local self-government withers the roots of democracy grow dry. If it is genuinely alive, it nourishes the reality of democratic freedom.'[3] The 'reality of democratic freedom' was apparently never seen as applying to the reorganisation process itself however. It is undoubtedly extremely difficult for a Minister to sound out public opinion in relation to a structural change, but it is debatable whether a system of government that is itself based on the democratic principle can be reorganised without taking into account popular preferences. If the process does so then the outcome must run the risk of being overtaken by the malaise which now afflicts the present local government system. This seems to have been the view in the past and the 1958 Local Government Commissions were required to take into account the wishes of the inhabitants when making their proposals.

A second possible reason for the apparent failure of the Walker Act is that it was not designed to suit the public so much as to suit the Conservative Party. The failure of the new system, so this argument runs, is derived from its being a party gerrymander rather than an attempt to create a better local government system.[4] Undoubtedly there were party political motivations underpinning the Act, and they are only too obvious in certain of its features, such as the narrowly-drawn boundaries of the metropolitan counties. More specifically, the division of Glamorgan into three parts is so flagrantly party-political that it evoked an unprecedented accusation of indefensible political gerrymandering from Lady Sharp, the former Permanent Secretary of the old Ministry of Housing and Local Government. *New Society* dubbed the Bill 'a pure political carve up, devoid of all justification in terms of social geography or of good planning'.[5] Even in more general terms, party bias is discernible for Mr Walker was resurrecting, albeit in an attenuated form, a very long-standing Conservative desire to neutralise the radical propensities of the cities by placing them under the umbrella of the Conservative-voting shires. This strategy was first attempted by Mr Ritchie in 1888, but came to nothing because of a backbench revolt which transformed his county-centred bill into the dual system of counties and independent cities – the county boroughs – which the Walker Act replaced.

Party advantage was, then, an important consideration in the Act. This is hardly surprising, however, because new boundaries mean a new basis for determining majorities and therefore which party will win. No party in power dares miss the opportunity to ensure that whatever the ostensible reasons for boundary change may be, its interests are not only protected but if possible enhanced.[6] Also, party advantage must be seen as one of the incentives for the party in government. Local government reorganisation is, after all, a very arduous and distinctly unglamorous legislative task. In a wholly area-based parliamentary representative system, too, party advantage may be decisive in winning over crucial numbers of back benchers in the majority party who are likely to face hostile electorates, and therefore may buck the party line unless there is an easily comprehensible motive for putting party loyalty first. In this sense the Heath Government was not fundamentally different from its Labour predecessor, who had initiated the reform process from which the Walker Act was derived, largely to protect their own party interests;[7] or, indeed, from an earlier Conservative administration which pushed through the London Government Act.[8] But, although party advantage must probably always be a major ingredient in the local government reorganisation process, it would be wrong to see it as the sole cause of the patent failure of the 1972 Act. As we shall see, in the sense that the pursuit of party advantage undermined the necessary relationship between diagnosis and remedy it was likely to be one contribution, but only a contribution, to the ultimate failure of the Act.

Another possible candidate for the source of public disillusionment with the Walker Act, if not its palpable failure, is that the Government when promoting the reform promised far too much for the new order, and thus raised public expectations beyond anything the new system could possibly achieve. We have already noted the large claims made on behalf of the new system in relation to democracy, but perhaps the most glaring disparity between promise and reality was the persistent claim by Mr Walker and his colleagues that one of their primary motives was to create a stronger system of local government which could then be given greater autonomy. This is a theme that all governments bent on reorganisation feel bound to introduce, presumably to soften the blow of change. It was a feature of the Labour Party's White Paper in 1970,[9] and of the then Prime Minister, Harold Wilson's, instant welcome to the Redcliffe-Maud Report on the day of its publication in June 1970.[10] For Mr Walker, however, giving greater autonomy to local government seems to have taken on the character of a primary objective of the reorganisation; for not only did it figure prominently in his public pronouncements on the issue after the publication of the Redcliffe-Maud Report,[11] it was also an important theme of his Second Reading speech on the Bill. Such was the importance he placed on it that one observer has concluded that from the 1970 General Election onwards local government reform which would involve 'a genuine devolution of power from central government . . . became the main plank of the Government's platform'.[12] Some indication of the emphasis the Government placed on enhancing local autonomy can be gauged from the following quotation from the 1971 White Paper that preceded the Bill:

> The Government are equally determined to return power to those people who should exercise decisions locally, and to ensure that local government is given every opportunity to take that initiative and responsibility effectively, speedily and with vigour. . . . A vigorous local democracy means that authorities must be given real functions – with powers of decision and the ability to take action without being subjected to excessive regulation by central government through financial or other controls. . . . And above all else, a genuine local democracy implies that decisions should be taken – and should be seen to be taken – as locally as possible.[13]

It became apparent soon after the Act was passed that, at the very time all these brave declarations were being made, Mr Walker and his Cabinet colleagues were busy preparing a series of legislative enactments that, taken together, probably constitute the biggest *subtraction* of power from local government in such a short space of time in the modern era. These enactments were, first, the Water Act, which transferred from local government the whole of sewerage and main drainage and water supply to new Regional Water Authorities; secondly, the Health Service Reorganization Act, which transferred practically all the local personal health services to the revamped National Health Service; and, finally, the Housing Finance Act, which took away from local authorities what was possibly one of their politically most important rights, that of determining the level of rents for their own housing.

Here were unquestionably solid grounds for disillusionment with the new system. But it is likely that it was largely confined to those within the local government system rather than the public at large, who do not normally read White Papers or worry much about local autonomy. Certainly one professional – Alderman Chester of Oxford City Council – was disillusioned very early on by this disparity between Mr Walker's promises and the reality of the Bill.[14]

Another possible reason for the failure of the Act could be that the new system has become the scapegoat for public discontent that has little to do with the new structure. Part of the discontent in question arose in 1974 following a sharp increase in rate levels. The reorganisation did, of course, involve additional costs both of a once-for-all and secular kind. One estimate for implementing the Redcliffe-Maud proposals put the total figure derived from an analysis of Merseyside at £200,000,000.[15] But it is also likely that inflation and changes in the distribution of the Rate Support Grant were at least of equal importance as causes for the upsurge of public discontent. This was the so-called 'rates revolt' of 1974: a new national association of ratepayers was formed in its wake and one of its results was the Layfield Committee on local finance.[16] There has also been a linked though much less widespread growth of public discontent with the increase in the number of local government employees.

However, real as both sources of public disquiet may have been as contributory factors in undermining public confidence in the new system, the 'rates revolt' had by 1977 almost disappeared, whereas dissatisfaction with the new system was, if anything, more intense. Public discontent with staffing levels did not abate so rapidly, and it has greater relevance to the possible effects of the new system, particularly for some services. Planning is a notable example since the new system has unquestionably generated a need for substantially greater numbers of planners.

In short, although they are almost certainly contributory factors, neither the rates revolt nor public concern about staffing costs offer a satisfactory explanation for the unpopularity of the Walker Act; let alone for its objective shortcomings. If we are to explain the failure of the new system we need to probe a little deeper into the actual functioning of the new structure in relation to the objectives it was established to achieve. This approach needs perhaps further emphasis since, in the nature of the case, provided it meets some very general conditions there can never be an inherently 'right', or indeed a 'wrong', reorganisation scheme. However, we can at least talk about a re-organisation scheme that is inappropriate in relation to the purposes it was established to achieve. In the case of the Walker Act we may identify these objectives fairly easily since they are set down in the opening section of the White Paper that preceded it.[17] They were also adumbrated by Government spokesmen during the passage of the Bill through parliament, and, further, most of these objectives have their origins in the lengthy statement of the case for reorganisation set out in the Redcliffe-Maud Report.[18]

THE OBJECTIVES OF THE WALKER ACT

The primary objectives of the Act may be briefly summarised as being to:

  (i) Increase the power of the local government system by giving it greater freedom from central control.
 (ii) Create a system that is sufficiently flexible to match function to area and to ensure that decisions are taken as locally as possible.
(iii) Create a system that is as coherent as possible and is 'understood and accepted as sensible by electors, by members and by officers'.
 (iv) Bring the boundaries of local authorities more into line with present-day population patterns and linkages by joining the built-up area of cities with their hinterlands.
  (v) Increase the population size of local authorities so as to enhance their capacity to provide services to present-day standards.

There would seem to be some conflict between objective (ii) and objective (iv), in the sense that it is difficult to see how a local authority can be more local and larger at the same time. The explanation of this apparent contradiction is that objective (ii) is not related to the then existing system so much as to the Redcliffe-Maud scheme which the White Paper was expressly conceived as superseding. We will return to this aspect of objective (ii) in a moment.

How has the new system lived up to these aspirations? We have already discussed objective (i) and found that not only has the new order not achieved any significant increase in autonomy, but the new system has actually lost an important clutch of functions to other agencies. So much for objective (i).

The second objective, or rather pair of objectives, which sought a better 'fit' between area and function and wanted decisions as local as possible, looks a great deal closer to achievement than objective (i). But if there has been no glaring disparity between intention and achievement, then equally it would be difficult to claim that the new system is better in relation to this objective than the old. The vast bulk of the country was covered by a two-tier system under the old order so that the function-to-area 'fit' argument was already as close to being met as the new. Where it was not – in the county boroughs – the successor districts are either larger than the county boroughs they superseded, or they are the same size. Either way, there has been no increase in local decision making. Moreover, it must be remembered that under the new system some major functions that were entirely the responsibility of the county boroughs have been transferred to the much larger counties. In short, it is difficult to see how objective (ii) has been achieved and it is *prima facie* something of a puzzle to know why it was ever cited as an objective in the White Paper until we remember that it was included to highlight the advantages of the proposed Bill over the dreaded unitary authorities of the Redcliffe-Maud Report. This is an important point to be noted because it is one reason why the Walker Act is deficient when measured against the *status quo ante*. Unlike most Ministers intent on institutional change, Mr Walker had the advantage that his plan replaced an even more drastic proposal that had been endorsed by the preceding Government so that those most adversely affected were willing to support the new proposals, not because they necessarily saw them as being an improvement on the existing system, but because they would be even more adversely affected by the Redcliffe-Maud scheme which had got as far as the White Paper stage barely a year earlier. The Walker Bill was therefore not only an attempt to eliminate the perceived faults of the old, but also to eliminate the perceived faults of the 'might have been'. These two aims were not necessarily compatible.

Objective (iii) is very difficult to assess. Its first part – the need for coherence – is taken directly from the Redcliffe-Maud Report where it was clearly achieved, for the Report's proposals involved a highly simplified system comprising single-tier unitary authorities throughout the country except in the conurbations. But the Walker system is far less simplified and in some respects may be regarded as being less coherent than the old system. The creation of a second tier in the old county boroughs where previously there was a single tier is one example.

Another example of increased complexity is the overlapping responsibilities in planning. The second part of objective (iii), which posits as a criterion of success whether the public regards the system as 'sensible', is something of a novelty in the long literature on local government reform and its fundamental ambiguity perhaps explains why. It seems likely that it found its way into the White Paper not so much as an objective, but rather as another sideswipe at the Redcliffe-Maud proposals designed to rally the party stalwarts in the shires who had consistently claimed that the Redcliffe-Maud proposals were substantially less than 'sensible'.[19]

The fourth objective – which requires that local government boundaries follow population settlement patterns – we may call the socio-geographic objective. The fifth objective – which requires that individual local authorities are big enough to provide services efficiently to currently acceptable standards – we may call the service provision objective. Both objectives bring us much nearer to the heart of the Walker Act than the preceding objectives and to its fundamental defects. They will both therefore receive more extended analysis. Before proceeding to that analysis, I must admit that I shall be a great deal less sympathetic to both objectives than I have been in the past.[20] The explanation is that ten years' experience of the application of these objectives, first in Greater London and since 1973 in the rest of the country, plus a little bit more scrutiny of what they entail, has made me change my mind.

AN ANALYSIS OF FUNCTIONALISM

The socio-geographic objective is based on the assumption that the basic settlement form is now the service centre and its hinterland. The service centre may be defined as the continuously built-up area of a town and its hinterland as the surrounding ring of satellite communities. These communities are embedded in a semi-rural and rural environment but, it is argued, they owe their existence to their proximity to the service centre and its accessibility to them in terms of employment, shopping and a myriad of private and public services. Thus the hinterland is said to be just as much a part of the town as are the suburbs that form the rim of the town's continuously built-up core.

The basic settlement pattern, so this argument continues, is, then, no longer one of urban entities that are sharply differentiated in socio-economic terms from their rural surroundings, but of a series of service centres and their hinterlands – spread cities – whose boundaries meet and overlap to cover most of the country and especially the central population core of England (where over two-thirds of the population live) that runs from Greater Manchester and Merseyside in the North West to London and the South East Region. In this, the so-called 'coffin', we may no longer talk of urban and rural but rather of different degrees of urban-ness.

Translated into local government boundaries, the socio-geographic objective implied the abolition of the old county boroughs, which, broadly speaking, did not usually embrace even the whole of the built-up areas of cities, and the creation of new authorities that embraced some approximation to the spread city.

The need to match the local government structure to this alleged reality rested on three grounds. First, the objective linkages of the town plus hinterland will have already generated a subjective community of interest among all the inhabitants of the spread city 'through the links of employment, shopping and social activities'.[21] Secondly, and more decisively, planning and the related functions of traffic management, highways and public transport can only be effectively and efficiently undertaken if their jurisdiction covers the whole of the spread city since in planning terms service centre and hinterland are interdependent.[22] The extent of settlement in the hinterland, for example, can directly affect the prosperity of the service centre economy, and, equally, the level and pattern of public and private services in the service centre – employment opportunities, car parks, shopping facilities, traffic control, public transport, cultural and educational services – affects those in the hinterland. Thirdly, retaining the old county borough boundaries was inefficient and irrational. Put in the more formal terminology of public goods theory,[23] we may say that the public goods services it provided had effects – they confer benefits or exact costs – over a much wider area than the built-up core. The extent of each service's externalities varied, but they were all well beyond the boundaries of the county borough. Extending the boundary was therefore an improvement on the *status quo* in the sense that it would come closer to internalising these service externalities and thus making possible a sharing of the costs and the benefits of the public goods more equitably among those affected.

How far does the new system fulfil these three socio-geographic aims? In one sense it never could, simply because the three aims conflict to some extent with other main objectives – for example with objective (ii), which seeks to keep decisions as local as possible. It also conflicts, one may suppose, with objective (iii), which seeks to ensure that areas seem sensible. But to the extent that the more localised second-tier authority of the new system, the district, meets both of these objectives it is possible to make a fairly straightforward judgement on the extent to which the Walker Act meets the socio-geographic objectives. It clearly fails in some of the metropolitan counties which do not even embrace the continuously built-up area. Elsewhere, too, the boundaries of the shire counties are only a very crude approximation to the actual influence areas of the cities they encapsulate. To some extent this is because the spread city model cannot be applied in many areas outside the 'coffin', simply because a distinctive rural society still persists there. Also, many influence areas overlap. For these reasons the question to be asked is not so much whether the Walker Act fits the centre plus hinterland model but, rather, whether it is better suited than the old for the delivery of the major services, and the verdict must be that under the terms of the spread city model the system is a clear improvement on the old. Whether the spread city model is appropriate for determining local government structure is another matter which we will discuss later.

We now come to the last objective of the new system inaugurated by the 1972 Act. This is the service efficiency objective which seeks to improve the quality of local government services by enlarging the average population size of local government units. The discussion of this objective in the reform literature is a little vague and it is necessary in order to achieve some clarity to introduce a more formal mode of argument. There are two assumptions implicit in the service efficiency objective. The first is that the scale of existing units is insufficient to enable them to provide services effectively; that is to say, to provide the service in its full range to currently accepted standards.[24] The second assumption is that the units in the old system were too small to reap all the possible economies of scale, especially economies of scale in management and cost control.[25] As with the socio-geographic objectives, it is very difficult to ascertain whether or not the service efficiency objectives have been achieved since the change in the structure itself and the distribution of functions, not to mention exogenous changes that have occurred since reorganisation, means there is no possibility of making a true comparison of service costs – to test the economies of scale objective – or of service quality, to test the effectiveness objective. All we can say is the conditions which will make it possible for the assumed effects to take place has been created in the sense that the new system does consist of units with larger average populations. Under the old system there were just under 1400 authorities, whereas under the new system there are only 422.[26]

However, both objectives are based on the assumption that the geographical distribution of the given population in a local authority does not modify the assumed relationship between population size and service effectiveness, or economies of scale. Yet the possibility that it does is a very strong one. Consider, for example, the different communication costs and the different needs of an authority based on a continuously built-up town and one with the same population but embracing a tract of marginal agricultural upland. Another questionable assumption of the effectiveness, if not the economies of scale objective, is that population is directly related to resources. That is to say, it assumes that an increase in population automatically implies an increase in resources. Obviously there is likely to be some relationship between population and resources, but since the major components of local resources – central grants, taxes on industry and households, and rents and charges – are themselves only very loosely related to population scale, we may claim with some confidence that the link will always be an indirect one. In extreme cases, such as the central London Borough of Westminster for example, the relationship is very indirect indeed. Westminster's rateable value alone is in excess of that of Birmingham, Liverpool and Manchester combined, yet its population is less than half of their combined population.

The economies of scale objective raises even more serious doubts. Although seldom spelled out in the reform literature and certainly not discussed in the White Paper that preceded the reorganisation Act, the claim that there were economies of scale to be reaped by reorganisation could only be based on the assumption that local services generate certain fixed costs irrespective of the population size of the authority. If the average population served by local authorities was increased it followed that unit costs of the service would fall. The difficulty with this assumption is, first, that these fixed costs have never been identified. They have only been assumed to exist and we may presume that the faith in their existence is derived not so much from evidence of their existence as the pervasive influence of the economic theory of the firm. Secondly, the assumption seems to be that the long-run cost curve declines at the same point and for the same level of output for all services – education, social welfare, highways, housing, police and so forth. Equally, too, they are assumed to operate over a very wide population range so that any enlargement of any existing authority would apparently reduce service costs. Finally, the belief in the apparently limitless fixity of fixed costs was matched by an equally firm belief in the absence of diseconomies of scale. All of these assumptions would be more plausible if there had been any evidence under the old system that they might be correct. But there was little or no evidence that scale did bring lower costs. There had, it is true, been a long line of official reports that preceded the reorganisation Act, mainly concerning individual local services, that to a greater or lesser extent recommended the enlargement of existing local authorities, either in terms of population or of area. The Redcliffe-Maud Commission with a perhaps pardonably elastic definition of enlargement, discovered forty-nine such inquiries that appeared between 1950 and 1968.[27] The vast bulk of these recommendations were, however, highly subjective and were in any case not concerned with cost reduction, but the somewhat different objective of devising optimum conditions for the operation of a particular service.

There had also been a number of more systematic and objective studies that had attempted to examine the effects of the population size on their service performance as measured by expenditure statistics of local authorities. The Redcliffe-Maud Commission itself conducted or commissioned some of this research. However, after carefully reviewing all of these studies, Newton has concluded that the search for a relationship between population size and service performance

> has been conspicuously unsuccessful, whether the performance measures have been spending patterns or the quality or type of services provided. . . . Of 73 different attempts to ascertain the effects of size . . . in 38 . . . the impact is statistically insignificant but substantively small, and in the remaining 17 cases the effects are significant and of medium strength. In no case is size a powerful or dominant variable which can explain as much as a quarter of the variance.[28]

To sum up the discussion of the two functionalist objectives, we may say that if the new system seems to fulfil them to a much greater extent than the other objectives which it was created to achieve, the functionalist objectives are based on a number of shaky assumptions. Not only are these objectives based on shaky assumptions, but they have been the prime determinants of what is perhaps the fundamental defect of the new system, and that is the enormous scale of the new authorities. Before discussing how the functionalist objectives have led to such large authorities it is worth while establishing just how big they are. Despite the claims of the 1972 White Paper that the new units would be created, 'above all else', on the basis that 'a genuine local democracy implies that decisions should be taken as locally as possible',[29] the local units, the districts, are *on average* in excess of 120,000 population. In some of the remoter rural areas this means 'genuine local democracy' operates in areas of 40 miles across, and districts where the seat of government is 20 miles from quite large population centres within the district are quite common. At the county level, which provides most of the major functions, the situation is even more extraordinary. The *average* population of the English and Welsh counties is in excess of one million and in some instances the seat of government is a half-a-day's travel time from the largest centres of population within the county. In Devon, for example, the largest city – Plymouth – is 40 miles from the county seat at Exeter.

Some further idea of how peculiarly large British local authorities are can be gauged from comparisons with some other West European democracies. These are set out in the table below and they reveal that in France, where the basic unit of local government is the commune, the average communal population is about 1300, that is to say some hundred times smaller than the English average. France for a number of reasons may be something of an exception, but even in West Germany the equivalent local unit has an average population of about 2700 and Sweden, which with the exception of Britain has just completed the most far-reaching restructuring of its local government among the industrial democracies, the average Kommune population is less than 30,000; that is to say some four times smaller than the English average. Nor is it likely that European democracies are exceptional for there are about three times as many local authorities in the New York City region as there are in the whole of England and Wales.[30]

One explanation for the enormous size of the new units as revealed in the table could be that in Britain people live in larger cities. This is an impossible characteristic to measure or compare in this instance since it is impossible to get population statistics that are not themselves prisoners of the local government system. Certainly by one indirect measure of general urban-ness Britain is exceptional, for the proportion of its work force engaged in agriculture is about $2\frac{1}{2}$ per cent, which is probably the lowest among industrial democracies. But by another more decisive measure, that of population density, Britain comes fourth behind the Netherlands, Belgium and West Germany.

The explanation for the huge local authorities in Britain is, then, unlikely to lie in the settlement pattern. Another factor which could account for larger local government units in Britain than elsewhere is the absence of an intermediate tier of government or administration between the localities and central government. The British system is neither a federal system like West Germany nor does it follow the prefectoral pattern of an intermediate level of the central administration. This means that in Britain there is no alternative other than local government itself for providing local services. It follows that there is much greater pressure on the local government system to be functionally appropriate. Moreover, in the absence of an intermediate tier the relationship between centre and locality is predominantly functional, every central department having its own link with the equivalent department at the local level. This enhances the tendency to view local government as first and foremost a provider of services. In France, by contrast, the small scale of the average commune is tolerable precisely because it is primarily a political unit, and is of little functional importance. The Commune is, in short, primarily a reflector of local interests, whereas it is the out-stationed civil servants under the nominal leadership of the prefect that, outside the largest cities, is the

Country	Total population	No. of basic units	Average population of basic units
Belgium (Communes, 1977)	9,788,248	596	16,255
Denmark (Kommuner, 1972)	4,995,653	277	17,963
France (Communes, 1968)	49,778,500	37,708	1,320
Italy (Commune, 1973)	54,136,547	8,059	6,717
Netherlands (Gemeentin, 1972)	13,599,092	841	16,170
Norway (Kommuner, 1973)	3,947,775	444	8,891
Sweden (Kommuner, 1976)	8,208,442	278	29,527
West Germany (Geminden and Kreisfrie Stadte, 1975)	60,650,600	22,510	2,694
England and Wales (Districts, 1972)	49,219,000	401	122,740

functional level of local government in France. With its political role overshadowed by its functional role, local government in Britain is that much more vulnerable to the charge of functional incapacity. The fact, noted earlier, that forty-nine official reports by looking solely at the optimal needs of a particular service all concluded that the enlargement of local units was necessary, exactly reflects this tremendous functional pressure on the local government system.[31]

This peculiarity of the British system could be a major factor accounting for the difference between the size of British local authorities and those of other comparable countries. But it has to be remembered that in the other unitary states listed in the table, other than France and Italy, the intermediate level is now very attenuated despite the much smaller scale of their local authorities. Bearing in mind the fact that the counties average over a million population, we may conclude that the relatively large scale of British local units is well beyond what may be attributable to the absence of an intermediate tier. A more likely candidate is the functionalist bias of the Walker Act. Too much weight, in short, was placed on the two functionalist objectives, the first of which, it will be remembered, sought units that would embrace town and country,

(a) so as to reflect a community of interest that already existed among the citizens of both;

(b) so as to create self-contained areas for planning and related services; and

(c) in order to internalise the externalities of the public services provided by the town.

The two aims of the second objective were to create units that were large enough to

(d) make service provision more effective; and

(e) to exploit economies of scale.

The feature that all five of the above aims share is concern for improving service performance, and it is the assumption that this improvement can be achieved by increased scale that is the hallmark of the Walker Act as it was of the Redcliffe-Maud Report.[32] This dominant emphasis on scale effects meant that the other major requirement of local government – that it should be democratic – is overwhelmed. The result is that the primary local authorities in the new system (the counties and the metropolitan districts) are too large to correspond to anything that anyone can recognise as a community in the sense that they can command the loyalties of the citizens, evoke a sense of identity among them, or correspond to their patterns of movement.

Not only is the democratic criterion overwhelmed, it is also undermined by the incorporation of functionalist criteria within it in the sense that making local government units functionally effective is also seen as making them more democratic. The reasoning behind this connection runs something like this: democracy implies the capacity of government to act. It therefore follows that enhancing the capacity of a local authority to act, making it more functionally effective that is, also enhances democracy. Bruce Wood has expressed this conflation of the democratic and functional objectives in the Walker Act thus:

'Responsive' government is government responding to public demands, and 'accountable' government is government seeking judgement on its performance. Both imply that a council has goods to deliver, that it is responsible for the provision of reasonably important public services. Here there is a clear link between the ideas of 'democracy' and those of 'efficiency' or 'effectiveness'. A responsible local authority is one with clear choices to make about the nature of its outputs: it is not one which is too small to be entrusted with a reasonable range of functions by Parliament.[33]

Now it cannot be denied that representative democracy does indeed imply that government has some capacity to act; such capacity is the essential prerequisite for ensuring that it is responsive.[34] However, making the government of a democratic polity functionally effective cannot be equated with making the polity itself functionally effective. In other words, *governmental* capacity is not the same thing as *system* capacity. A parish council is no whit less democratic than the Greater London Council because its capacity to act happens to be very considerably less. As Barry has put it, 'system capacity is, surely, in itself neither democratic nor undemocratic, since it refers to the range of options open to those who set the policy of the country'.[35] In short, system capacity is a 'given' and has no bearing on the way in which power is distributed within the system.

Here, I think, lies the root of the overemphasis on functionalism in the Walker Act that has produced such inordinately large local authorities and in turn kindled such dissatisfaction with the new order. This brings us back to our starting-point, which was the extraordinarily low public support for a new system that was supposed to do so much to improve local life and the quality of local democracy. If the high level of public discontent with the new order continues, there will almost certainly be moves to change it. At the risk of attempting to predict or advocate what the alternative scheme might be, there is a good case for exploring further what the prerequisites of an alternative structure ought to be, for in so doing we may also be able to pinpoint more closely the weaknesses of the present system.

PREREQUISITES OF AN ALTERNATIVE SYSTEM

The first prerequisite of any alternative to the present structure is the restoration of the democratic desideratum, not just in terms of casting out system capacity as a democratic criterion, but also to give the maintenance of democracy equal status with the improvement of functional provision in any alternative system. This will entail a much greater willingness to accept conventional definitions of the settlement pattern. It may mean, for example, a return to drawing a distinction between town (the continuously built-up area) and country (the rest) when not to do so involves the creation of units that are so big that they have no meaning to the inhabitants and, in addition, weaken the operation of the democratic process. To put it another way, the hypothetical advantages of pushing out the boundary on functionalist grounds must always be set against the palpable costs of scale to democracy. For if we take the most basic definition of democracy – that government acts in accordance with the wishes of citizens – then democracy is undeniably a diminishing function of scale. We must of necessity talk in highly generalised terms, but other things being equal, we may say that a small unit is likely to be more democratic than a larger unit for at least three reasons. First, because in small units leaders are more likely to be responsive to citizens' views; second, because a smaller unit makes it more possible for citizens to participate in decision making; and, thirdly, in smaller units there is a greater likelihood of political homogeneity among the citizenry, thus making possible more clear-cut majorities on issues and more popular control of leaders.[36]

Another way of looking at the democracy criterion is to view the nation state as being, in socio-economic terms, arbitrary. It is, however, made up of definable sub-national entities which are not arbitrary. Because these sub-national communities are definable and relate to individual patterns of life, they command a sense of identity and allegiance among their citizens. They are, in other words, a 'given' which has to be recognised in any local government structure which has any pretensions to reflecting popular wishes. Such recognition may be necessary irrespective of their scale. This is a conception of local government that was recognised by J. S. Mill long ago:

> There are local interests peculiar to every town whether great or small, and common to all inhabitants; every town, therefore, without distinction of size, ought to have its municipal council.[37]

Today we may not be able to go the whole hog with Mill and make every town a separate unit, but his insistence on the primacy of the urban entity ought to be the starting-point for designing any local government system and not the hypothetical requirements of the functions it happens to provide.

Another prerequisite of any alternative to the present system is the recognition that functionalism, whatever its defects in democratic terms, may not even be *functionally* appropriate. The pursuit of self-containment, service externalities and economies of scale leaves entirely out of account the positive relationship between urban-ness and the need for public services. If we imagine a rural-urban continuum running from the remote farm to the centre of the central business district (CBD) – let us say Piccadilly Circus – the need for public services is substantially less at the rural end than at the CBD end. This link between population density and government is derived mainly from three factors. The first is to do with self-sufficiency. Our isolated farmer does not need, or can provide for himself, a wide range of services that the central city dweller needs but can only obtain through local government Such services include refuse collection and disposal, main drainage, street cleansing, cultural services, traffic management, full-scale policing services, and public transport. The isolated farmer does, of course, get some of these services but most of them are not usually provided to isolated farms. Secondly, the need for more government as density increases is also derived from the greater need to control, manage and plan the environment. This aspect of the need for more government is closely linked with the decline in the self-sufficiency factor just discussed, but it is possible to discern two senses in which it is distinct from it.

In the first place, there is the need to regulate the impact of the negative externalities of individuals, households and firms as population density increases. As Mancur Olson has put it, 'As population, urbanization and congestion increase, external diseconomies almost certainly increase too.'[38] The isolated farmer can breed pigs, burn old tyres, park his tractor on the highway, and dig a hole to dump his refuse in. If the Piccadilly flat dweller, office manager or shopowner did any of these things it would have intolerable effects on his neighbours. In some cases, digging a hole for example, the action might bring the whole of the CBD to a halt.

The second sense in which government is needed to regulate inter-action in the central city in ways which are not needed in a remote rural area is derived from the fact that some externalities generated by individuals and firms are beneficial. These are the scale externalities that separate firms undertaking part of a single productive process exploit, or other externalities generated by some central city activities which other firms can exploit by locating in the central city. Government enhances the capacity of such firms to reap such externalities by planning land use and providing, regulating and policing the communication system – roads, traffic, public and quasi-public transport.

The third and final reason why more government and more inte-grated government is needed in urban than in rural areas is derived from the fact that as we move nearer to the centre so the tendency increases for the area to take on a collective functional role on behalf of the whole built-up area and its hinterland by providing common services that are not obtainable outside the central city. The larger the urban area the wider the range of such services provided. Many of these services are, of course, provided by the private sector, others by central government. But there remains an important range that are usually the responsibility of local government. Such services include higher and further education, art galleries, libraries, museums, theatres, car parks, markets, shopping and recreation centres, parks and so forth.

These links between urban-ness and the need for government have important implications for local government modernisation. In the first place, they place a large question mark against the town-plus-country thesis that underlies the present system and they do so on purely functional grounds. An urban area has distinctive needs not only in terms of requiring more collective action, but also in terms of more integrated government than a rural area. The advantages of creating a distinctive form of government for urban areas is for this reason powerful. They may even outweigh the planning advantages of extending the boundary of urban authorities to embrace the outer limits of the hinterland. They may also outweigh the other hypothetical advantages of boundary extension such as internalising public goods externalities and potential economies of scale. Moreover, if we also take into account the likely possibility, discussed earlier, that such enlarged units weaken the democratic quality of the system then even the modified city-plus-hinterland solution of the Walker Act looks very doubtful. The extreme form advocated by Derek Senior takes us out of the realm of local government.[39]

One way of exploiting the benefits of the extended boundary but at the same time retaining as strong a democratic element as possible is to create a two-tier system. This was the solution adopted by Senior and by the Walker Act. But if the second tier is to perform that purpose it must retain politically important powers. If it does so, however, there must inevitably be functional overlapping between the tiers. In the case of the Walker Act this has meant that there are two planning, two traffic and two highways authorities in every urban centre despite the fact that this is precisely the place where, as we have seen, integrated and effective government is most needed and where in the past there has always been integrated government since the inception of urban local government. Under the two-tier centre-plus-hinterland model vertical integration is sacrificed to horizontal integration. It is precisely this problem that led Redcliffe-Maud to the unitary authority.

There may be other aspects in which a certain scepticism about the functionalist case is appropriate. Let us look at the functional effectiveness claim first. This, it will be remembered, seeks to achieve a larger unit in order to provide the resources and the case load to make it possible to provide the full range of a given service to currently demanded levels. This looks a reasonably straightforward aim, but when it is translated into concrete terms it usually is transformed so that what is being assessed is not only the main aspects of the service, but also those relatively marginal innovations to professional orthodoxy that naturally exercise the professional groups who operate the service. But these emblems of professionalism, as it were, can hardly be said to constitute the fundamentals of the service. Anyone examining the evidence of the professional groups to the Redcliffe-Maud Commission could not fail to notice this tendency,[40] and it is perhaps best illustrated in the report of a national survey on the quality of local education authorities in relation to population size submitted to the Commission by the Department of Education and Science.[41] This survey was derived from the subjective assessments of Her Majesty's Inspectorate and its two principal conclusions were:

good authorities can be found through all size ranges but the weak ones are entirely below a population of 100,000 and others below an acceptable level are heavily concentrated in the size group up to 200,000.

and

the probability of good performance from an education authority increases with size and the probability of below-acceptable performance decreases rapidly with size.[42]

These are unambiguous conclusions, yet the twelve performance indicators on which they are based could hardly be said to measure comprehensively the principal components of an education service. It is notoriously difficult to get complete agreement either among laymen or professionals as to what precisely those components are. None the less, it is difficult to see how the following performance criteria (which comprise a third of those used by the HMI in arriving at their conclusions) are central to any assessment of the relationships between scale and educational performance, although it is perfectly conceivable that they are very important to an inspectorate intent on *raising the level* of the education service:

* 'Adequacy of specialist advisory staff
    (*a*) Range
    (*b*) Quality.'
* 'Encouragement of modern educational methods'
* 'Willingness to experiment'
* 'Relations with other authorities

    (*a*) "Free Trade" in pupils and students
    (*b*) Consultation over common problems.'
* 'Arrangements for assistance to pupils and
discretionary awards to students'.[43]

Doubts as to the validity of the HMI's conclusions are reinforced since each of the sixteen criteria were weighted according to their relative importance and the seven just listed make up no less than 44 per cent of the scoring.

There is another reason for scepticism about the functionalist case for reorganisation and the need to look more carefully at the advantages of not pursuing hypothetical scale advantages. It also underlines the advantages of restoring something more durable like urban-ness as a criterion of boundary drawing. This is the inevitable impermanence of functionalist criteria. Functions themselves change in their character; new ones arise and others are transferred to other agencies of government; and professional opinion changes as to what is the optimal population or area of administration. Moreover, new forms of transport or better roads can extend the commuting boundary. Functionalism, in short, is a recipe for the constant rejigging of the system. Obviously, local government cannot expect to enjoy as permanent boundaries as the nation state. Nevertheless, it is difficult to see how a local government system can operate effectively under a permanent state of impermanence. This is broadly the situation that the British local government system has faced since the end of the war, beginning with the Boundary Commission in 1945, continuing with the Local Government Commissions and the Redcliffe-Maud and Wheatley Commissions. For reasons discussed earlier (see p. 94) there has always been a special concern with population minima in Britain which other countries might find puzzling and this tendency goes back at least to the 1888 Act. In the last twenty years, however, under the pressure of functionalist arguments this tradition has verged on an obsession with a consequent rapid increase in the minima. Even as late as the early 1960s, the Local Government Commission was willing to make Torbay with a population of 100,000 a county borough, and the Herbert Commission on London government in 1960 proposed 'most-purpose' boroughs in the range of 100,000 to 150,000. The government subsequently upped these limits to 200,000 and a third of a million in the 1963 London Government Act. With the advent of the Redcliffe-Maud Commission, Whitehall increased the minimum and the central departments were strongly advocating population minima of 300,000, with a range of up to three million. The Commission itself settled for a range of 250,000 to one million. The counties under the Walker Act range from 109,000 to 2,700,000 and the districts from 24,000 to one million. It would be reassuring if we could say that, whatever its merits or demerits, the thirty-year period of uncertainty has come to end with the passing of the Act. But within two years of the passing of the Act another scheme with even larger top-tier units, this time on an economic region basis, was being enthusiastically promoted by the former Chief Planner of the Department of the Environment.[44]

Another prerequisite for any new approach to local government modernisation concerns the attitudes of the central departments and their Ministers. It is clear that the London Government Act of 1963 marked a watershed in the post-war reorganisation saga for it revealed to the Government and the Shadow Front Bench that it was possible to effect quite radical change without allowing the local authorities affected to take any part in the formulation of the terms of reference of the inquiry preceding change, or in the process following the inquiry but preceding Ministerial decision. Thereafter it was always possible that should a Minister or Cabinet desire to do in the rest of the country what Sir Keith Joseph had achieved in London there was little to stop them. Such a Minister soon made his appearance when Richard Crossman assumed the helm at the Ministry of Housing and Local Government. In his historic announcement in September 1965 that he would set up a 'powerful and important committee' to work out a set of principles 'according to which a commission would proceed to re-shape the areas and functions of local government so to enable it to do its job in modern terms'[45] he was, as Jane Morton has so perceptively noted, marking a crucial turning-point. For it meant the 'total rejection of the principle that local authorities had a right to define the scope and nature of change themselves'.[46] In the event, Mr Crossman changed his mind about the need for a ground-rules committee to precede the setting up of a Royal Commission. Instead he set up a Commission and charged it with the task of defining its own principles.

The implications of the new approach were not lost on Whitehall and the central departments were now in a position not merely to be passive spectators in the battle of wits between the local authorities and some reorganisation commission (as they had at the three preceding post-war inquiries), but active participants, despite the fact that their respective Ministers were to sit in judgement on the Commission's final report. The departments, in other words, could now for the first time put forward proposals without being accused of prejudging the issue for a system of local government which would suit *them* as well as meeting the requirements of the various functionalist arguments. It is therefore hardly surprising that they took up their new role with enthusiasm and provided the Commission with some of the most forthright and radical proposals of any put to it. Moreover, they all spoke with virtually one voice. The scheme they favoured involved a massive upheaval that effectively reduced the number of local authorities from about 1400 to between 30 and 40 city regions.[47]

That such a drastic reduction in the number of local authorities suited the departments there can be little doubt, for whatever the potential risks of creating such large authorities in terms of their ability to thwart central policy, they had undoubted advantages. First, there was the need to head off what appeared to be a growing interest in creating elected councils at the level of the economic planning regions that had been sparked off by the creation of the Economic Planning Boards and Councils in 1964 – that is to say, a growing interest in something that from the central government viewpoint went well beyond local government reorganisation and looked like the beginnings of quasi-federalism, or what, since the Kilbrandon Commission's report and the later upsurge of Scottish and Welsh nationalism, has come to be known as devolution. If local government were transformed into thirty to forty regional authorities then most of the functional arguments for devolution (and they were then the dominant ones) would disappear and with it the dangers of what was seen as a fatal weakening of the national body politic. As the Treasury evidence in making the case for the city region solution to the Redcliffe-Maud Commission put it:

> With this structure a further regional tier of government would be unnecessary. In a country of the size of England there seems to be no need for more than one tier below the Central Government with electoral responsibility for control of expenditure and powers of local taxation. The interposition of a further regional tier would probably lead to administrative complexity which is wasteful certainly of staff and probably of resources too. There is also the danger that such a course would lead to the disintegration of broad national policy and to very great difficulties for Whitehall in arbitrating between the claims of the regional authorities so constituted.[48]

The second reason for central government's enthusiasm for the city regional solution was perhaps rather more decisive. In a word it meant a radically reduced task for them. Dealing with thirty to forty authorities rather than 1400 for, say, housing and 140 for planning and education obviously meant a substantial reduction in workload. We may assume that reduction in workload has become an important objective of the centre in a world where its responsibilities have been expanding at something like an exponential rate in an ever more hostile environment, and where the local government sector absorbs something like a third of all public expenditure which itself is periodically in need of rapid and delicate management. Central government, in short, has just as urgent a need to aggregate public-sector agencies as it has private-sector ones. Naturally, this motive for local government reorganisation is not one that is usually discussed in public, although it was stated reasonably explicitly by the Treasury in its evidence to the Redcliffe-Maud Commission thus:

> For the future there will be need to be much closer working and more frequent exchange of views between the central government and local authorities collectively, in order to secure satisfactory results. This closer working would be greatly facilitated by a reduction in the numbers of the major spending authorities.[49]

Perhaps the best statement of the case for reforming local government so as to reduce the central workload was made by Mr Walker himself to the House of Commons Expenditure Committee when it was investigating transport planning in June 1972. Mr Walker was discussing various aspects of national transportation policy and Mr du Cann, a member of the Committee, asked how he was going to ensure that local authorities would actually carry them out. This is Mr Walker's reply,

> After reorganization I shall have six metropolitan areas and 39 counties and this will be my total relationship in that sphere with the major transport authorities. This does mean that both at regional office level and in terms of our office in Whitehall we are able to establish a relationship which I think will be very effective. The ultimate power, of course, which we have is in the expenditure, and I believe that we can develop with local authorities this block grant system so that we can see that the best knowledge is applied to try to bring a total solution to the areas involved. This will mean that we get basic co-ordination in central and local government thinking and few difficulties.[50]

Whatever view is taken of Mr Walker's command structure conception of central local relations, we may readily sympathise with him as with any other Secretary of State for the Environment who wants to ensure his policies are carried out. Nevertheless, reducing the central workload ought not to be a criterion for redesigning local government. The number of local units must be a function of the needs and conditions of the sub-national communities whose existence justifies the creation of a local government system in the first place. If the structure of local government is also to be determined by the needs of central government then it is difficult to see the justification for a local government system, as opposed to some form of deconcentrated central administration. The essence of local government, it cannot be emphasised too sharply, is that it is local; but almost all the reformist pressure over the past twenty years has been designed to transform it into something else. *Its major defining characteristic has come to be seen as its central defect.* This seems to be an intellectual trend that is common to all the heavily urbanised Western democracies: As Forstall and Jones have put it, 'The great anathema is the under-bounded political or administrative area.'[51] The problem is that it has gone very much further in Britain, to the point where it has become a self-defeating process. Glancing back at the table on p. 95 with its gross disparity in scale between Britain and the rest (which is even wider for the counties) we must question whether we now *have* local government in many areas of the country. That is to say, even the district, which is supposed to be the democratic counterweight to the inevitable remoteness of the county, is merely an arbitrary tract whose *only* rationale is the size of its population. These populations have therefore no possibility of identifying subjectively with their local government. Nor can such districts reflect the objective indicators of community or be accessible to their electorates. Yet it is these three factors which together are essential for democracy. The very notion of an elected local authority with a fixed boundary implies the pre-existence of a distinctive common interest.

The obsession with functionalism not only dresses up arbitrary tracts as local authorities, it also denies identifiable communities the chance to undertake important collective tasks themselves. Even the most enthusiastic functionalist would be hard put to explain why the city of Nottingham with a population of 305,000 is considered incapable of providing its own education, health and welfare services; or why towns that would be major civic authorities in their own right anywhere else in the world, such as Leicester, Stoke-on-Trent, Plymouth, Derby, Southampton and Portsmouth, are also considered to be similarly incapable.

Perhaps one last possible prerequisite for any new approach to local government reorganisation is the creation of an intermediate tier at the regional level between the centre and locality. Lacking one, we are it seems constantly tempted into the pursuit of the ever-larger local government unit, either for irrelevant motives like that of central workload reduction just discussed, or to achieve some functional capacity that is either unattainable or should properly be the task of the missing intermediate tier. There may be a number of reasons for creating such an intermediate tier, not least the need to make more accountable the growing number of non-departmental organisations that at present exist in a limbo between central and local government proper.[52] There may also be a need to create an intermediate level in response to Scottish and Welsh nationalism. But so ingrained is functionalist thinking that there may be an equally important need to create an intermediate tier so as to head off at least some of the functionalist claims and in the process both protect local government from further 'reform' and, hopefully, correct the more glaring faults of the Walker Act.

NOTES AND REFERENCES

1 For one rare exception to this see Lord Redcliffe-Maud and Bruce Wood, *English Local Government Reformed* (Oxford University Press, 1974) chas 4 and 11. For some general discussion and analyses of the Redcliffe-Maud Report and the Walker Act, almost all of them critical or neutral, see:

J. Bowen-Rees, *Government by Community* (Charles Knight, 1971).

J. A. Brand, *Local Government Reform in England, 1888–1974* (Croom Helm, 1975).

Jane Morton, *The Best Laid Schemes?* (Charles Knight, 1970).

Geoffrey Smith (ed.), *Redcliffe-Maud's Brave New England* (Charles Knight, 1969).

H. Victor Wiseman, *Local Government in England: 1958–69* (Routledge, 1970).

Bruce Wood, *The Process of Local Government Reform: 1966–74* (Allen & Unwin, 1976).

Douglas E. Ashford, 'Reorganizing British Local Government: A Policy Problem', *Local Government Studies* 2, 4 (1976).

S. L. Bristow, 'The Criteria for Local Government Reorganization and Local Authority Autonomy', *Policy and Politics* 1, 2 (1972).

C. J. Davies, 'The Reform of Local Government with Special Reference to England', *Studies in Comparative Local Government* 7 (winter 1973).

W. Hampton, 'Political Attitudes to Change in City Council Administration', *Local Government Studies*, Apr 1972.

G. W. Jones, 'The Local Government Act 1972 and the Redcliffe-Maud Commission', *Political Quarterly* 44, 2 (1973).

—— 'Varieties of Local Politics', *Local Government Studies* 1, 2 (1975).

—— 'Intergovernmental Relations in Britain', *The Annals of the American Academy of Political and Social Science*, Nov 1974.

R. Newman, 'The Relevance of "Community" in Local Government Reorganization', *Local Government Studies*, 6 Oct 1973.

Roderick Rhodes, 'Local Government Reform: Three Questions', *Social and Economic Administration* 8, 1 (1974).

Derek Senior, 'Metropolitan Planning and Local Government Reform', *Town and Country Planning* 40, 2 (Feb 1972).

L. J. Sharpe, 'The Weak Points of the Bill', *Municipal Review*, Feb 1972.

2 *Royal Commission on Local Government in England. Research Study 8, Community Attitudes Survey: England* (HMSO, 1969) pp. 127–9.

3 *Royal Commission on Local Government in England: Short Version*, Cmnd 4039 (1969) p. 2.

4   See the claims made by Labour MPs in *House of Commons Debates, 1971–2, Official Report of Standing Committee D – Local Government Bill.*

5   *New Society*, 18 Feb 1971, p. 259.

6   Ashford, 'Reorganizing British Local Government', p. 7.

7   For a discussion of what these interests were and how they influenced the setting up of the Redcliffe-Maud Commission, see R. H. S. Crossman, *The Diaries of a Cabinet Minister, Vol. 1: Minister of Housing, 1964–66* (Hamish Hamilton and Jonathan Cape, 1975) pp. 64, 91 and 380.

8   The party-political background to the London Government Act is discussed in L. J. Sharpe and D. Hill, *The Politics of a Changing Metropolis*, ch. 1 (forthcoming).

9   *Reform of Local Government in England*, Cmnd 4276 (1970) para. 60.

10 *Hansard* (Commons) vol. 784, col. 1462.

11 See the report of his speech to the 1970 Conservative Party Local Government Conference, *Sunday Times*, 1 Mar 1970.

12 Wood, *The Process of Local Government Reform*, p. 100.

13 *Local Government in England*, Cmnd 4584 (1971) p. 6.

14 See Norman Chester, 'Restoring Power to the People', *The Times*, 16 Feb 1972.

15 *Costs of Reform* (Cheshire County Council, 1970).

16 Its full title was *Inquiry into Local Government Finance*, and its *Report* was published in 1976, Cmnd 6453.

17 *Local Government in England*, pp. 5 and 6.

18 *Report of the Royal Commission on Local Government in England*, Cmnd 4040 (1969) vol. 1.

19 See, for example, *The Democratic Alternative to Maud* (Rural District Councils Association, 1969).

20 See, for example, 'Why Local Democracy?' (Fabian Tracts, 1965).

21 *Local Government in England*, para. 8.

22 For a succinct account of this argument see *Royal Commission on Local Government in England: Written Evidence of the Ministry of Housing and Local Government* (HMSO, 1967) pp. 60–6.

23 One of the earliest academic discussions of local government reorganisation to employ public goods theory is Vincent Ostrom *et al.*, 'The Organization of Government in Metropolitan Areas. A Theoretical Enquiry', *American Political Science Review*, LV (1961). Also see J. Stefan Dupré, 'Intergovernmental Relations and the Metropolitan Area', in Simon R. Miles (ed.), *Metropolitan Problems* (Toronto: Methuen, 1970).

24 For a discussion of the service-effectiveness case see *Royal Commission on Local Government in England: Written Evidence of* (i) *Ministry of Housing and Local Government*, paras. 256–62; and (ii) *Department of Education and Science*, paras. 83–102.

25 For a discussion of such economies, see *Royal Commission on Local Government in England: Written Evidence of H.M. Treasury*, paras 8–10.

26 This figure is for England and Wales less Greater London and the composition of the various types of authority before and after reorganisation is as follows:

Old System		New System	
English County Boroughs	79	Metropolitan Counties	6
Welsh County Boroughs	4	Metropolitan Districts	36
English Counties	45	English Counties	39
Welsh Counties	13	Welsh Counties	8
English Boroughs and Districts	1086	English Districts	296
Welsh Boroughs and Districts	164	Welsh Districts	37
Total	1391		422

27 *Report of the Royal Commission on Local Government in England*, vol. III, Appendix 9.

28 K. Newton, 'Community Performance in Britain', *Current Sociology* 22 (1976) p. 54. Also see R. A. Dahl, 'The City in the Future of Democracy', in L. Feldman and D. Goldrick, *Politics and Government of Urban Canada* (Toronto: Methuen, 1972) who concludes that, 'there is no worthwhile evidence that there are any significant economies of scale in city governments for cities over 50,000', pp. 420–1.

29 *Local Government in England*, p. 6, para. 8.

30 Robert C. Wood, *1400 Governments* (Cambridge, Mass.: Harvard University Press, 1961).

31 For a more detailed discussion of this point see L. J. Sharpe, 'Modernizing the Periphery: Local Reorganization in Britain and some French Comparisons', in J. Lagroye and V. Wright (eds), *Local Government in Britain and France* (forthcoming).

32 The Report lists ten principles on which its proposals were based, seven of which are functionalist, see *Report*, vol. 1, pp. 3–4.

33 Wood, *The Process of Local Government Reform*, p. 24.

34 For a more detailed discussion of the link between functional effectiveness and democracy, see L. J. Sharpe, 'American Democracy Re-considered, Part 2', *British Journal of Political Science* 3, 2 (1973).

35 Brian Barry, 'Size and Democracy', *Government and Opposition* 4, 9 (1974) p. 495.

36 Barry, 'Size and Democracy', p. 497.

37 J. S. Mill, *Representative Government* (Dent, 1968) p. 350.

38 Mancur Olson, *The Logic of Collective Action* (New York: Schocken, 1971) p. 171.

39 *Royal Commission on Local Government in England, Vol. II: Memorandum of Dissent by Mr. Senior*, Cmnd 4040–1 (HMSO, 1969).

40 See, for example, the evidence of the Association of Child Care Officers, the Town Planning Institute, the Association of Medical Officers, and the Institute of Municipal Treasurers and Accountants in *Royal Commission on Local Government in England. Written Evidence of the Professional Associations* (HMSO, 1967).

41 *Report*, vol. III, Appendix 11.

42   *Report*, vol. iii, p. 231.
43   *Report*, vol. iii, p. 232.
44   J. James, Address to the 25th Anniversary Conference of the Town and Country Planning Association, 1974.
45   R. H. S. Crossman, Address to the Association of Municipal Corporations Annual Conference, Torquay, September 1965.
46   Morton, *The Best Laid Schemes?*, p. 17.
47   The departments which gave the most detailed evidence (Transport, and Housing and Local Government) did also contemplate second-tier authorities in addition to the 30–40 main authorities. But they were very shadowy entities and it is reasonably clear from their written evidence, if not from their oral evidence, that these second-tier authorities would have no functions of any importance.
48   *Royal Commission on Local Government in England, Written Evidence of H.M. Treasury* (HMSO, 1967) para. 5, p. 2.
49   *Written Evidence of H.M. Treasury*, para. 18, p. 5.
50   *House of Commons, Second Report of the Expenditure Committee. Urban Transport Planning, Vol. II: Minutes of Evidence* (HMSO, 1973) p. 507, para. 2444.
51   Richard L. Forstall and Victor Jones, 'Selected Demographic, Economic and Governmental Aspects of Contemporary Metropolis', in Miles, *Metropolitan Problems*, p. 47.
52   See D. C. Hague *et al.* (eds), *Public Policy and Private Interest: the Institutions of Compromise* (Macmillan, 1975) for a discussion of the growth of non-departmental bodies.

8 Management and Politics: A European Dimension

UWE KITZINGER

Norman Chester's concern for the practical applicability of social studies has marked Oxford in many ways. One was his encouragement of European political studies, another his decisive contribution to the founding of the Oxford Management Centre.

It was he who, in 1956, negotiated with the Ford Foundation to endow a Fellowship at Nuffield in European Politics and to finance what was meant to be a ten-year programme of research and conferences but which in fact, by proper husbanding of investments, has become a permanent activity of the College. The special relationship between Nuffield and the Fondation Nationale des Sciences Politiques in the rue St Guillaume has been cemented with two regular conferences a year comparing the evolution of French and British politics and a whole series of problems common to both countries. A number of books and a great number of articles written by successive Ford Fellows on French, German and other national politics, but also in particular on Community problems, helped British understanding of political and institutional developments on the other side of the Channel. Few had, in the mid-fifties, the vision to recognise just how closely these developments would, by degrees, come to affect the fate of the United Kingdom itself. When, at the time of the 1975 referendum, Norman Chester became Chairman of 'Oxford in Europe', he could look back on twenty years of work in the College which sought to ensure that the practical interdependence between Britain and the new Europe would not be neglected in academic research.

European political studies, in the Nuffield context, remained essentially a small-scale operation which never involved more than four or five people at a time. Within the college structure the generosity of the Ford grant, while satisfying the requirements of individual researchers doing their own thing, allowed little more than that, and the University felt no need for any major teaching programme, let alone any special centre of research, on European contemporary affairs. Not so in the case of management education. In 1964 the University had established a Certificate and a B.Phil. in Management and in 1965, on the initiative of Norman Chester and a small group of economists and businessmen, the Oxford Centre for Management Studies was founded as Oxford's contribution to improving the quality of British management. It set out to foster research into management and business economics, to provide teaching for post-graduates in management, and to organise a small high-level course for practising executives.

Norman Chester remained Chairman of its management council and guided it through the crucial first ten years of its life. He saw it grow and prosper to its present scale – a zinc and concrete building with accommodation for twenty-four executives, a fine library, research facilities and a teaching staff of twelve Fellows, on a 30-acre site two miles south of Carfax. He helped it build close and fruitful relations with some twenty British firms and a number of distinguished visiting Fellows. But what, one may then ask, was the head of a social science research college, himself an expert on political studies and public administration, doing when he set out to establish a business school? For what have the study and teaching of politics to offer to the study and teaching of business management, or for that matter what has the study of management to offer to politics? So was this not, really, another Football Commission, essentially extrinsic to a Warden of Nuffield's main professional concern?

It is on the contrary the object of this brief chapter to argue that, if ever there was any clear divorce between management and politics (and even that question might be debated), today they are so closely linked that even to formulate the dichotomy is to be in danger of committing what our Oxford philosophy colleagues call a 'type fallacy'. It is to assume that the two words 'management' and 'politics' describe distinct entities of analogous type. The relationship is surely far more complicated than that. It is not just that the techniques of business management have become some of the techniques of politics in our societies at large. That is the first, but a minor, aspect. The affinity is wider than that. Business management may entail some highly specialised skills with their own disciplines. But so do educational management, hospital management, the organisation of police forces, the running of a civil service, of a navy, or of a major medium of communication. Each of these has something to learn from – and perhaps also something to give to – business management; and they certainly draw on many of the same skills.

Second, there is the recognition that the management of business enterprises and other social organisations is a part, an integral part and an important part, of the whole way in which we organise our living and earning our living together. It is not simply as a matter of ethical prescription that we talk of 'the public responsibility of business': it is a sheer description of objective function that top management in industry and commerce and finance forms today part of the governance of our total society. That also is why, thirdly, the way in which even private businesses are managed and organised is becoming increasingly a subject-matter of political debate and decision. The acceleration of social changes symbolised by 'the events' in Paris in 1968 and in this country by the recent Bullock report, the economic changes symbolised by 'the crisis' of 1973–4, national suspicions of transnational enterprises, consumerism and ecological concerns are seeing to that. Fourthly – and it is on that aspect above all that this chapter seeks to concentrate – the task of managing any enterprise is becoming less and less the science of the technical optimum, and more and more the art of the humanly and socially possible.

No doubt some people still have at the back of their minds a paradigm contrasting traditional concepts of 'management' and of 'politics'. They may think the two differ in at least four respects. Management, some people think, is a science which:

–selects a minimum of pre-existing resources of various kinds;
–then feeds them into a finite process, a sort of 'black box';
–which has knobs on the outside, through which it is subjected to rational external managerial control;
–in order to achieve a maximum output of a single, predetermined good – return on investment, or value added or whatever it may be.

But, if we take these four aspects in reverse order:

–in politics there is no single given output target: there is a welter of conflicting goals and demands to satisfy;
–in politics there is no black box to be controlled from the outside by pressing the right button: there is only an open arena, and in that arena the participants find themselves acting and reacting rationally or irrationally in conflict and in shifting coalitions, by personal influence, social pressure and uneasy compromise;
–then again, the process itself is not a finite one, whether in time or in any clearly delimited system boundaries: it is a permanently unstable, continuous and almost seamless process;
–nor is there a set tray of inputs from which to choose: there is only a confusing total environment with multifarious facets of different and changing relevance and intrusiveness.

Now for some of the time in the classroom we may still abstract from reality and pretend that we can isolate inputs, black box, control buttons, and final success and failure. But, in practice, whether or not modern politics is becoming more 'managerial' by the use of more 'scientific' and more quantitative methods of appraising and managing a whole society, certainly modern management is becoming far more political in essence and in character. This is happening first of all even within firms, corporations, and other organisations; secondly, of course, it is also happening in the relations between any organisation and its environment. But I also want to make a third point, and ask how far we can realistically still maintain that distinction between any firm or specific functional organisation and the totality of its social and political environment.

First, within organisations, there is the decline or death of Adam Smith's 'economic man'. He never quite existed even in Adam Smith's day. But now affluence, taxation and social security – not to mention broad changes of attitudes – have killed him stone-dead. People no longer see maximising their gross earnings as their overriding aim. The more consumer durables we have, the greater the relative scarcity of evenings with the family, the greater the desire for professional recognition, for job enrichment, for cultural and environmental satisfactions. Our motivations are clearly multidimensional. The effective manager recognises that fact – in himself as well as in others – and then he plans accordingly. One can still run a factory with workers who, rather than earn more money, do not want to fall out with their mates. But a manager will make more money if he adapts his investment decisions to this world of shifting values in advance, and he will run his business with less frustration if he is realistic about what this whole trend has done to the old organisation chart and to the traditional concepts of power and responsibility within the firm.

In the classical model, hiring and firing are the ultimate sanctions and rewards. How easy it must have been when operating in the single dimension of the cash nexus: the successful firm could promote its effective employees, the unsuccessful one was forced in any case to lay off its workforce. In that sort of world the organisation chart had a fairly clear meaning: there is power downwards, and responsibility upwards, delegation and accountability, and middle management acts as the transmission belt both ways. Today power is diffused throughout the firm and seeps out into its environment to the point where two kidnappers can bring a factory to a halt. Today one cannot fire without bringing the union out on strike, promote without rigmaroles of competition and consultation, raise wages without falling foul of parities and differentials (and even, now, of the law); the addressees of the old rewards and sanctions half the time have become unresponsive, indeed almost indifferent to either. The very top layer of management can take decisions on financing and location and on product policy, but

the margin of manœuvre for active middle managers is becoming more
and more restricted. Part of their job may still be to decide and to
execute, but increasingly their role is to cajole, to compromise, and
their fate to be ground between the upper and the nether millstone – so
no wonder there is alienation. But both at the top and in middle
management within the firm today, the rigorous sciences of taking the
hard facts, working out the right decision, and then controlling its
execution, are still necessary skills, but they are no longer sufficient.
There is more to decision-making than the decision that is made: there
is also, and not least, the manner of its making. Increasingly the name
of the game is consensus and the soft facts of attitudes and personalities,
the sensitive antennae of the politician have to be called in as well, even
within the outwardly so cut-and-dried, comfortingly hierarchical
pyramid of the single firm, directed as an organisation to a single
objective.

But is the modern corporate enterprise really directed only to any
one single objective? One may argue – convincingly – that while
individuals may be multidimensional in their motivation, a functional
institution like a firm (after all, and not only in Tönnies' German, a
Gesellschaft, not a *Gemeinschaft*) has – and ought to have – but one aim:
maximising the financial return to its owners, whether measured in
terms of its balance-sheet or the discounted present value of its dividend
payouts or its Stock Exchange capitalisation.

Let us leave aside the question of whether or not it 'should'. Even
if, in the very long run, it does only have that single objective, the long
run is long indeed. On the way to it, in any short or medium-term
strategy the modern corporate enterprise – whether it likes it or not –
finds itself reasoning – and forced to reason – in a number of other
dimensions as well. Customer satisfaction, workers' loyalties, management's own rewards, market share, the reduction of financial uncertainty, its public image, international and product diversification,
avoidance of non-commercial risks – all these compete with the profit-
and-loss account in the allocation of scarce resources and the setting of
medium-term goals. (What is true in private commerce or industry is,
of course, even truer in any form of private non-profit, quasi-public or
public enterprise, where the management has permanently to weigh
against each other, e.g. medical efficiency, patients' psychology, staff
overstrain and budget constraints, or the rival claims of practice,
teaching and research.)

Whether or not private enterprises have any legitimate criteria of
success other than maximising the return to the shareholder in the long
run, in practice managements have constantly to make incalculable
trade-offs between different short-term objectives in incommensurate
dimensions. In each case there may be a variety of correct solutions,

and the choice between them is essentially a qualitative, discretionary matter of political judgement.

Again, when we look beyond the firm itself, there is the second phenomenon: the dominant feature in the firm's environment today is public policy. Every firm has one partner who matters more than its suppliers, more than its customers, more even than its labour force, because it acts on all of these as well as acting on the firm directly: and that is government at all its levels, from the local hospital board to the Brussels Commission. By its laws and its taxes, its purchasing policies and its *ad hoc* decisions, by pressures and incentives and exhortations, government has powers or weighty influence on location and pollution, on pricing policy and dividend distribution, on safety standards and on labour relations. The trade unions, too, have gained weighty influence on wages and personnel policies, on rationalisation and productivity: they, too, impose shifting constraints on business policy. But the unions, like business, are in turn limited by law, and government is limited both by business and the unions; and then the Greek chorus of public opinion, and even popular opinion from time to time, has its own contribution to make. In fact, the mutual dependence, indeed symbiosis, of business, unions, and government, citizens, producers and consumers, resembles the mutual veto powers of feudal barons and kings, and their reciprocal power struggles fought with disparate, but not ineffectual weapons in shifting coalitions against each other. When Walter Hallstein, as President of the European Commission, said of the European Community, 'We are not in business, we are in politics', the counterpoint may have been meaningful in the fifties. In the seventies, to be in business *is* to be in politics, just as surely as Monsieur Jourdain, whether he knew it or not, in fact spoke prose.

Moreover, thirdly, can one still talk about what is 'within' and what is 'outside' the firm? Have we not rather reached a point when a firm, however large (and perhaps the larger the truer this is for it), has to be considered not only as an autonomous system, but also as a point of intersection between vast different systems – of oil politics and labour relations, of ideological conflict and monetary turmoil – or as having to survive somehow in the interstices between them? This becomes a matter of boundary consciousness, of awareness of what is intrinsic and what is extrinsic to a situation – and even over the past decade or two, depending on where any organisation finds itself in space and in its total social context, much of the social and political evolution that was extrinsic even a few years back has now, in effect, become intrinsic to the problems of enterprise. We can deplore that, but management consists of realistically facing and coping with the facts of here and now, the trends of there and tomorrow – not of weeping over them, but of understanding them, and turning them to our advantage.

So more and more today we need not just optimal technical solutions
to clearly defined present problems: we have to extend and refine our
concepts to cope with overlapping political processes between inter-
lacing social sub-systems. And precisely because of the impact, which
we cannot but recognise more and more, of the human and social,
political and cultural facts intrinsic to the enterprise and its environment, it becomes more and more problematic simply to graft on to a
different social stock techniques and indeed philosophies of management that were conceived in and for a different culture. Which is why
management education is too serious a matter to be left to the
professors of business schools.

Until a decade or two ago, 'business schools' were an American
invention. Even today, the bulk of teachers at European management
centres have had the bulk of their own training in management (and
in the techniques of teaching it) at American institutions, and it is to
America they tend to return on their sabbatical leaves of study. Of
course we have every reason to be grateful for the pioneering efforts of
American thinkers and American educational establishments in
developing the study and teaching of management. Without their
asking the relevant questions and seeking to find the answers in the
world around them, European management centres might never have
been started, and would certainly have gone nothing like so far. But on
the other hand, we do neither ourselves in Europe, nor the cause of
management as a subject of study and teaching anywhere, any service
by simply taking over lock, stock and barrel the objectives and the
assumptions, the methods and the conclusions that may have worked
well in the past – even the recent past – in the United States. North
American society is as untypical of the rest of the world as one could
imagine, and the fact that some of its consumption habits have proved
infectious the world over is no proof – any more than Japanese productive efficiency is proof – that management organisation based on
American, or Japanese, assumptions would prove ideal in Britain or
France. It is thus one of the first tasks of management centres in Europe
to ask themselves searching questions as to the relevance and applicability of inherited American premises and precepts to the tasks
confronting us in the Europe of the 1980s.

But there are several more conclusions to be drawn from that train
of reflection. Certainly we have a responsibility towards less developed
countries to aid them in matters of management education. But just as
we must beware, in using American methods in Europe, of automatic
admiration, so must we beware, in helping Asian and African and
Latin American countries, of an industrial or managerial absolutism of
our own. It is up to us to cultivate a cultural humility that recognises
that what would work in Britain or France could prove far from ideal

in Ghana or Indonesia, India or Brazil, where we cannot presuppose the ambitions of nuclear families, the time-is-money syndrome, the judgement of individuals by what they do rather than by what they are, and all the rest of puritan industrial ideology.

But cultural relativism applies not only between continents. Just as America is a special case in the world, so is Britain in Europe. So, for that matter, are Western Germany, Sicily, and Switzerland. Where much of American thought could, in the past, presuppose American managerial superiority and almost assume therefore its exclusive claim to single universal truth, we in Europe, from seeing the cultural inappropriateness of tenets self-evident in the United States, can also recognise the geographical and cultural limitations of any attempts at a European managerial dogma of our own. The question, 'Can there be a European teaching of management distinct from the American body of doctrine?' must therefore be answered in the negative: though not because American insights are universally applicable, but because, on the contrary, wherever we find ourselves confronted with human and social issues, even any attempt at a 'European' solution would break down in the face of the remaining manifold cultural differences between our different societies even within a single Economic Community. Only internationally comparative studies will – in business as in politics – do justice to current realities and provide the most fruitful basis for theoretical analysis.

To operate in modern business on anything except the smallest scale, a purely nationally-oriented management education would thus prove as sadly inadequate as any attempt to confine oneself to universally applicable verities. Even where business operations are not yet international, the options usually are, and so certainly are the parameters that govern profitability. One cannot, these days, run even a dairy farm without being acutely aware of international perspectives – oil negotiations and fertiliser prices, overseas crop failures and Brussels directives. How much more necessary then is an international perspective to the managers of any firm that wants to break into overseas markets when the home economy is stagnating, wants to create a stream of hard currency earnings for itself and the national economy, or wants merely to protect itself against blindness to international factors that may catch it unawares when it could, with knowledge and foresight, have built overseas opportunities and overseas threats into its investment, production and marketing decisions from the start.

Certainly most major firms, whether in manufacturing or in financial services, would regard it as old-fashioned these days to think in anything less than European or world-wide dimensions in their marketing. But how many of them have, in their personnel recruitment, training and development policies, followed that logic through? Certainly the

British economy needs men and women managers who can operate in French, in German and perhaps in some other language as well, who can work with Brazilians, Japanese and Saudi Arabians, who can cope with an Egyptian civil service, a Polish trade authority, or an African dictatorship. This is not simply a matter of reading the right periodicals, though that is part of the story. It is a matter of awareness of the types of factor involved, the means of information and the styles of contact abroad: it requires managers who have been steeped in at least one foreign culture, had some exposure to several more, and have practiced sensitising themselves to societies other than their own. Top management in a big modern firm cannot afford not to know when it has to learn (and how to set about learning) the relevant aspects in the cultural background and political systems of competitors like the Japanese, or of potential sources of finance like the Arabs, or of vast potential markets like China. Perhaps not every internationally-oriented businessman has to have read Descartes and the Koran, or to have studied Shintoism and Mao Tse-tung. But he should at least have reached the point at which he seriously asks himself if he should. Certainly it is by sensitivity to international political and cultural factors that the young executive today reveals the boardroom baton in his engineer's or accountant's knapsack.

But the renunciation of absolutism is required of us, not only in culture and geography, not only in space but also, and increasingly, in time. Not only have private values and public environment changed over the past decade, not only has the separation of economic life from political, of national from international, been eroded, but the changes continue and they are most likely still accelerating, possibly at an exponential rate, but certainly in different and incoherent degrees and directions. We are in the middle of an explosion of technology, of an explosion of population, of an explosion of expectations here and overseas as to the psychological and social and material needs that the social system is meant to satisfy. At the same time we are faced by a more or less finite environment, and the costs and limitations of human adaptability. Our perception lags behind events, the very concepts with which we try to apprehend and order our environment lag behind reality, and our ideologies and our institutions are subject to increasing built-in obsolescence. If history was ever cyclical in the past, it certainly seems to have broken out of that pattern now. So if as pragmatists we reject the comforting thesis (common to Christian and Marxist mythology) of a new stable equilibrium on the other bank of the maelstrom, then our choice is really only between a cataclysmic nightmare – that the system is bound to spin out of control altogether – and a sceptical Heraclitean view: history is one damn thing after another, only more so, bigger if not better, probably worse. Either way, we can no longer rely on the fundamental premise of inductive reasoning: that the future will be like the past. And once that assurance has gone – and I think in strategic respects it has – then we really live in a very uncertain world in which all our knowledge, all our disciplines, all our presuppositions are open to challenge and management education, so far from being a once-and-for-all process of absorbing a defined corpus of certain knowledge, stands clearly revealed as a perpetual process of continuous up-dating, endless questioning, and permanent intellectual dialogue.

From this progressive interpretation of politics and economics, of public and private sectors and of national and international operations, and, last but not least, from the acceleration of change in our techno-logical and human environment, there follow certain lessons for management education itself.

First, in our teaching, we have a double responsibility. On the one side we must be rigorous in our disciplines and tough in our standard procedures. But there is also a second responsibility: not only to answer some questions, but also to take good care to keep certain others open; for there are some questions, and not the least important, to which we have just have no pat answers or routine solutions. And the higher the successful manager goes up the ladder, the more will he need, not only the techniques that can be taught, but also those elusive and uncertain arts which can, at best, only be learnt. More and more what matters is the ability to spot when our beautifully logical and coherent tech-niques simply cease to be applicable, are in fact dangerous and counter-productive: what matters is the flexibility – and the guts – to abandon them. Certainly society has never been in greater need of this sort of self-criticism and consequent corrective innovation than today. Our means are relative to fast-changing circumstances, and there is no agreed absolute even as to ends. It is as if events were forcing us to move from Euclid's concepts of space into those of Einstein. We have, at one and the same time, implacably to impose excellence in Euclidean drills, and also to admit the concept of relativity and the vast uncharted domains which our social sciences have yet to probe and to conquer.

That, secondly, is also why teaching is not enough. Just as one cannot have systematic teaching without rigorous conceptual analysis, so one cannot achieve realistic teaching without empirical research. Each is needed to fructify the other. Only thus can we forge new intellectual tools to cope with current dilemmas. Our management centres must intensify their research firmly rooted in current realities, focus on up-coming strategic policy options, and explore alternative scenarios for the constraints on business decisions and the opportunities for management action in the future.

That also, thirdly, is why management centres must look to the practical world of business for intellectual support. We need practising managers in all sorts of enterprises to guide us to the burning issues, to advise us on what has been tried and failed, to share with us hunches as to where possible solutions may lie. And by asking us to help them solve their problems, they will force us to keep up-to-date with their most acute concerns. Only thus can management education really fulfil its social and political mission. For a modern management centre not to be simply a business school, transmitting to tomorrow's managers yesterday's tired intellectual capital, it must be a forum for facts and ideas, a place of dialogue between those hard pressed to take urgent practical decisions and those with the privilege and the concurrent obligations of longer time-spans and wider comparisons.

The Oxford Management Centre, on the green slopes at the edge of the city of which he was an Alderman, drawing on the economists, sociologists, and industrial relations experts of the University of which he was a Councillor, was designed as a resource for British industry, commerce and finance in their efforts to raise the productivity of the British economy and to work Britain out of her persistent balance of payments difficulties by more successful exports to the European Community and the rest of the world. That concept falls squarely both into what used, after all, to be called 'Manchesterism', and also into Norman Chester's own concept of what a university should be doing in the modern world. The three activities of academic teaching, practical problem-solving, and scholarly research are mutually rein-forcing parts of a single whole. Their combination must be at the service ultimately of ordinary workers and football-fans all over the country, to help raise their standard of living and the quality of their living and working together. It thus aptly expresses the profoundly liberal and social, North Country and internationalist, ideals for which Norman Chester worked within and beyond the College.

9 The Public Corporation: An Ambiguous Species

NEVIL JOHNSON

> Generally, I feel that it is inconceivable under our parliamentary system, that, if a Public Board, appointed by a Minister and associated in the public mind with his Department, goes seriously wrong, the Minister will not be held accountable, however precisely or indefinitely relations between him and the Board are laid down by statute. [Major Gwilym Lloyd-George, in a memorandum of June 1943 supplementary to the report of the Cabinet Sub-Committee on the Future of the Electricity Industry, R44(3)]

Public corporations of the trading variety can be treated either as agencies for the supply of goods and services or as experiments in public administration. The applied economist is most likely to approach them from the first of these perspectives. His concern will be to consider the extent to which a public corporation is able to produce goods efficiently and economically[1] and if it is hindered from so doing, what economic reasons account for this and under what economic conditions performance might be optimised. For the student of government and administration the public corporation is a particular type of administrative institution which engages in commercial activities (the aspect of the matter which really interests the economist), but does so subject to certain constraints set by its position within the political and administrative system as a whole. These constraints are in essentials at least embodied in statute: they find expression in the powers and duties of the different public corporations and in the powers exercisable by Ministers in relation to their boards. In total these constraining conditions define the institutional framework within which a corporation must conduct its commercial operations. It is to these conditions that the student of administration will direct his attention and in so doing he will hope to arrive at a characterisation of this particular species in the administrative world. Of course, the interests of the economist lead him on to the analysis of institutional conditions and the administrative scientist cannot ignore the economic factors at stake in the operations of commercial public corporations. An area of overlap between the two perspectives is inevitable. But the rough distinction already made still seems to remain valid. The economist is concerned with economic analysis in relation to the public corporations, though he has to recognise that economic behaviour is seriously 'skewed' by conditions of a non-economic nature. The administrative specialist needs to know something of the economic factors at stake, but his focus is on the conditions which 'skew' the commercial operation of public corporations, thus distinguishing them in important ways from a private business concern.

For over forty years now Norman Chester has been fascinated by the administrative perspective on public corporations. The species existed before 1945, but it was rare and not too hard to characterise. 'The London Passenger Transport Board was to Lord Ashfield, its first Chairman, the London General Omnibus Company much enlarged and given a monopoly, with a muted Minister of Transport in place of equity shareholders.'[2] In the years after 1945 the public corporation became the chief instrument for managing several basic industries transferred into public ownership – coal, railways and much of road haulage, gas, electricity, iron and steel. Though after 1951 the frontiers of public ownership were pushed back here and there, as, for example, through the repeal of the Iron and Steel Act 1949, the tide has more recently rolled forward again. But the administrative devices for nationalisation have remained to a significant degree unchanged: it is the public corporation which is regularly resorted to.[3]

The public corporation as established after 1945 was, however, by no means unproblematical. Its characterisation and the definition of the terms on which a public corporation is intended to operate have presented many problems and puzzles for the student of British public administration. It is to their elucidation that Norman Chester has made such a major contribution, notably in his masterly analysis of the passage of the legislation bringing into existence the immediate post-war crop of public corporations. In the founding statutes, in the terms in which they are written and the conditions under which they were passed, are prefigured many of the problems which have continued ever since to beset the operation of public corporations as well as to obscure our understanding of the species. As Herbert Morrison acknowledged in 1950: 'In some respects, however, the Boards have not fulfilled our hopes. . . .'[4] The student of the species must sadly agree, even whilst noting that its continued proliferation must express that triumph of hope over experience once said to be embodied in the institution of marriage.

E

In the light of the uncertainty which still persists about the status and duties of public corporations it seems worth considering yet again what kind of administrative species we have to do with here. This concern means that we must look at some of the familiar weaknesses of the public corporation as it has been used in the UK, weaknesses which appear to be inherent in the institutional definition of a public corporation and in the ambiguities affecting its relations with Ministers. This takes us on to a brief consideration of some of the remedies proposed, notably by the Select Committee on Nationalised Industries in 1968 and very recently by the National Economic Development Office. Finally, I shall raise the question whether the problems stemming from the institutional ambiguities of the public corporation in its relationships with Government, its progenitor, are ever likely to be resolved. In other words, can the circle be squared or, to change the metaphors, must the species remain an unsatisfactory hybrid?

A public corporation of the kind with which I am concerned here is basically a body corporate established by statute and appointed by Government with the function of producing specified goods or services. It is a trading organisation which is expected to operate in such a way that, 'taking one year with another',[5] its revenues cover the costs it incurs. Thus in principle it is supposed to operate as a commercial enterprise. According to one official source this type of corporate body is distinguished from other public trading bodies (e.g. within the sphere of central or local government) by the fact that it is 'publicly controlled to the extent that . . . a Minister appoints, directly or indirectly, the whole or the majority of the board . . .', and secondly that it is 'a corporate body free to manage its affairs without detailed control by Parliament . . .; in particular, its financial independence includes the power to borrow within limits laid down by Parliament, and to maintain its own reserves'.[6] In fact it is not at all certain that these criteria allow us to distinguish the public corporation from other similar species as clearly as is implied. Nevertheless, this quotation does point to two of the continuing problems in defining the public corporation in practice: it is a statutory body, required to act in certain ways, but at the same time it is both subject to external controls and entitled to claim a certain autonomy. But how much external control and how much autonomy?

The morphology of the public corporation as an administrative institution is set out in detail in Norman Chester's history of the post-war nationalisation legislation. Though each industry taken into public ownership was recognised as having its own special characteristics and as a result no attempt was made to apply across the board a uniform pattern of public corporation organisation, nevertheless there evolved a recipe and the public corporation assumed a distinct administrative shape. The board is appointed by the sponsoring Minister, subject to varying conditions as to his paying regard to certain qualifications for membership and consultation with the designated chairman. The duties of the corporation are prescribed by statute and it is required to operate on commercial terms, though at the same time the statutes imply or state in different ways that the corporations shall have regard to the public interest. The responsibilities of management are vested in the boards of the public corporations, though even in formal terms these are qualified in various ways, e.g. certain measures of internal reorganisation would require statutory change and therefore ministerial support. The corporations are not autonomous either in determining investment programmes or in deciding how much to borrow: in the former respect they are subject to ministerial approval and in the latter to limits approved by Parliament and Ministers. But in theory they can fix prices charged to customers and the earnings of their employees. Additionally Ministers were given the power to prescribe the form of accounts and in some cases to approve programmes of research and development and of training and education. A ministerial power of great symbolic significance was that of general direction 'in the national interest'. This was to be important not as a consequence of its frequent use, but because it provided the basis for a substantial degree of ministerial intervention designed precisely to avoid resort to formal directions.

Though there are numerous and often puzzling differences in detail as between the nationalisation statute for one industry and that for another, the 'founding' statutes do specify in reasonably clear terms the intended character of the public corporation as an administrative institution. It was to be an instrument of professional commercial management, committed to the achievement of efficiency; and this in itself would express the corporation's chief contribution to the public interest. But the political rationale of public ownership required that the public corporations collectively should act in such a way as to further a wider concept of public interest, the nature and content of which would be determined from time to time by Ministers accountable to Parliament. However, the theory assumed that such a determination of the public interest would present no serious problems. It would be set out in such decisions as Ministers made establishing the claims on resources which as representatives of the shareholders, the sovereign people, they thought could reasonably be attributed to each industry. Within these limits the corporations would manage their industries independently, enjoying an 'arm's length' relationship with government. Thus would the imperatives of efficiency and social responsibility be satisfied.

In practice things have not turned out like this and Norman Chester alludes to some of the reasons in the closing sections of his work on the post-war nationalisation measures. The relationship between the form of public administration chosen and the purposes of nationalisation was neither clear nor simple. For some, nationalisation was justified in terms of the prospect of running certain industries more efficiently and of achieving rationalisation; for some the desire to eliminate the profit motive was paramount; for others nationalisation opened the way to the coherent planning and control of the economy, a concept which could embrace control of investment, maintenance of full employment, regional development, redistributive wages policies and so on.[7] Though most of those who put through the initial nationalisation programme attached great importance to the idea of efficient and autonomous management, it also turned out to be relatively easy to accommodate a variety of views of the purposes of public ownership within the terms of the statutes. This proved to be possible because the degree of independence which in practice the public corporations would be allowed to claim was left uncertain and even confused, to say nothing of the extent to which the principle of covering costs was to be applied.

Experience quickly revealed that the degree of independence enjoyed by the public corporations depended on the manner in which Ministers interpreted their powers, and even more on the readiness of Ministers to claim what might be called 'implied powers'. The right to issue general directions came to be seen as exercisable only 'in exceptional circumstances',[8] that is to say as a means of resolving some serious conflict of opinion between a board and a Minister. Instead, there developed a network of informal relationships between Ministers and board chairmen and between departmental officials and public corporation staff which enabled governments to acquire a major influence over many aspects of the activities of the corporations. True, the pattern of intervention varied substantially from industry to industry, being most intense in the deficit industries such as railways and perhaps for a time least extensive in electricity and gas. Moreover, during the years of Conservative rule in the fifties economic circumstances still appeared sufficiently favourable to justify a certain restraint on the part of Ministers. But as the general weakening of the economy became more serious, so from a mixture of practical and ideological motives the inclination of governments to intervene in the nationalised sector of industry grew stronger.

Intervention might not of itself have been so harmful had it not been dominated by short-term considerations. But far from governments setting a firm policy framework within which public corporations could operate, they tended to chop and change their policies for public investment, thus imposing on the nationalised industries a high degree of uncertainty and constraining them from time to time to take decisions which on commercial grounds could not be justified. This policy instability – which has persisted for at least two decades – affected not merely particular industries. It affected, too, large sectors of the economic environment within which the public corporations have to work, and thus the factual basis on which their corporate planning might be based. More recently the interventions have extended extra-statutorily to pricing and to levels of pay, an inevitable consequence of the resort to overall prices and incomes policies. Admittedly this evolution has also been marked by a continuing attachment to the ideal of the 'arm's-length' relationship, symbolised perhaps most vividly by the 1967 White Paper setting out guidelines for the fulfilment by the nationalised industries of their economic and financial obligations. In principle this was intended to give clear guidance to the corporations on pricing policies (long-run marginal costing), on investment appraisal (test discount rates) and on financial targets (varying rates of return on capital employed).[9] But though praiseworthy in intention and to some extent useful in practice, the attempt to delimit the respective spheres of the boards and of Ministers through the commitment of both to such operating guidelines did little to remove the confusion of responsibilities which had grown up. And indeed it is the years since 1967 which have witnessed an even wider extension of ministerial 'guidelines' and intervention.

What has just been described in very summary terms is a double failure. No firm conclusions were reached on the economic criteria for the operations of nationalised industries and – this being the point under discussion here – there was a concomitant failure to develop a 'clear and precise doctrine as to the relations which should normally prevail between the Boards and their appointing Ministers'.[10] Nor was this absence of doctrine confined to the relations between Ministers and boards. It extended also to the role of Parliament and to the mediated relations with the public corporations which the House of Commons sought to establish both by exploiting the answerability of Ministers to it and later by establishing the Select Committee on Nationalised Industries. However, the parliamentary aspects of the problem will not be pursued here. Our concern is with the Minister–board relationship and in particular with the question whether the difficulties affecting it and, therefore, the status of public corporations as administrative devices are susceptible of solutions.

Over the years attention has frequently been focused on the extent to which the boards can be expected to operate independently. But the perspective in which this issue is seen has changed. In the early years of the post-war wave of nationalisation the political pressures were chiefly exerted in the direction of making Ministers more accountable, a course of action which would have reduced substantially the managerial autonomy of the boards. These pressures were on the whole successfully resisted, notably by Herbert Morrison, who was determined to sustain the doctrine that Parliamentary Questions should be confined to matters of importance for which Ministers had a statutory responsibility. Morrison also opposed the setting-up of a Select Committee, though on this matter his views did not prevail and the Conservative Government conceded such a committee in late 1951.[11] In the event it turned out to be a kind of lightning-conductor, absorbing much of the energy in the House of Commons which had threatened to strike at the public corporations in other ways. Indeed it is not unreasonable to conclude that the gradual establishment of the Select Committee, combined with the decline in Conservative hostility to nationalisation as a principle,[12] contributed to a deflection of external political pressures away from the boards. And it was precisely in these circumstances that the intricate network of informal relations between Ministers and departments on the one hand and boards on the other could develop towards an intimacy which, if not always cosy, nevertheless provided grounds for suspecting that the public corporations were becoming something like tenants in the great ramshackle mansion of central government administration.

Undoubtedly it was the difficulties of the transport industry, revealed in several inquiries and prompting the appointment of a ruthless and independent-minded chairman in 1961, which acted as a catalyst in bringing about a renewal of active political interest in the terms on which the corporations should operate. Unfortunately, though governments attempted through guidelines on financial and economic objectives to establish a revised basis for a more autonomous managerial role for the corporations,[13] this policy had to be pursued at a time when mounting economic difficulty and the extension of government intervention in economic life which this produced worked against the genuine re-establishment of a clear boundary-line between the responsibilities of the public corporations and those of the Government. This was the context in which the Select Committee on Nationalised Industries pursued its first full-scale inquiry into the institutions and procedures through which ministerial control was exercised in relation to the whole nationalised industry sector.[14] The inquiry was long and complex, yielding both a detailed report and a vast collection of evidence.[15] In essentials the Committee concluded that there was confusion of responsibilities. There was also confusion about purposes, e.g. of ministerial control of investment, and about methods, e.g. how to apply a pricing policy. Yet the basic confusion was in the allocation of responsibilities. The Treasury, the sponsoring departments, certain other government agencies and finally the public corporations themselves were all involved, but nobody seemed to know the limits of his powers and competence. The result was lack of confidence, poor decisions and loss of a sense of direction.[16]

The British are said to be highly pragmatic and perhaps they are in practice. Yet over the past twenty years or so whenever they have turned to the analysis of governmental institutions they have been tempted into a curious kind of rationalism. This finds expression in the belief that if only the allocation of responsibilities can be clarified and above all a suitable organisation devised to accommodate their subsequent distribution, then successful operations will be ensured. The Select Committee's report, though admirable in its presentation of the evidence about the ministerial impact on public corporation autonomy and often perceptive in its analysis of the reasons for ministerial actions, was also infected by this tempting rationalism. It accepted that the efficient management of the nationalised industries called for a substantial degree of board independence – here was the Morrisonian component. But it recognised, too, both the legitimacy of and the need for ministerial intervention. This led to the conclusion that what had to be done was to define more precisely the content of ministerial responsibilities. The Committee emphasised two points in this regard. 'They [i.e. the responsibilities of Ministers] are, first, to secure the public interest, and secondly, to oversee and to seek to ensure the industries' efficiency.'[17] The Committee was of the opinion that the real problem lay in the institutionalised confusion of these two responsibilities, and it was for this reason that it recommended that overseeing the efficiency of the nationalised industries should be entrusted to a new Ministry of Nationalised Industries, whilst the responsibility for safeguarding the public interest would, broadly speaking, remain with the sectoral sponsoring departments. By these means, so it was argued, greater cohesion and better co-ordination would be achieved in the exercise of those ministerial powers which were directed essentially towards facilitating efficient performance by the boards, whilst the separation of 'public interest' considerations would, it was believed, encourage clearer definition of sectoral policies (e.g. in transport or energy) and sharper identification of responsibilities. Within such a framework the boards would have some prospect of knowing where the limits of their independence were to be found.

Much could be said about this diagnosis and the therapy proposed. However, only two points will be made here. The first is that when the Select Committee came to spelling out the responsibilities of the proposed new Minister for the Nationalised Industries, they looked suspiciously like those of the existing sponsoring departments which in turn were derived from the statutes and extra-statutory practice. In other words, the Committee came near to treating a bundle of powers which had up to then been justified by reference both to ensuring efficient performance *and* to protecting the public interest as simply concerned with the encouragement of efficiency. Thus there was an element of cheating in its analysis. If the idea of a single ministry was to be sustained, then it would have been more straightforward to have argued for it entirely on the case for co-ordination of the treatment of publicly-owned industry, coherence of methods of oversight and the desirability of building up professional skills in the central administration. It was not difficult for the Government subsequently to reject the recommendation on the grounds, *inter alia*, that the Committee was making unrealistically sharp distinctions.

The second point is in reality the obverse of the first. The report was obscure in its treatment of the public interest. Obviously, in some sense the enhancement of efficiency is a public interest. But beyond that the Committee appeared to think that the public interest should be defined in terms of interests 'wider than the purely commercial interests of the industries or their consumers, as judged by these industries'.[18] Presumably this means in fact any purpose which those in political authority judge to be socially desirable and which would either not be pursued if commercial criteria are applied or would conflict with the continued application of such criteria. Subsidies to financially non-viable railway lines come to mind as an obvious example.[19] Additionally, however, the Committee appears to have believed that the formulation of sectoral policies was a public-interest responsibility which should rest with at any rate some of the functional departments, though one of them, the Ministry of Power, was recommended for dissolution. Whether sectoral policies could in most cases be realistically formulated by departments so sharply cut off from the public corporations which contributed massively to these policies is a question which received little attention.

The Government did not act on the Committee's recommendations, chiefly because it did not welcome the organisational upheaval proposed, nor did it accept that the distinctions drawn by the Committee were valid. In retrospect what is most striking about the Committee's approach is that it tried to tackle the problem of demarcating areas of responsibility not by referring directly to the boards and their powers, but instead by a clarification and redistribution of responsibilities within the central government machine itself. It is in this connection that the limits of administrative rationalism stand out most starkly. Was it plausible to believe that merely by reallocating responsibilities in Whitehall, the relations between boards and government would have been significantly changed? Can ministerial preoccupations, nearly all of a highly political nature, as well as civil service working habits, be modified simply by adjusting the machinery? Was not the confusion of responsibilities in part at least a reflection of the weakness of the boards? If it was, then surely it would follow that one possible remedy would have been to strengthen the boards? But such a course of action could hardly be followed without some readiness actually to circumscribe in certain ways the powers and responsibilities of Ministers. To contemplate that possibility would at the least have implied taking a more sceptical view of the necessity of so much ministerial influence on behalf of the 'public interest' than the Committee was prepared to countenance. No doubt in 1968 faith in the beneficent effects of central government management of the economy was still intact. Let us on that note turn to a much more recent diagnosis of the problem of public corporation and ministerial responsibilities, one produced by an agency of central government economic management, though at a time when faith in the central government's capacity to guide the path of economic development has waned.

Arising out of a report on Capital Investment Procedures by the Select Committee on Nationalised Industries in 1973[20] the Government in 1975 asked the National Economic Development Office to enquire into the role of nationalised industries in the economy and the way in which they should be controlled in the future. This request resulted in a report published in late 1976 under the title *A Study of UK Nationalised Industries: their role in the economy and control in the future.*[21] It is the control aspect which is of interest in the present discussion.

NEDO's Study Team reached much the same diagnosis as the Select Committee: 'there is a lack of trust and mutual understanding between those who run nationalised industries and those in Government . . .'; 'there is confusion about the respective roles of the boards . . ., Ministers and Parliament, with the result that accountability is seriously blurred'.[22] The psychological treatment which it recommended consisted of an injection of 'trust, continuity and accountability'.[23] Here the NEDO is plainly expressing its own preference for 'concertation', for getting everyone involved together in a friendly atmosphere in which sensible compromises can emerge. But psychological prescriptions have to be transmuted into institutional arrangements and it is in this sphere that the NEDO study strikes off in a different direction from that recommended by the Select Committee. It is recognised realistically that the 'arm's-length' relationship has not worked out satisfactorily and that, given the scale and strategic significance of the nationalised sector,[24] it is difficult to see how the range of the Government's concern can be narrowed or defined precisely. Some of the dangers of what is called the 'concerted solution' are recognised, e.g. the risk of weakening board responsibilities for efficient management and further blurring of accountability. As a result the report proposes a solution which, it claims, would secure the advantages of both

approaches. On the one hand it should be possible to define more
clearly the aims and strategic policy appropriate to each nationalised
industry as well as performance criteria. On the other it is necessary to
engage the Government itself in the determination of those conditions
under which, it is hoped, the boards will be able to discharge indepen
dently and effectively their management functions. The institution
proposed to achieve this is a Policy Council for each industry consisting
of a president along with members drawn from government depart
ments, trade unions in the different nationalised industries, and the
management of the corporations themselves. There would also be
independent members. Apart from the president, who would be
appointed by the relevant Minister, the other members would be
appointed by their constituencies or by the president himself.

Clearly this device has a number of sources. It is reminiscent of the
supervisory board of Continental company law and it reflects too the
example of the National Enterprise Board established in 1975. The
intention is to set up a buffer between the Minister and the executive
board of each public corporation, but at the same time to involve the
Minister through his agents in the decisions of the buffer institution. In
this way it is hoped that the departments might really be held at arm's
length from the corporations themselves, for the implication of the
proposals is that Ministers would no longer be entitled to intervene at
all in the decisions of the corporation boards. But, perhaps to render
this prospect more palatable, it is suggested that the Minister's powers
of specific direction should be extended and those of general direction
widened in relation to the new Policy Councils.[25] Presumably it is
assumed that Ministers would, through their representatives on the
Policy Councils, be ready to make more frequent and explicit use of the
power of direction, though it is not explained why this should be so.
Indeed the report shows some signs of being confused on this point,
since it discusses the power of direction in the context of persuading the
Policy Council to adopt policies which 'the government feels to be
imperative'.[26] Here we seem to be back in the period 1945–50 when it
came to be acknowledged that the power of direction was an
exceptional one, to be used only *in extremis*. But if that is so, then the
normal pattern of relations is that of the informal exercise of influence.
And against that the Policy Council could hardly be a barrier.

It is clear that implementation of anything like this study's proposals
would require a substantial statutory upheaval. And there must remain
many doubts about whether, at the end of the day, the degree of
independence to be enjoyed by public trading corporations *would* have
been defined and stabilised. Ministers would be deeply involved in the
affairs of the new Policy Councils which, like the regulatory boards of
which Bentham wrote, might turn out to be screens covering with a

decent measure of consultation the ministerial capacity for direct intervention in the affairs of the public corporations themselves. There are many other question-marks too. How far would this new buffer in fact undermine the sense of responsibility of boards, bearing in mind that there have been strong and courageous chairmen who have on occasion stood up to Ministers and at least made it evident where the responsibility for particular decisions lay? To what extent is there indeed enough managerial talent available to man not only the boards, but another supervisory layer as well? And above all, how far can institutional devices of the kind proposed be expected to withstand successfully the pressures which stem from the political prerogatives of Ministers, their claim (and some would say their right) to interpret the public interest, their concern with the survival of a Government, their accountability to Parliament? It all sounds just a little reminiscent of the title of a play by J. B. Priestley, *I Have Been Here Before*. Or, as Norman Chester expressed it rather sadly at the end of his 1967 memorandum to the Select Committee: 'It is not easy to see a simple solution to this problem.'[27]

Let me now in a few concluding remarks pose a basic question. Is the semi-independent public corporation concept viable in the United Kingdom? For thirty years students of nationalised industry have pursued essentially the same problem. Here were corporations set up by statute to conduct a variety of commercial operations. The broad principles on which they were to do this were set out and the powers of Ministers in relation to the corporations were similarly prescribed, though in a manner which left room for uncertainty about what was intended. In theory it ought to have been possible to establish a stable division of responsibilities, but in practice this has not happened. The reasons are to be found only in part in the economic difficulties which have affected particular industries and in the failures of economic performance which have increasingly been revealed in the country at large. Nor has the technical difficulty of defining financial targets, investment appraisal methods or criteria for monitoring performance been decisive, important though these factors have been. At root the problem has been political. It is the terms on which political authority is exercised in Britain which have constantly frustrated the attempt to allow to the public corporations that 'large degree of independence' of which Morrison spoke thirty years ago.[28] As another scholar with great knowledge of public enterprise once wrote: 'So long as the Minister is held by Parliament to be *generally* responsible for the performance of the nationalised industry under his supervision – and there is no likelihood that Parliament will discharge him of that responsibility – he will continue, I believe, to try to ensure, by predominantly informal means, that its activities are such that he feels he can reasonably defend before the House of Commons.'[29] Professor Hanson may, writing ten years ago, have underestimated the extent to which Ministers want to defend themselves before audiences other than the House of Commons. Nevertheless, he put his finger on the key issue – the infinite temptations to which Ministers are exposed, the infinite flexibility which their relations with Parliament allow them to claim.

Now it may well be that, for the reasons just stated, the problem is insoluble and that the public corporation is destined to remain an ambiguous and frustrated administrative species. But let us for a moment imagine a few conditions under which the capacity of public boards to claim a more substantial autonomy might be greater. First, there is the matter of security of tenure, particularly for board chairmen. Were they appointed for seven or even eight years and removable only through the application of some cumbersome procedure analogous to that required for the removal of High Court judges, their relations with Ministers might well change. True, such conditions might tempt Ministers into appointing nonentities, though if they did the resulting penalties for those in government might be severe. But greater security of tenure might on the whole be expected to encourage boards to stand up for their own interests and policy preferences more strongly.[30] It is remarkable how much confusion of responsibilities in British administration occurs simply because people like to be nice to each other, and nowhere does the tendency operate more powerfully than in the relations between Ministers (together with their civil servants) and non-central government administrative bodies. It follows that any provision which reduced the costs of not being nice and accommodating might at the minimum contribute to clarification of uncertain and variable administrative relationships.

Second, it has to be remembered that there is neither political nor bureaucratic cement holding the corporation boards together. Thus they have a very limited ability to consolidate defensive mechanisms which might be deployed in relation to Ministers and departments. What is meant by political and bureaucratic cement? Political cement is to be found in relationships of interdependence, the disturbance of which by one party to them would be associated with a serious political cost. It might be provided in several ways, for example by conferring more importance on the political affiliations of board chairmen (and members) and by considering ways in which Parliament might become more of a patron of the public corporations, much as Congress in the USA is patron to a large number of regulatory agencies. Of course there are well-known objections to such overt political patronage, and no doubt it would be desirable for it to be exercised on a 'fair shares' basis as between parties and with regard to the need to secure technical competence as well.[31] This would certainly not be easy to achieve and many would find it distasteful. Yet it would be a way of buttressing the corporations, giving them a bit of what is vulgarly referred to as 'political clout'. To achieve a bureaucratic form of cement would call for different policies. For example, a policy of appointing relatively young civil servants to board membership might be followed, people who would after a fixed term have some guarantee of return to Whitehall should they desire to do so. Here again would be a means of establishing in the public corporations a certain kind of interest which might be resistant to the pressures of transitory Ministers and their advisers.

A third possibility for moving towards greater board autonomy might be found in an abandonment (admittedly improbable) of the pervasive belief in the virtues of centralised management of the economy by direct government intervention. Obviously the central political authority must determine to a large extent the framework of conditions, fiscal, monetary and regulatory, within which economic activity generally is to take place. But it is by no means self-evident that it is beneficial for it to assume as well an almost unlimited discretion to intervene whenever it seems expedient to do so in the particular decisions of the innumerable agents, public and private, who are engaged in the activities of production. With a different understanding of the economic role of government the underlying concept of the public corporation as a responsible commercial undertaking might begin to make the kind of sense which it clearly did to some of those who did most to shape it. It would become easier for a public corporation to defend its judgement of what constitutes a sound decision precisely because there would be a context of decentralised economic decision-making which would tend to legitimise a plurality of such judgements. Unlikely though a change in this direction might be, it should at least be noted that the pleas made by the Select Committee and by the NEDO for more effective clarification of the guidelines on which public corporations should operate make little sense unless they can be set within the context of a far more modest and more sceptical view of the role of government in the economy than has so far been accepted in Britain. Perhaps it is the tendency to see the problems of nationalised industries in isolation from the general terms on which the economy is guided that goes some way to explaining the meagre results so far of such pleas as have been made for establishing a framework of principles for the operation of the public corporations.

Fourth, we might contemplate the prospect of a different kind of legal framework. It is possible to envisage a general statute defining in consistent terms the duties of a public trading corporation, its legal status as a body corporate, the terms of appointment of its board, the financial conditions to which it is subject, its general obligations towards corporation employees and their status, the supervisory powers of Ministers and so on. This would represent an effort to define the whole species, rather as happened long ago in the case of local authorities. Subsequent legislation, perhaps by statutory instrument, could deal with those points of species difference requiring formal regulation. Now it may well be argued that putting the public corporations into a new (and standardised) set of legal clothes would do little good: informal practice would still be decisive in shaping the terms on which boards related to their supervising Ministers. Moreover, it is a peculiarity of the nationalisation statutes that many of the duties of the corporations are either expressly unenforceable[32] or could not in practice be made the object of any judicial proceedings. Nevertheless, there is the possibility that a serious attempt to define in comprehensible and reasonably consistent terms the characteristics common to *all* public trading corporations would clear the air and give to all members of the species a firmer basis on which to conduct their external relations. Were such a measure combined with a policy of attracting a degree of non-public finance, perhaps through the issue of preference stock at a fixed yield,[33] the prospects of making the corporations more self-reliant might be further improved.

These suggestions should not be taken as recommendations for immediate action. They are too sketchy and too impressionistic for any such purpose. They amount to no more than a number of signposts, pointing to possibilities of change which would go beyond a mere redrawing of organisational boundaries and adjustments to administrative structures. They indicate the kind of changes in the underlying conditions of the administrative system of which the boards are a part and in the terms on which it operates which, in my view, would have to be contemplated if the dilemma under discussion here is ever to be resolved. Additionally, they throw some doubt on the practical wisdom of merely readjusting the existing organisational structures. It is widely recognised that the public corporation has remained ambiguous in concept and sometimes ineffective in operation. Yet we continue to want (quite understandably) as effective and responsible management of the basic industries in public ownership as can in principle be secured in private industry under the stimulus of market conditions and of the necessity of paying to shareholders an adequate dividend. Not even the most committed advocates of more nationalisation have recommended that Ministers and departments should directly manage industries on the pattern of the Post Office before 1970.

Thus the ideal remains that of a substantially independent board of management. It is the refusal to recognise that this ideal is incompatible with the exalted claims made on behalf of Ministers and Parliament to exercise *their* political discretion at will, which has made it impossible to achieve that stabilisation of administrative relationships which was originally hoped for in the process of nationalisation, and which is still rightly regarded as a necessary condition of successful economic performance by the corporations themselves. It follows that the ambiguity which has characterised the nationalised industry corporations can hardly be removed unless, as the proposals just sketched out suggest, some breaches are made in the underlying political assumptions on which central government in Britain operates. Ultimately a choice will have to be made. Either we must recognise the need to impose limits on Ministers and Parliament by establishing effective and legitimate countervailing powers, or we must reconcile ourselves to making do with a continuation of centralised muddle – necessarily a muddle since its basic principle is that Ministers should respond as they see fit to the pressures exerted through Parliament or to such demands as they legitimise by invoking their parliamentary accountability.

NOTES AND REFERENCES

1 'Efficient and economical supply' is a phrase which recurs in the sections of the nationalised statutes setting out the duties of various public corporations.
2 D. N. Chester, in a Memorandum, 'The Nationalised Industries – External Organisation', submitted in July 1967 to the Select Committee on Nationalised Industries (SCNI, First Report, 1967–68, *Ministerial Control of the Nationalised Industries*, Minutes of Evidence, HCP 371–II, p. 522.
3 This statement needs qualification to the extent that in the case of companies threatened with financial collapse the Government has acquired 100 per cent of the shares and retained the company board structure. Rolls Royce (1971) and British Leyland (1975) are, of course, leading examples of this mode of nationalisation. The National Enterprise Board has since 1975 come on to the scene as the Government's shareholding agent.
4 Quoted in Sir Norman Chester, *The Nationalisation of British Industry 1945–51* (HMSO, 1975) p. 922.
5 A familiar phrase to be found in all the nationalisation statutes, but omitted from the Aircraft and Shipbuilding Bill 1976. There is in that measure only a reference to 'an adequate return on capital employed' (Clause 10).
6 Central Statistical Office, *National Accounts Statistics – Sources and Methods* (HMSO, 1968) p. 237. It is to be noted, however, that since 1969 Passenger Transport Executives and since 1973 Regional Water Authorities have for statistical purposes been brought within the public corporation category, though their boards are appointed wholly or partly by local authorities. The Select Committee on Nationalised Industries has also brought the latter into its remit.
7 In February 1947 the Minister of Transport, countering an amendment

to the Transport Bill to delete the power of the Minister to issue general directions, explained that the new legislation differed constitutionally from the London Passenger Transport Board legislation in that at the time of the latter it was not contemplated that such bodies as the LPTB 'should be part of the economic organisation of the state to secure, or to give their contribution towards, a policy of full employment and the maximum output of consumer goods for the purpose of consciously improving the general standard of living in the country' (quoted in Chester, op. cit., p. 902). This remark vividly encapsulates a dilemma which has beset the public corporations and governments ever since.

8   Herbert Morrison's phrase, used in 1947, quoted by Chester, op. cit., p. 1036. Two directions were issued, one in 1951 to the doomed Iron and Steel Corporation, another in 1952 to the British Transport Commission (on fare increases outside London). No direction was issued thereafter.

9   *Nationalised Industries: A Review of Financial and Economic Objectives*, Cmnd 3437 (1967). This improved upon and modified the earlier White Paper, *The Financial and Economic Obligations of the Nationalised Industries*, Cmnd 1337 (1961). The latter was methodologically far less developed than the former, though for political reasons more overtly committed to the commercial view of public corporations.

10   Chester, op. cit., p. 1038.

11   It should, however, be remembered that the Select Committee did not really operate effectively until 1956 and after.

12   I refer here to ideological objection to the nationalisation already effected, subject to the exceptions of iron and steel and road haulage.

13   Chiefly through the 1961 and 1967 White Papers already referred to.

14   Two other accompanying circumstances are worth noting. In 1967 iron and steel were nationalised again and in the same year the Government decided to refer certain questions of efficiency and prices to the National Board for Prices and Incomes.

15   *Ministerial Control of the Nationalised Industries*, Report and Evidence, HCP 371–I–III, 1967–68.

16   For the conclusions of the Select Committee's report, see op. cit., Part III, Chapter xviii, pp. 189–90.

17   SCNI, op. cit., p. 191, para. 884.

18   Op. cit., para. 900, p. 196.

19   No doubt this case influenced the Committee, as the Transport Bill 1968 was going through Parliament when it reported. This provided for explicit public subsidies for services kept open by British Rail on social grounds.

20   First Report, 1973–4, HCP 65.

21   Published by HMSO, November 1976 (no price shown).

22   'A Study of UK Nationalised Industries', p. 8.

23   Ibid., p. 10.

24   Note that by 1976 the scale of publicly-owned industry had been significantly extended, though not always by the creation of public corporations.

25   Only in a few cases do the statutes confer powers of specific direction,

e.g. in the Iron and Steel Act 1967, Sections 6(1) and 30(6), and in several clauses of the Aircraft and Shipbuilding Industries Bill, which also contains a general direction power in Clause 4.

26 Op. cit., p. 49.

27 Op. cit., para. 20, p. 526.

28 *HC Deb.*, 4 Dec 1947, c. 566.

29 'Parliament, Minister and Board', Memorandum submitted by Prof. A. H. Hanson to the Select Committee on Nationalised Industries, 1967, HCP 371–II, 1967–68, p. 528, para. 7.

30 The NEDO study does in fact recommend that presidents of Policy Councils should have substantial security of tenure, though it does not specify any details.

31 It is not entirely irrelevant to note that the West German Federal Bank has for nearly thirty years been notably independent, yet nobody would deny that political considerations have entered into the appointment of its board and in particular of the president and vice-president.

32 As provided, for example, by Clause 2 of the Aircraft and Shipbuilding Industries Bill 1976 and by Section 3(4) of the Iron and Steel Act 1967.

33 A proposal of this nature is set out by Prof. J. Heath in a discussion paper on Financial and Economic Control, published as item E in the Appendix to the NEDO study referred to above.

10 Nationalised Industries: Government Intervention and Industrial Efficiency

AUBREY SILBERSTON

Political considerations have of course played a large part in the motives for nationalisation. Given the existence of nationalised industries, however, economists have been much concerned with such questions as the pricing and investment rules that such industries should follow. These are important subjects, but I do not propose to discuss them here. This chapter concentrates above all on the overall pressures for efficiency (and inefficiency) in British nationalised industries under present conditions. In what I say I shall be drawing on a number of sources, including my own experiences in the British Steel Corporation, where I was a part-time board member from 1967, soon after nationalisation, until 1976.

What is said here will scarcely be a surprise to observers of nationalised industries, especially since the publication in 1976 of the NEDO report on this subject (see note 21 to Chapter 9 above). I hope, however, that I may be able to add some points of interest. I will not try to be comprehensive, but will discuss a number of problems which seem to me to have a bearing on the attainment of industrial efficiency.

This paper is on the whole critical of government intervention in nationalised industries, but it is important to say at the outset that the problem of the relationship between government and nationalised industries is a difficult and intractable one. It has been actively discussed for very many years,[1] and the White Papers of 1961 and 1967 in particular were serious attempts to think out and specify appropriate guidelines for the industries.[2] There are certainly no easy solutions to this problem, and the present paper does not claim to find any.

CHARACTERISTICS AND LEGAL STATUS

The members of nationalised industry boards are appointed by the appropriate Minister. Tenure is comparatively short – five years or less – and reappointment at the end of a period of tenure is by no means a foregone conclusion. All finance is from public sources, or raised privately with government consent. Even bank borrowing must be within approved limits. The Treasury may guarantee loans from private sources and typically does so. There is an overall statutory borrowing limit, and any proposal for an increase in the limit must be placed before Parliament. This inevitably means that there is a debate, which typically ranges widely over the affairs of the nationalised industry concerned.

The relevant nationalisation Act lays down the financial duty of the corporations: in all cases to break even, taking one year with another. In addition the Minister may specify a minimum rate of return to be attained. This is drawn up with the particular circumstances of each industry in mind, and differs from corporation to corporation.

The Minister may give directions to the boards of nationalised industries, and these may be specific in character. The general programme of investment must be agreed by the Minister. The range of activities undertaken by the corporation may be laid down by the Minister. This means that any new activities, or any proposals for mergers, must gain ministerial approval. Whether this approval is forthcoming or not is likely to depend on the political colour of the government of the day, as well as on narrower considerations.

In addition to the controls derived from the nationalisation acts, the Minister may place other obligations on boards, although these are not always derived from his specific legal powers. For example, he may lay down the test rate of discount to be earned on new investment projects, or he may moderate suggested price increases. Such obligations can be imposed under the Minister's powers of direction, but Ministers are reluctant to use these powers, except in formal cases, and this is well known. Nevertheless, the powers are in the background, and have on occasion been used (e.g. in the BSC's case in 1971, when a proposed price increase was halved). This is very much in the minds of those in charge of nationalised industries, and affects their actions. One may try to resist pressure from the Minister or from civil servants, on the ground that legally the power resides in the board, but it takes a determined chairman and board to oppose a Minister's wishes on an important matter. Driving a Minister to issue a directive is a hostile act, and is likely to sour relations between the board and the administration concerned for a considerable time. What is more, any confrontation of this sort is likely to become public knowledge. It is surprising how easily leaks occur, and the press is always interested in nationalised industry conflicts. Some issues are debated more in public than in private, e.g. the conflict between Tony Benn and Sir Monty Finniston over redundancy in steel, and nationalised industry chairmen have to grow accustomed to becoming public figures. The contrast in this respect with the chairmen of even the largest private companies is very marked.

STRUCTURE AND DEVELOPMENT OF THE INDUSTRY

I have said that the Minister must give his consent to mergers. This causes delay, sometimes in circumstances where an opportunity is missed. It also causes hesitation in putting forward proposals for merger or for expansion into new areas, since a detailed case will be necessary, and argument may occur. More important than this is that nationalised industries must stick to their last: they have been set up to undertake a given activity and it is almost inconceivable that they would be allowed to abandon it. A private steel firm may decide to refine copper and other non-ferrous metals, and may even choose to move gradually out of steel altogether, but the nationalised steel industry is not free to take this kind of decision, except to a limited extent. In this respect there is a great difference between private and public industry.

The initial structure of a nationalised industry depends on the terms of the relevant nationalisation acts. Just as with private mergers, all sorts of fringe activities may be caught up on nationalisation. As compared with a private merger, there are exceptional problems over divestiture and tidying up generally, as ministerial consent is required. This may not be easy to obtain, since political considerations may be involved. The same applies to proposals for reorganisation; the Minister's consent is again needed, and once again political problems may arise, e.g. over the relocation of a regional headquarters.

Following the initial merger, a nationalised industry is likely to be easier to reorganise or rationalise than would be the case with a merger of private firms. Drastic changes in structure are likely to be expected by politicians, and desired also by many members of nationalised industry boards. Existing managers may well resist such changes, as with a private merger, but in the end a strong chairman and board can overcome such opposition, since it is known that the Minister is there to be appealed to, and that his word is law. It is well known that severe difficulties of this sort occurred in the early days of the BSC, when Lord Melchett was faced with strong opposition from some of the chairmen of the old steel companies. It was obvious he would have to win in the end, although at the time the episode was a fraught one.

In the light of the problems faced by the BSC, it is easy to see why Austin and Morris had the merger problems that they did, and why the later merger of BMC (Austin/Morris) with Leyland gave rise to major difficulties. In a nationalised industry it is difficult to believe that these problems would not have been resolved a good deal sooner. This is not of course to say that the initial form of organisation arrived at by a nationalised industry is necessarily the best one. The experiences of the National Coal Board and the British Steel Corporation, among others, bear this out. But at least the process of merging – often a matter of great complexity in itself – is bound to have a great deal of impetus behind it.

Nationalised industries are much less well placed in comparison with private firms when it comes to rationalising production, and especially when it comes to closures. In a private firm, the fear of bankruptcy may force through a closure (though admittedly the Government may intervene in important cases), while bankruptcy is not normally a possibility for the nationalised industry. There is nearly always political opposition to closures, and, in the absence of rigid financial constraints, long battles may ensue. The situation has become much more difficult in the 1970s. In the 1950s and 1960s there were many nationalised industry closures, above all in the coal industry. These would not go through so quietly today.

In the case of the BSC, major plans were drawn up after nationalisation for the rationalisation and expansion of steel production, involving heavy investment expenditure. These plans were finally accepted by a Conservative Government early in 1973. Steel production was to be concentrated on five coastal sites by the early 1980s, and many centres, including Shotton in North Wales, were to cease making steel, although they might remain as processors of steel. When the Labour Government came to power in 1974 it was pledged to review all projected steel closures. A long process of review and discussion followed, during which ample time was given for every threatened centre to organise opposition to the BSC's plans. In the end, with one important exception, virtually all of the BSC's plans were endorsed, with minor concessions to local interests. There were delays in timing but some of these could be attributed to the fact that demand was in any event rising more slowly than had originally been foreseen by the BSC. The important exception concerned the plans for Port Talbot in South Wales, and Shotton in North Wales. Shotton had been due to run down its steel making, while Port Talbot had been destined to double its capacity. The decision over this case was repeatedly delayed – well beyond the time it should have been made for market reasons. During 1976 the Government said it would allow all developments to go ahead on the Port Talbot site that did not pre-empt the Shotton decision, but the BSC argued that, in the absence of a decision, final plans could not be made for Port Talbot. In the end, an agreement between the BSC and the Government was announced in March 1977. Port Talbot was to be expanded in the first instance by less than originally envisaged, while Shotton was to continue to make steel. New investment at Shotton in steel making was not however announced, and it therefore seems likely that eventually steel production there will be discontinued. This agreement was reached well after I myself had left the BSC Board, and I know nothing of the inside story. I am not sure whether the decision is one that the BSC would have reached on its own, but in any event the BSC itself would certainly have reached a decision very much sooner.

Government views on the structure of a nationalised industry, and of its investment plans, may be influenced by industrial, social or political considerations. As regards industrial considerations, my experience is that civil servants and Ministers are naturally a good deal less well informed than those in the industry itself. I am doubtful whether they are much better informed than those in the industry on general industrial trends, or on relevant interconnections in the economy, or on general foreign trade matters. They are certainly less well informed on specific technical and market matters. It is true that on occasions those in central government have succeeded in tempering the enthusiasm of optimists within the nationalised industries. But such instances have probably not been numerous or important, especially as changing market conditions have necessarily led to reductions in over-ambitious expansion plans. In my experience, the major plans of the nationalised industry are endorsed eventually, although often after much delay. Even the Shotton decision seems to me to be no exception to this.

It could be argued that the knowledge by nationalised industries that their plans will be scrutinised by government leads to these plans being exceptionally carefully prepared. On the other hand, it may be that the knowledge that time will elapse before projects are approved sometimes leads to plans being rather hastily presented. On balance, the former influence probably preponderates, with some beneficial effects.

As regards social considerations, my experience suggests that nationalised industries are, if anything, more aware of the social implications of their actions than governments. They are after all in the front line, and in addition their nationalised status makes them particularly sensitive. The BSC has certainly leaned over backwards to pay regard to social effects. Two years' notice of closure have been given for closures involving one hundred or more employees, and considerable efforts have been made to attract alternative employment to closure areas. In practice, the efforts of government in these areas often seem ineffectual. Private firms, indeed, have sometimes made impressive efforts to provide alternative employment, e.g. the Steel Company of Wales, when it decided to change from open hearth to basic oxygen steel making, but the longer purse of a nationalised industry certainly helps in cases of this sort.

From time to time governments draw the attention of nationalised industries to social considerations, such as the unemployment that would be caused by closures, and the costs of alleviating the effects of this. Difficulties of this sort may indeed arise, with their attendant political problems, but it is noteworthy that narrower political considerations appear to loom large in certain cases – for example when marginal constituencies are involved. One cannot help suspecting that on a number of occasions the narrow political aspects dominate the broader social and political ones. This is understandable from the point of view of government, but it does little to encourage industrial efficiency on the part of the nationalised industry concerned.

It is often argued that if a government feels strongly that a particular 'uneconomic' course of action should be taken on grounds of national interest, it should require that action to be taken but should compensate the nationalised industry concerned by giving it an explicit subsidy. There may be instances where this can be done without serious harm to efficiency, but I suspect that such instances are rarer than at first appears. A major problem with a policy of this sort is that its effects may run throughout the industry concerned: a decision about Shotton, for instance, will affect not only Port Talbot but also projected investment in Scotland, as well as in other parts of the country. The appropriate subsidy would not be easy to calculate, since industrial efficiency in the industry concerned may be adversely affected for many years to come. Even if the effect could be localised, there is the danger that one intervention could easily be followed by others. The ultimate effect of a series of piecemeal interventions of this sort might be that there would be a considerable loss in efficiency. For these reasons, many nationalised industries have not welcomed subsidies for 'social' reasons. What is more, governments themselves have not liked to propose explicit subsidies (even when no EEC problems have arisen), especially as the case for intervention may not always be easy to justify. What happens in practice is that the government puts on pressure for particular policies, but then expects the industry concerned to bear the cost of any subsequent losses. This type of policy is common, and may have particularly serious effects where investment is concerned, since the consequences are likely to be long-lasting. Private firms are not free from pressures of this sort, but can escape from them a good deal more easily than can nationalised industries.

Having said all this on the negative side, one must add that once nationalised industry investment plans have been approved they are normally carried through. A nationalised industry's investment programme may be held up to some extent by a reduction in government expenditure, but this factor may not be quantitatively important. Funds for approved projects are made available from the exchequer even when the industry is making losses or the economy is depressed. Unlike much private industry investment, that of nationalised industry tends to be geared to the trend rather than to the cycle, and in this respect provides a valuable stabilising element in the economy.

ACCOUNTABILITY AND PLANNING

Nationalised industries have to produce many statistics and forecasts for government. There are five-year development plans, annual operating plans, investment programmes and cash flow statements, among many others. It must be shown that major investment projects will earn the test rate of discount, and that prices bear some relation to long-run marginal cost (though in practice I have seen little stress on this last criterion). All this requires the nationalised industries to have good systems of accounting, both financial and managerial. They must also have good, or at least respectable, methods of demand forecasting and of investment appraisal. They know that their plans will be subject to intense scrutiny, by Parliament, the press and the unions, as well as by central government, and that it would be difficult to get away with poorly-based investment decisions or sloppy profit forecasts. In these respects, they have to maintain higher standards than private firms are called upon to demonstrate, and there is little doubt that in these matters they are more advanced than many private firms.

The other side of the coin is that nationalised industries are required, or urged, to produce many figures which are not vital to the running of the business. Much work is involved, and some figures are produced, such as five-year profit forecasts, which are so conjectural that nobody has any faith in them. What is more, the need to produce more and more figures may do harm internally, in that, apart from the work they cause, they may mislead managers into thinking that producing consistent numbers is a substitute for taking correct strategic decisions. Initiative may be stifled, and major matters of principle may be submerged in a mass of detailed figures and reports.

Another aspect of the continual checks imposed by government is that a great deal of top management time is taken up, especially that of the chairman and chief executive. Additional time is taken up when crises occur. Since steel was nationalised in 1967 there have been a number of major problems in the relationship between the Government and the BSC. These have occurred irrespective of which government has been in power. The demands they make on top management have made it very difficult for those concerned to concentrate on running the business. Most nationalised industries are enormous and complex businesses by any standard, and impose great burdens on those in charge of them. Quite apart from the planning and execution of investment programmes, with all the technical and labour problems involved, there is the sheer scale of the day-to-day task of keeping the business running. This would tax the resources of men of the highest ability, but those actually bearing the responsibility can find it hard to concentrate on what might reasonably be said to be the primary aspect of their jobs. What is more, the decisions they actually reach may well be adversely influenced by the continual pressure on them, and the resulting need for semi-public justification. Sometimes the effects are unconscious ones: one cannot say what would have been decided if a more arm's-length relationship had been possible.

It has been argued that in matters of this sort there is little difference between nationalised industries and large privately-owned firms: there is much contact with government by large private firms, and there is pressure on them to fall in with government wishes. I believe that it is fallacious to argue in this way. The pressures on private firms are tiny compared with those on nationalised industries. Only when private firms run out of money and have to turn to the Government for survival can such an intense relationship be approached in their case.

PROFITS

As was said earlier, nationalised industries have to break even financially, over a period of years, and also to meet target rates of return. The industries are generally keen to make profits if they possibly can, because this improves their standing with the public, and also gives them access to internally generated funds. They do not like to be driven into unprofitability by constraints like price controls. At the same time, governments exert pressure for profit targets to be met, and may even impose sanctions, such as temporarily withholding access to the exchequer, if they are dissatisfied with performance. From all these points of view, the drive for profits is likely to be a factor making for efficiency.

At the same time, the pressures from government that have already been mentioned, especially pressures from Ministers and other politicians, tend to work in the opposite direction. Ministers are particularly likely to be affected by short-term political considerations, while nationalised industry boards need to take a longer view. But pressure from government looms so large that action which is loss-making, such as keeping open marginal plants, may be taken by boards without any overt government action.

One paradox of the situation is that officials and Ministers sometimes – although not always – appear to be on opposite sides of the fence, the officials pressing for profits, and the Ministers pressing for action which would make profits unattainable. This is another source of strain on those in charge of nationalised industries.

If one asks why some nationalised industries do not seem to try as hard for profitability as they might, it is not always clear whether the answer is that they themselves are not highly motivated to do this or whether they behave as they do because of spoken or unspoken pressure from government. In these circumstances a situation arises where those running nationalised industries find it natural to blame the Government for almost everything that goes wrong. While this may sometimes be justified, it is not healthy to work in an atmosphere where it is so easy to find a scapegoat for what may be one's own short-comings.

If a nationalised industry is determined to make profitability its objective, it may well have to fight the government of the day in order to achieve this. The BSC certainly fought strongly during much of the period I was with it to be allowed to reach the profit targets to which governments themselves had agreed.

One would be more sympathetic to government interference in nationalised industries if one could believe that governments always had the long-run efficiency of the economy and of the industry at heart, and that they genuinely took social considerations into account. My belief, however, is that these attitudes are more likely to be adopted consistently by the boards of nationalised industries than by governments. But in the end the Government has the power, and is likely to prevail. This is frustrating for those in charge of nationalised industries, especially when their efficiency tends to be judged by government, as well as by the general public, by the profits that they make.

Having said this, it is necessary to add that the performance of nationalised industries frequently has shortcomings which cannot be attributed to government intervention. These industries are by no means free from the all-pervading disease of British industry – the inability to use existing equipment as productively as comparable firms and organisations overseas, whether in the USA and Japan or in Europe. The Central Policy Review Staff has produced detailed evidence for this in the motor car industry,[3] which contains one nationalised firm in British Leyland (although admittedly only recently nationalised). The BSC itself has pointed to the differences in productivity between its Llanwern plant and a comparable plant in Belgium. Neither lack of investment nor government intervention can be held to be the root causes of failures of this sort. It is only too easy for government to be blamed for shortcomings such as these, however, when relationships between government and nationalised industries are as fraught as has often been the case.

CONCLUSION

What has been said here cannot be encouraging for those concerned with the efficient use of resources by nationalised industries. One must not, however, forget the good effects that have been mentioned – the emphasis on sound planning and on systems of control, the social concern, and the fact that investment is geared to the trend, and not to the cycle.[4] Can anything be done to retain these benefits while avoiding the adverse effects?

One answer is to encourage competition with nationalised industries, thus imposing external pressures for efficiency. There is already much competition in steel from home as well as from abroad, and the now publicly-owned British Leyland has to meet plenty of competition. Competition may well have good effects, since failure to match up to competitors is humiliating, but good effects cannot come about if the Government stands ready to cover losses caused by competition. In such cases, it is the competitors who may suffer, and the pressure on nationalised industries is reduced.

Another possible policy is to avoid nationalisation wherever some other solution is possible. In the case of the Chrysler rescue bid, for example, the company was left in private hands, and the fear of bankruptcy was not therefore removed. Nor was there any guarantee of continued, as opposed to temporary, government financial aid. The number of such possibilities is, however, limited. We have many industries already nationalised. It would be virtually impossible to denationalise most of them, and would in any event be undesirable – at least in my view. What can be done about these?

A solution which would be possible for those industries, or sectors of industries, which have prospects of continuing profits, would be for a substantial proportion of their capital to be offered to the public. If this were done in the form of equities which carried votes, it is probable that the nature and frequency of government intervention would change appreciably. The 'BP solution' may have much to commend it.

As against this, it can be argued that British Petroleum is a special case, since the greater part of its business is overseas. This is bound to reduce the temptation for government to intervene in its affairs, because the domestic economy, where political problems are greatest, may be relatively unaffected by BP's decisions. This may indeed explain why the BP arrangement seems to have worked so well, but if one wishes to reduce political interference with nationalised industries generally, a comparable arrangement in other sectors might bring with it similar advantages, although the problems would undoubtedly be greater.

Even in the absence of private equity holders, there is at present a certain amount of pressure against 'uneconomic' government intervention from sources other than the British Government. Foreign lenders, for example, have exerted such pressure, although they need not fear for their money, backed as it is by government guarantee. The EEC banking institutions have also exerted pressure of this sort. In addition, the ECSC has general powers over the coal and steel industries, and is much concerned that nationalised corporations should compete fairly with privately-owned firms. In this sphere, the EEC can be held to have had beneficial effects on efficiency, although possibly these pressures will not be continuing ones.

Apart from external sources of pressure, one would like to think that it should be possible to forge a relationship between government and nationalised industries which is less close and continuous than the present one. The government must of course be concerned when major calls for funds are made, and must act as a highly interested and expert banker in such cases. Given the inescapable need for such funds by most of the nationalised industries, it is not easy to see, political considerations apart, how further disengagement than at present can be brought about. The NEDO proposal for inserting an additional layer, in the form of Policy Councils, has found little favour with anyone, including the nationalised industries. One can see why state industry chiefs should be against a scheme which reduces at the same time their access to government and the power of their boards. Nor can one believe that this device would do much to reduce political pressures on the industries themselves. We seem to be almost as far as ever from solving the problem, although it may be that some other form of the 'membrane' solution will in the end turn out to be the least unsatisfactory arrangement.

At the very least, the situation could be much improved, even in the absence of institutional change, if decisions could be reached by government much more speedily than at present. One recognises that political considerations are often involved, but quick decisions can sometimes be less politically painful than slow ones – and the industrial arguments against delay may often be very strong.

What tends to be forgotten in the discussions of these issues that have taken place for so long is the great importance of the nationalised industries in the economy. These industries account for more than a tenth of the national product and nearly a fifth of total fixed investment. What is more, the nationalised sector is growing, with the addition of aircraft and shipbuilding. It is one of the many depressing features of the British economy that the efficient utilisation of so massive a proportion of its resources should be bound up with political considerations, often short-term in their nature.

NOTES AND REFERENCES

1 Norman Chester has recently drawn attention to the early post-war discussions in his *Nationalisation of British Industry, 1945–51* (HMSO, 1975).

2 Cmnd 1337, *The Financial and Economic Obligations of the Nationalised Industries* (HMSO, 1961); Cmnd 3437, *Nationalised Industries: A Review of Economic and Financial Obligations* (HMSO, 1967).

3 Central Policy Review Staff, *The Future of the British Car Industry* (HMSO, 1975).

4 There is also the speediness of the initial merger, but this is not of course a continuing gain.

11 A Profits Test for Public Monopolies[1]

M. FG. SCOTT

In the summer of 1948 the writer, having just completed two years of study for a first degree in Philosophy, Politics and Economics at Wadham College, was elected to a Studentship at Nuffield College. Although he had specialised as much as he could in Economics, taking four out of six papers in that subject in the 'shortened schools' permitted at that time for ex-servicemen, his knowledge of the subject was rudimentary. He believed, however, that the best way to improve it was to work as an applied economist outside the academic world, and therefore was anxious to limit his stay at the university to one further year. He accordingly decided to read for a B.Litt., which would give him a year's experience of academic research.

At that time, the economics of nationalised industries, and especially their optimum price and output policies, had attracted much attention, stimulated by the Labour Government's nationalisation programme which was still in full swing. Articles and books on the case for and against marginal cost pricing had appeared by economists such as Henderson, 1948; Lerner, 1944; Lewis, November 1946; Meade and Fleming, December 1944; Vickrey, June 1948; and Wilson, December 1945. Economists evidently had something to say on the subject, but it was not clear to the writer what practical conclusion emerged from it all. The problem, as it seemed then (and as it still seems today) could be put as follows.

The managers of private enterprises face difficult problems of price and output policy. In static textbook terms, far removed from complex reality, it is bad enough, since they have to determine at what point marginal revenue equals marginal cost, and in order to do this they need to know the demand curves for their outputs and the supply curves for their inputs; and that is quite a tall order. Allowing for a real world where everything keeps changing, and where the future is uncertain, makes a difficult problem seemingly impossible. How, then, do managers take their appallingly difficult decisions?

The answer is that they do the best they can, and that they undoubtedly make many mistakes, but that there is a mechanism which rewards the better decisions and punishes the worse ones, and that is the profits system. Successful firms, the ones which grow fastest and can attract most capital, are, on the whole, those which make the most profits.[2] So long as this system operates reasonably effectively, we do not have to worry too much about the theoretical problems faced by management. We can leave them to find out the best practical solutions, though, as academics, we must of course be interested to learn what those solutions are, and may even sometimes be able to suggest ways of improving them. There is an analogy with the process of natural selection. It seems at first sight unbelievable that an apparently blind process of trial and error can have led to the evolution of such incredibly complex and wonderful systems as we find all around us, yet that is the best explanation for them that has yet been found. Human beings have a better capacity for forethought than other living species, and so their institutions (such as private enterprise) develop by a process that is more sophisticated than pure trial and error. Nevertheless, the trial and error component is still very important.

When we turn to public monopolies, however, the profits mechanism breaks down.[3] We do not want the Electricity Generating Board, or the Post Office, for example, to try to maximise their profits, and they are not instructed to do so in the Acts which set them up. The result of their doing so would be prices for electricity, or the telephone, which would be far too high, and which would greatly hamper other industries. The super-normal profits of public monopolies are equivalent to taxes. It is a well-known proposition in public finance that taxes on intermediate goods – the inputs of other industries – are best avoided, and that it is preferable to tax final consumption goods. Even then, it is preferable to impose a uniform tax (such as VAT, if applied at a uniform rate on all economic activity), and to reserve especially high rates of tax for goods such as alcohol and tobacco where there is some reason to believe that consumers tend to buy more than is good for them. The case for high taxes on electricity and the services provided by the Post Office seems very weak.

If, however, we do not want public monopolies to maximise profits, what do we want them to do? No really satisfactory answer to this question has yet been found. The White Paper of 1967,[4] for example, instructed the nationalised industries to earn target rates of return on their net assets, and to undertake investments which would earn at least as much as a test rate of discount (originally 8 per cent per annum in *real* terms, but soon adjusted to 10 per cent, where it still remains at the time of writing). Some attention was paid to the principle of marginal-cost pricing, but one could not be sure that it was compatible with the target rate of return, nor was it clear how the latter related to the test rate of discount. The target rate of return suffered from various disadvantages. It could be achieved, for example, by earning large profits in some activities which offset large losses elsewhere, although, to be sure, the White Paper frowned on this practice. The definition and measurement of the net-assets base on which the return was to be earned was rather arbitrary, and some industries have in practice had their targets adjusted from time to time by large write-offs of debt. While the system was reasonable enough for those public enterprises facing strong competition (e.g. British Steel, British Airways or British Leyland), and who could, therefore, be treated rather as if they were private enterprises, it was quite inadequate for public enterprises in a strong monopoly position. For they always had some 'slack' which could be taken up by raising prices. Hence they could always hit their targets, no matter (within reason) how inefficient in other respects they might be, provided they were given a free hand in fixing their own prices. Realising this, the Government has not in practice given them a free hand, but that has not provided a happy solution to the problem. For if the targets are not hit, the management can always blame the Government's price control. Furthermore, there is no good way of deciding how prices *should* be controlled. In principle, and even to some extent in practice, it is possible to make estimates of long-run marginal costs, but it is almost certainly impracticable for the Government to attempt to second-guess every pricing decision these enterprises need to make.[5] This is a recipe for delay and frustration of the kind depicted by Aubrey Silberston in Chapter 10. It was precisely this failure to relate the theoretical case for marginal-cost pricing to a practical procedure which would ensure that correct price and output decisions would be somehow 'rewarded' that was the flaw in the academic literature of the late 1940s.

What was (and still is) very much needed was some substitute for profits which could be used as both a test and an objective for public monopolies. It was with this idea in mind that the writer decided, long ago in 1948, to attempt a B.Litt. thesis on 'Criteria of Efficiency for Nationalised Industries'. The problem was partly theoretical – what criterion would in theory lead to an optimum price and output policy? – and partly practical, since it was no use devising a criterion which could not be applied in practice. His University supervisor had a happy blend of interests in both aspects, had recently published the invaluable *The Nationalised Industries: a Statutory Analysis*,[6] and was none other than Norman Chester. The thesis was not completed in the year, and the writer had to take it away with him to work at it in his spare time in

Paris, where he was employed by the Organization for European Economic Cooperation. But with much help and sympathetic encouragement from his supervisor it was eventually written and successfully submitted. By then (as, one suspects, must often happen), the writer was heartily sick of the subject – which was in any case going out of fashion, as a Conservative Government had replaced a Labour one. He therefore promptly forgot all about it, and it has been collecting dust in Bodley ever since.

Every now and then, however, he has felt that he ought to resurrect the one novel[7] idea it contained, but other claims on time have always seemed more urgent. Perhaps the delay has been providential, since the subject is returning to fashion, and what could provide a better occasion than the present volume?

The idea alluded to above can be very simply explained. Let us abandon for the moment (we return to it in Part II) the idea of looking at the *level* of profits, or any related magnitude, achieved by a public monopoly. Instead, let us ask how we can judge whether there has been a *change* in its performance which is for the better or the worse. We want to know, for example, whether this year's results are better or worse than last year's. Let us then calculate profits for last year using this year's prices to revalue all inputs and outputs. So we now compare this year's actual profits with last year's recalculated profits. The change in profits will then be a result of quantity changes only. Profits, as recalculated, will increase if, for example, the quantities of outputs, valued at this year's prices, have risen by more than the quantities of inputs, also valued at this year's prices. Let us call such an increase, for short, an increase in *volume profits*, so as to distinguish it from an increase in the *value* of profits as conventionally measured.[8] A public monopoly will not always be able to increase its volume profits merely by raising its prices. In fact, this could well reduce them. If, for example, prices in general exceeded marginal costs, raising prices would lead to a fall in sales and output which would reduce their value (measured at constant prices) by more than the saving made in costs. This is a tautology. Hence, in these circumstances, a public monopoly would reduce its volume profits if it raised its prices, and it would increase its volume profits if it reduced its prices. The effects on actual profits could, however, easily be the exact opposite of this. Consequently, a public monopoly which strove to increase its volume profits would tend, by trial and error, to adjust its prices to marginal costs, and one would normally regard this as a much better approximation to optimal output than, for example, that which would result from the pursuit of maximum actual profits, at least if the monopoly were a strong one.[9]

Of course, in any actual year, the public monopoly's results might

F

be affected by 'chance' factors which would make it difficult to judge whether its underlying efficiency had improved. For example, there might be a bad strike, or a temporary rise or fall in demand due to the weather or to the usual ups and downs of the trade cycle. One would therefore need to 'take one year with another' (as the nationalisation Acts prescribe) and consider the cumulative increases in volume profits over a number of years.[10] Even then it would be, in the nature of things, very difficult to allocate responsibility for changes in volume profits between the management, for example, and other factors. The same problem exists in private enterprise and the solutions, in so far as there are any, are the same. By and large one has to be a bit ruthless and judge management by actual results, even if one is not sure who is responsible. This is the doubtless unfair test of the profit mechanism (and of natural selection), but it is hard to improve upon it.

It might be objected that if a public monopoly were judged by its performance in increasing volume profits, it would lose all interest in trying to keep its input prices down, or in getting the best prices it could for its outputs. There would, admittedly, be a weaker incentive in this matter than if the public monopoly were trying to maximise actual profits. But then, public monopolies do not in fact try to do this, and can hardly be permitted to do so. Hence their incentive is inevitably weakened. Furthermore, it is untrue to say that there would be no incentive at all. To take the case which probably springs most immediately to the reader's mind, a public monopoly which acquiesced in an unnecessarily large[11] wage increase would thereby reduce its opportunities for investment and the expansion of its volume profits. For such increases would tend to raise marginal costs and so make it necessary to cut back output and employment. Few managements would enjoy doing that. It may also be desirable to measure changes in volume profits in such a way as to subtract increases in costs due to increases in wages or other input prices, just as one would in measuring conventional profits, and the reasons for this are explained in Part III. This would considerably weaken the objection.

There are doubtless other objections which could be raised against the proposal, and there are many aspects of it which would need more detailed consideration before it could be applied in practice. The problem of measuring changes in sales and purchases at constant prices is not a trivial one, although it should be possible to make adequate estimates. Complete precision is not required, since any test of performance is bound to be imperfect. Some further points of a more technical nature are made in Part II, and an arithmetical illustration is given in Part III for those who (like the writer) find such things helpful. Nevertheless, the above is the central idea. It is not intended as a panacea for all the problems of the control and operation of public monopolies. It is merely a belated contribution to the debate which reflects the writer's particular interests and knowledge, and one which Norman Chester greatly assisted when it was originally formulated. If, by forming part of the present volume, it succeeds in catching some interested reader's eye in a way which would not be remotely probable were it to remain as a forgotten thesis in Bodley, then that is just one more debt which the writer must owe to his old University supervisor.

PART II

This part explains the volume profits criterion in a little more detail, mainly for the benefit of economists. The algebra is simple, but may nevertheless deter non-economists. The latter may prefer, therefore, to go straight to the arithmetical example in Part III.

It is convenient to start with a private enterprise's accounts, and then to show how these may be adapted to provide a criterion for a public monopoly which is comparable to profits for the private enterprise.[12] Many of the points we shall make are common to both, and are most easily grasped in the more familiar context of profits maximisation.

A private enterprise's net profits or revenue, R, may be regarded as consisting of two parts: its net current receipts, Y, and depreciation, D, so that:

$$R = Y - D \qquad (1)$$

Net current receipts are 'net' in the sense that current expenditures are subtracted from current receipts, and they are also net of maintenance expenditures. The latter may be regarded as the expenditures required to keep the enterprise *physically* intact (*not* economically intact), producing a constant physical flow of outputs from a constant physical flow of inputs. We can allow for inflation and refer to it below, but to simplify matters let us first assume that the general price level (say the retail price index) is constant and is expected to remain so. *Relative* prices will still be changing, however, and a typical enterprise can expect that they will be changing in such a way as to reduce the value of net current receipts. Typically, input prices (especially wages) will be rising relatively to output prices. Hence, not all of Y can be prudently distributed as dividends, for if it were, and if the enterprise consequently remained physically unchanged, it would find that its net current receipts would dwindle away eventually to nothing. In order to counteract the adverse changes in relative prices, the enterprise must continuously change itself, typically increasing its physical output per unit of input, and that requires a certain rate of gross investment expenditure. Suppose that D is the gross investment expenditure which is just sufficient to offset the adverse change in relative prices, so that $Y - D$ is the maximum amount which the enterprise could distribute as dividends and still expect to be able to distribute the same real amount each year indefinitely into the future. This is then its net profit, income or revenue, and it is net of D, which is depreciation.

Next let us consider rates of change in these magnitudes. We shall refer to rates of change at a point of time, rather than to differences between one year and the next, as this simplifies the algebra. However, in practice one would have to consider year-to-year changes, and we do this in the example in Part III. Differentiating (1) with respect to time we have:

$$\frac{dR}{dt} = \frac{dY}{dt} - \frac{dD}{dt} \tag{2}$$

If $\dfrac{dR}{dt}$ is positive, i.e. if R is increasing, does that necessarily mean that the enterprise is efficient? No, because the increase might have been achieved at too great a cost in terms of savings. Suppose that the rate of gross savings invested in the enterprise is S, and that we require a minimum net rate of return on these savings of r per unit per annum. A return of less than r is deemed to be inefficient (for a public enterprise, r is the test rate of discount). Then, for the enterprise to be efficient we require that:

$$\frac{dR}{dt} \geqslant r\,(S - D) \tag{3}$$

Thus, if gross investment just equals depreciation, the enterprise is efficient so long as R does not fall. If there is positive net investment, net profits must increase at a rate which is at least equal to r times the rate of net investment.[13]

The reader's attention is drawn to two features of (3). First, it sets, so to speak, a *base line*. If the left-hand side is equal to or greater than the right-hand side, the enterprise is efficient. If not, it is inefficient. Secondly, it provides a *measure of the degree of efficiency achieved*. The bigger the excess of the left-hand side over the right the better. Our profits criterion for a public monopoly should have both these features if it is to be satisfactory, but, as we shall see, it is easier to reproduce the second one than the first.[14]

The criterion suggested in (3) can be applied on a cumulative basis so as to 'take one year with another'. Thus we can add up, or integrate, the changes in net profits over a period as long as we choose and compare them with the net investment made during that period. Thus we get, between times t_1 and t_2, and assuming a constant[15] r:

$$\int_{t_1}^{t_2} \frac{dR_t}{dt}\, dt \;\;\geqslant\;\; \int_{t_1}^{t_2} r\,(S_t-D_t)\, dt \qquad (4)$$

or

$$R_2 - R_1 \;\;\geqslant\;\; r \int_{t_1}^{t_2} (S_t-D_t)\, dt \qquad (4A)$$

If t_1 was the start of the enterprise, and so there was no net investment before it, then the sum of net investment since t_1 would simply be the capital stock of the enterprise. R_1 would then be zero, and our criterion for the whole period since the enterprise was founded would take the familiar form:

$$\frac{R_2}{K} \;\;\geqslant\;\; r \qquad (4B)$$

That is, the ratio of profits to capital stock should at least equal the required rate of return, r, for the enterprise to be deemed efficient. It is a mistake, however, which is widely made, to regard this as a test of the *current* efficiency of the enterprise. As we have seen, it is really a test of its average efficiency over the whole period since it was founded. If we want a test over a more recent period we must use (4) and choose the limits of the period, t_1 and t_2, for whatever purpose we have in mind (for example, a new manager may have taken over at t_1).

If there is inflation, this somewhat complicates matters, but not as much as some might imagine. The writer has argued elsewhere that the best way to allow for inflation is to use only one price index, say the retail price index, to adjust all figures.[16] Thus (4) becomes:

$$\int_{t_1}^{t_2} \frac{1}{\pi_t}\, \frac{dR_t}{dt}\,.\, dt \;\geqslant\; \int_{t_1}^{t_2} \frac{r}{\pi_t}\, (S_t - D_t).\, dt \qquad (4C)$$

where π_t is the price index at t for an arbitrarily chosen base period. The rationale of this procedure is a simple one. The ultimate objective of economic activity being consumption, what one wants to know is one's income, R, in terms of its command over consumption. Likewise, one's net savings, $S - D$, represent a sacrifice of consumption. Hence these magnitudes in different periods are made commensurable by deflating by a suitable consumers' price index. It is incorrect to deflate savings (or investment) by, for example, a price index of capital goods (as is frequently done). The capital stock, K, in (4B) should measure accumulated consumption forgone, and *not* the replacement cost of capital goods. The latter is quite irrelevant for the purpose on hand (though possibly relevant for fire insurance![17]).

So much for a private enterprise. We start our consideration of a public monopoly by expanding equation (2):

$$\frac{dR}{dt} = \sum \left(\frac{p.dq}{dt} \right) + \sum \left(\frac{q.dp}{dt} \right) - \frac{dD}{dt} \tag{2A}$$

This merely subdivides the change in the value of net current receipts into two components: that due to quantity changes only, and that due to price changes only. Following the idea presented in Part I, it might at first sight seem that all we have to do, in order to compute the change in volume profits, is to strike out the second of these, thus leaving the change in volume profits as the sum of the first and last terms on the right-hand side of (2A). This was, in fact, the conclusion the writer reached in his B.Litt. thesis. One advantage of waiting about a quarter of a century before publishing anything on the subject is that he now realises that this was a mistake. Merely striking out the second term does provide a criterion with the second feature to which we drew attention on p. 158 above. That is, it is the case that the bigger the public monopoly can make the increase in volume profits, so defined, the better. However, it fails to provide the first feature. The base-line is incorrect, and in general is too easily crossed. In other words, were we to use this definition of the increase in volume profits in (3), and were it to equal the right-hand side (which would be the test rate of discount, r, multiplied by the rate of net investment, $S - D$) we would be generally mistaken in concluding that the public monopoly was (just) efficient. In general, it would be inefficient.

In order to see why this is so, we must further subdivide that part of the change in net current receipts which is due to price changes into two parts. The first of these, (a), consists of price changes *due to the quantity changes* of the monopoly's outputs and inputs. These are, in effect, the movements *along* the monopoly's demand curves for its outputs or supply curves for its inputs. This first component, (a), of the price change must be struck out. It would not exist for a competitive private enterprise, and so we want to remove it for our public monopoly, too. Secondly, (b), there are the effects of all other price changes, and these must be left in, since they would exist for a competitive private enterprise. The practical problem is now very clear. How can we possibly, in practice, make such a distinction? To do so would seem to require a knowledge of demand and supply curves which is certainly beyond the ability of any supervisory central government department whose task it is to monitor the performance of the public monopoly.

Fortunately, there is a way of approximating the distinction, but before we explain it we should point out that this is undoubtedly the less important feature of our volume profits criterion. Even if we draw the base-line in the wrong place, we shall still have a workable means of judging performance and a useful objective for the management of the monopoly. It can still strive to increase volume profits as much as possible, even if we are no longer very sure what constitutes an acceptable performance. The situation with this imperfect criterion will be much better than the existing situation of no clear criterion at all. Nevertheless, it obviously is desirable to draw a reasonable base-line, and in the remainder of this part we shall endeavour to show how this may be done. Those readers who find the argument difficult or tedious may prefer to skip directly to equation (9), p. 163.

The clue to the solution lies in our previous discussion of depreciation. We showed that depreciation was fundamentally due to adverse changes in the relative prices of inputs and outputs. These adverse changes would occur for a competitive enterprise, and would, in fact, be the *only* kind of price change that would occur,[18] since price changes of the first (*a*) kind, representing moves *along* demand and supply curves as opposed to shifts of those curves, would not occur. Can we, therefore, base our estimate of the (*b*)-type price changes somehow or another on depreciation? Given that all we need is a reasonable approximation, the following method has the virtue of simplicity.

At time *t*, the net present value of a particular asset may be written as:

$$A_t = \int_0^\infty Y_{t+\tau} \, . e^{-r\tau} . d\tau \tag{5}$$

where $Y_{t+\tau}$ is the value of net current receipts or quasi-rent from the asset at the time τ after t. We shall assume that the asset is fully maintained until the date of its 'death', so that the physical outputs and inputs associated with it are constant. However, because of adverse relative price changes, Y falls continuously, and the asset is scrapped when Y becomes zero.

Differentiating (5) with respect to time, we get:

$$\frac{dA_t}{dt} = \int_0^\infty \frac{\partial Y_{t+\tau}}{\partial t} \, . e^{-r\tau} . d\tau$$

$$= \int_0^\infty \left\{ \frac{p.\partial q_{t+\tau}}{\partial t} + \frac{q.\partial p_{t+\tau}}{\partial t} \right\} .e^{-r\tau}.d\tau \qquad (6)$$

where we have omitted the summation signs in front of the price and quantity terms for simplicity.

Now, as we have assumed that the asset is fully maintained, so that the quantities do not change, the first term in brackets is zero. The second term clearly is the price effect (*b*) which we are seeking, only we need the first term in the series, that is, $q.\partial p_t$ rather than the discounted
$\overline{\partial t}$
sum of the whole series to the end of the life of the asset, which is what we have got in (6).

Given our assumptions,[19] the rate of change in the net present value of the asset at *t is* (the negative of) its rate of depreciation at *t*. Hence, to find $q.\partial p_t$ all we must do is to make some assumption about the way in
$\quad\overline{\partial t}$
which the series of changes in net current receipts declines through time. The simplest is to assume a constant proportionate rate of fall at the rate, *g*. If this occurs, the asset's quasi-rents, Υ, will also fall at the rate *g*, and it is easy to show that the correct depreciation formula is the declining-balance method. Depreciation is then simply *g* times the net asset value, and both depreciation and the net asset value decline at the constant proportionate rate *g*. That being so:

$$\frac{dA_t}{dt} = -D_t = -gA_t = \frac{q\,\partial p_t}{\partial t} \int_0^\infty e^{-(g+r)\tau}.d\tau$$

$$= \frac{q\,\partial p_t}{\partial t} \cdot \frac{1}{(g+r)} \qquad (7)$$

Hence:

$$\frac{q\,\partial p_t}{\partial t} = -(g+r)\,D_t \qquad (8)$$

This, then, is a reasonable approximation to the (*b*) price term we require (it is only an approximation because the assumptions of the declining balance method and the assumptions mentioned in note 19 are unlikely to be precisely fulfilled). We may accordingly write out the volume profits criterion in full as follows:

$$\sum_{(} \frac{(p \cdot dq)}{dt)} - (g + r) D_t - \frac{dD_t}{dt} \geqslant r(S_t - D_t) \qquad (9)$$

Taking the terms in order from left to right they are:

$\sum_{(} \frac{(p \cdot dq)}{dt)}$ is the change in quantities of current outputs and inputs valued at constant prices.

$(g + r) D_t$ is the rate of depreciation multiplied by the sum of, first, the ratio of depreciation to net capital stock, g, and, second, the test rate of discount, r.

$\dfrac{dD_t}{dt}$ is the rate of change of depreciation (adjusted for inflation as already described).

$r(S_t - D_t)$ is the test rate of discount multiplied by the rate of net investment.

When this criterion is expressed in terms of year-to-year changes, the change in quantities may be valued either at later year prices or earlier year prices, or at some compromise. We have nothing to add here to conventional index number theory. The method of cumulating the results for successive periods, and of adjusting for inflation, are as already described for a private enterprise.

The criterion in (9) is not as good as (3), the corresponding criterion for a private enterprise. This is because our approximation to the (b) price term is less satisfactory than having the actual change in prices, as does (3). Our public monopoly might try to cheat by underestimating depreciation and so exaggerating the excess of the left-hand side of (9) over the right-hand side. With a private enterprise, this kind of cheating would not be possible. However, there would be some check on it for a public monopoly. The rates of depreciation used for different assets would have implications about their useful economic lives,[20] and these could be checked. Nevertheless, just because it is unsatisfactory, it seems worth while considering alternative ways of estimating the (b) price term, and one such is described in Part III.

III

In this part we present an arithmetical example to illustrate the calculation of changes in volume profits, and the application of the suggested criterion. The figures are entirely hypothetical.

We assume that the retail price index, our chosen measure of inflation, increases by 10 per cent from Year 1 to Year 2. We re-

calculate everything in terms of Year 2 prices, although it would i■
general be desirable to make comparisons at both years' sets of prices
and possibly to use some compromise between them as 'the' criterion
We assume the test discount rate is 10 per cent p.a. in real terms (a
it is at the time of writing) and that depreciation is 5 per cent of th■
net book value of assets (adjusted for inflation).

Item	Actual (1)	Year 1 Adjusted for inflation (2)	At Year 2 prices (3)	Year 2 Actual (4)
Sales				
Price (£/Unit)	0·9318	1·0250	1·0000	1·0000
Quantity	100	100	100	105
Value (£)	93·18	102·50	100·00	105·00
Purchases				
Price (£/Unit)	0·8920	0·9812	1·0000	1·0000
Quantity	80	80	80	81
Value (£)	71·36	78·50	80·00	81·00
Net Current receipts (£)	21·82	24·00	20·00	24·00
Net capital stock (£) at start of year	181·82	200·00	200·00	210·00
Depreciation (£)	9·09	10·00	10·00	10·50
Gross investment (£)	18·18	20·00	20·00	25·00

Let us first treat the enterprise as if it were private, to be judged b
its actual profits, adjusted for inflation. The latter adjustment simpl▶
requires multiplying all prices and values in col. (1), the actual Year
results, by 1·1 to bring them to the same general price level basis as th▶
Year 2 results in col. (4). This calculation is performed in col. (2
Comparing it with col. (4) we then have:

Increase in net current receipts $\quad = \quad £24 - £24$
$\qquad\qquad\qquad\qquad\qquad\qquad\quad = \quad £0$
Increase in depreciation $\qquad\qquad = \quad £10.50 - £10$
$\qquad\qquad\qquad\qquad\qquad\qquad\quad = \quad £0.50$
So increase in net profits $\qquad\quad = - £0.50$
Net investment in Year 1 $= £20 - £10 = £10$

So required rate of return multiplied by net investment $= £1$.
The test of performance is to compare the increase in net profits wit▶

the required rate of return multiplied by net investment, and, since

$$- £0.50 \quad < \quad £1$$

the enterprise has had a bad year, judged as a conventional profit maximiser.

Next, let us apply the volume profits test. For this purpose we need col. (3), where the values of sales and purchases have been further adjusted to Year 2 prices. Col. (3), unlike col. (2), assumes that *relative* prices of sales and purchases are the same in Year 1 as in Year 2. However, there is no further adjustment required for the other figures, since they all refer to consumption sacrificed at Year 2 prices already – and that is, so to speak, our unit of account for them. We now have:

Increase in net current receipts from Year 1 to	
Year 2	$= £24 - £20$
	$= £4$
Increase in depreciation, as before,	$= £0.50$

Price offset to be deducted[21] in arriving at increase in net profit = $£(0.10 + 0.05) 10 = £1.50$. So increase in net profit = $£4 - £0.50 - £1.50 = £2$. As this is greater than the test rate of discount multiplied by net investment, i.e. than $£1$, the enterprise has had a good year, judged by the volume profits test.

We have chosen our illustration so as to point up the contrast between changes in conventional profits and volume profits. The example can also be used to show a second way in which the 'price effect' (i.e. the $£1.50$ deduction) might be estimated, and one which has some advantages over the method used above. If we can assume that the monopoly is not a monopsony, so that, so far as its *purchases* are concerned it is a price-taker, and in the same position as a competitive enterprise, then we can leave *in* the whole of the price change on that side of the accounts. If, further, we can assume that no change in the quantity of output would have resulted in no change in its price (apart, that is, from rising in line with the general price level),[22] then we can take *out* the whole of the price change on that side. In our example we have chosen the figures so that the results of following this procedure are just the same as those of the one used above. Thus we would no longer have the $£1.50$ price deduction, but in its place we would put a deduction equal to the rise in the cost of purchases due to price changes, and that is also $£1.50$ (compare the value of purchases in cols (2) and (3)). We would still calculate the change in the value of sales as in the example, giving an increase at constant prices of $£5$, and everything else would be the same as well. Hence, in this example there is no difference between the two procedures. However, the second has the advantage of confronting the management with the actual increase in prices of purchases in a more direct way than does the first. It might therefore strengthen their resistance to wage increases, or other increases in the prices of their inputs. Whether this is a conclusive argument in its favour depends on how good an approximation we believe the assumptions on which it rests are to actual circumstances, and this would have to be looked at carefully.

NOTES

1 The writer is grateful to John Flemming and Aubrey Silberston for comments and suggestions.
2 For an illuminating account of the working of the system, see Downie 1958.
3 It also breaks down, from society's point of view, when there are strong private monopolies. The ideas discussed here may have some relevance to this problem as well, but we do not wish to pursue this line of thought further at this point.
4 Cmnd. 3437, Nov 1967. See also Cmnd. 4027, May 1969.
5 See, for example, Turvey 1968, p. 59, where, after explaining how long-run marginal cost for electricity supply may be estimated, he remarks: 'The same fact of technical progress makes long-run marginal cost a much more complicated concept than any economics textbook allows. There is no escaping an element of judgement in its calculation. . . . Finally, it cannot be emphasized too strongly that any estimate of long-term marginal cost has no significance *in abstracto* but only in relation to a specified load increment. There are as many marginal costs as there are conceivable load increments.'
6 D. N. Chester, July 1948.
7 Novel at least to the writer. No doubt someone else had already thought of it!
8 We have here, for simplicity, neglected interest and depreciation, although our definition of volume profits is net of both (see Part II).
9 It might be thought that the widespread existence of imperfect competition would mean that marginal cost pricing would not be optimal. In general, with prices higher than marginal cost elsewhere, prices equal to marginal costs in a public enterprise would be too low. The writer is doubtful whether this is an important objection to the use of volume profits, partly because he is not convinced that prices in private enterprises are appreciably higher on average than they ought to be in any relevant sense, and partly because the most important pricing decisions for a public monopoly may often be those relating to close substitutes, all produced by the monopoly itself. The most important thing may be to get these *relative* prices corresponding as nearly as possible to relative marginal costs. In any case, if it was thought that prices were too low, the Government could always impose a sales tax on the monopoly's output.

10   See Part II for further explanation of how this might be done.

11   That is, larger than was necessary to secure the supply of labour required.

12   In what follows, we make use of similar concepts and notation to those in Scott, Nov 1976. However, it is not assumed that the reader has also read that article.

13   Some readers may feel at this point that time-lags between the incurring of investment expenditure and the resultant increase in net current receipts should be allowed for. So far as the theory of the matter is concerned, time-lags should be taken care of by the estimate of depreciation. During the gestation period of investment the enterprise should experience *appreciation*, not *depreciation*, since the time at which net current receipts are going to increase is approaching, and the discounted present value of those receipts is therefore increasing – which is the opposite of the more usual case considered in the text in which net current receipts are expected to fall. Because of this appreciation, $\frac{dD}{dt}$ will become negative and so R will increase even if Y remains constant. This increase in R should equal at least r times net investment, as the text statement above implies. In practice, however, conventional methods of charging depreciation do not allow for this effect, and so it will be necessary to allow for time-lags. However, if investment is growing reasonably smoothly, and the time-lags are fairly constant, and especially if we 'take one year with another', the difficulty is not too serious.

14   A third feature of (3) which is worth noting is that it refers to the *absolute* increase in *net* profit. It is a measure of (change in) pure surplus, and not a measure of profit per unit of capital.

15   A variable r could be allowed for along the lines described in Scott, Nov 1976.

16   See Scott 1976 and Nov 1976.

17   *Inflation Accounting* [the Sandilands Report] (HMSO, Sep 1975) mistakenly, in the writer's view, argued that the correct way to value an enterprise's capital stock was generally at replacement cost. The Report's argument was based on the following quotation from Bonbright 1937: 'The value of a property to its owner is identical in amount with the adverse value of the entire loss, direct and indirect, that the owner might expect to suffer if he were to be deprived of the property' (paras 208 and 209). While this seems a useful definition for insurance purposes, it is not useful for the purpose of estimating profits, which was the main concern of the Report.

18   Of course, the price changes need not necessarily be *adverse*! Land and minerals, for example, may appreciate as well as depreciate. However, for most of the assets of a typical enterprise depreciation would be more likely than appreciation, and in what follows we shall, for simplicity, only consider that case, although the analysis can easily accommodate both. Appreciation may, in fact, be very important for some public enterprises, notably coal, gas and oil, and for them depletion should also be taken into account.

19   That is (implicitly or explicitly), a constant rate of discount r, which

equals the return on the investment of depreciation funds, and the fulfilment of expectations on average. For further discussion the reader is referred to Scott, Nov 1976, especially pp. 340–8.

20   Strictly speaking, the declining balance method implies that assets last for ever. However, the above formula can easily be adjusted to refer to straight-line depreciation if that is desired. Furthermore, one could use the formula in the way suggested above, that is, with any system of depreciation that seems useful, and with g measuring the current ratio of depreciation to net asset value.

21   Those readers who have omitted Part II may not understand this term. Broadly speaking, it shows the effect of price changes between Year 1 and Year 2 which *should* be shown, that is, which would show up even in the accounts of a competitive enterprise.

22   This amounts to assuming that the demand curve for the product has not shifted in real terms, which would not generally be a plausible assumption to make.

REFERENCES

Bonbright, J. C., *The Valuation of Property* (McGraw-Hill, 1937).

Chester, D. N., *The Nationalised Industries: a Statutory Analysis* (Institute of Public Administration, July 1948).

Downie, J., *The Competitive Process* (Duckworth, 1958).

Henderson, A. M., 'Prices and profits in state enterprise', *Review of Economic Studies*, vol. 16, no. 1 (1948).

Her Majesty's Government, *Nationalised Industries. A Review of Economic and Financial Objectives*, Cmnd 3437 (HMSO, Nov 1967).

—— *Ministerial Control of the Nationalised Industries*, Cmnd 4027 (HMSO, May 1969).

—— *Inflation Accounting*, Report of the Inflation Accounting Committee, Cmnd 6225 [the Sandilands Report] (HMSO, Sep 1975).

Lerner, A. P., *The Economics of Control* (Macmillan, 1944).

Lewis, W. A., 'Fixed Costs', *Economica*, Nov 1946.

Meade, J. E., and Fleming, J. M., 'Price and output policy of state enterprise', *Economic Journal*, Dec 1944.

Scott, M. FG., *Some Economic Principles of Accounting. A Constructive Critique of the Sandilands Report*, Institute of Fiscal Studies (London, 1976).

Scott, M. FG., 'Investment and Growth', *Oxford Economic Papers*, Nov 1976.

Turvey, R., *Optimal Pricing and Investment in Electricity Supply* (Allen & Unwin, 1968).

Vickrey, W., 'Some objections to marginal cost pricing', *Journal of Political Economy*, June 1948.

Wilson, T., 'Price and output policy of state enterprise', *Economic Journal*, Dec 1945.

12 The Machinery of Economic Government: Some Personal Reflections

DONALD MACDOUGALL

It may seem presumptuous for an economist to write about an aspect of the machinery of government in a volume in honour of such an expert as Norman Chester. My only excuse is that for a good half of the last forty years I have been a practitioner in the field of economic government – in war and peace, under Conservative, Labour and coalition administrations, on the fringes in Neddy and the CBI; only service in the TUC would have been needed to complete my education, and my contact with the last has been fairly close and continuous for the past fifteen years.

Thus, though I am no expert in the machinery of government, it may be of some interest to those who are, and perhaps to others, to go through my various periods of experience in and with government and say what views, or perhaps I should say prejudices – and changing ones at that – they implanted in my mind, often without my conscious knowledge (because I am not given to thinking deeply about matters of administration when concentrating on economic problems) in regard to the most appropriate machinery of economic government, and in particular central policy formulation.

It is not easy to be objective. One tends to think an organisation appropriate if one happens to be where there is at the time a good deal of the power and influence. I have been lucky enough to have been in this situation a good deal, and the reader will no doubt discount as he thinks fit for any bias.

My first experience was during the Second World War, from 1939 to 1945, working for Professor Lindemann (later Lord Cherwell), commonly called 'the Prof', when he was in turn advising Churchill. This was first in the First Lord of the Admiralty's, then in the Prime Minister's, so called 'Statistical Branch'. (The Prof was appointed Paymaster-General in December 1942.) I wrote a chapter on this branch – the activities of which in fact reached far beyond the realms of statistics – in *Lessons of the British War Economy*, edited by Norman Chester and published in 1951. This volume was written by those who had been personally involved while events were still relatively fresh in their minds and, despite the limitations of the thirty-year rule, it tells us a lot about the widespread ramifications of what may loosely be called 'economic government' during the war. I was concerned with a small, but very central, neck of the woods. Another small but important central body – on floors just above us in the 'New Public Offices' adjacent to Great George Street for a good part of the war – was the Economic Section of the War Cabinet Secretariat, of which one D. N. Chester was a distinguished member, seconded for part of the time to work for William Beveridge on his famous report on Social Insurance and Allied Services.

My next sortie into Whitehall was for two years in 1951–3 when Churchill again became Prime Minister and once more asked Cherwell to advise him as Paymaster-General. I was given leave of absence by Nuffield and the University to join them. The 'branch' this time was smaller – but perhaps made up for this by quality, with three out of its four economists being Nuffield men – and it dealt with very different problems.

Then after eight years or so back at Nuffield, I joined the newly formed National Economic Development Office early in 1962 as its first Economic Director and stayed there until October 1964 when Labour won the general election and set up the Department of Economic Affairs (DEA) under George Brown. I was appointed Director-General of the new department and saw it both in its early heyday and as it was gradually losing some of its powers to other departments and a good deal of its influence generally. But before its actual demise I was transferred to the Treasury on New Year's Day 1969 as Chief Economic Adviser and Head of the Government Economic Service. I thus saw a little of life in the Treasury while there was the DEA at the other end of the corridor, as well as a much longer period without a DEA. My spell at the Treasury was first under a Labour Government then under a Conservative one, and I saw both the non-interventionist and the interventionist phases of the Heath Government's economic policy before I retired from the Civil Service in October 1973 and crossed the road to be Chief Economic Adviser at the CBI a few hundred yards away. This propinquity to my old haunts has not been unimportant.

WAR

During the war I worked for a Prime Minister who in the last resort was pretty well supreme on major strategic economic decisions and who, alone among those in authority, was in possession of the wide range of information necessary as a basis for making such decisions. He also took a great deal of interest in the details of many aspects of economic policy.

Strategic economic decisions mainly concerned the allocation of resources between military and civilian uses, but he was also enormously interested in the efficiency of the use of resources in each of the two sectors.

Thus, for example, on the civil side he campaigned endlessly for the substitution of steel imports for imports of iron ore. This was repugnant to the steel man because the final product was more expensive, but clearly in the national interest when shipping space rather than money and foreign exchange became the overriding bottleneck.

He was equally concerned not to waste resources on the military side. Thus, to take another example of the use of shipping space, in the early days of the war in North Africa, lorries were driven on to ships, wheels and all, in Britain and went that way on the very long trip round the Cape of Good Hope to Suez, with a ludicrously small number of vehicles per ship. There was obvious scope for great economies by dismantling and crating (or 'boxing' as it was called) in various forms. This the military resisted because it would be inconvenient in a number of ways, but when we were able to show convincingly how much shipping could be saved and what this was equivalent to in terms of imports into hard-pressed Britain the Prime Minister finally directed that it was to be done; and it was done, with monthly reports to him to prove it.

Turning from the Prime Minister's interest and intervention in matters affecting efficiency in the use of resources in both the civilian and military sectors, the following are a few examples of strategic economic decisions relating to the balance between the two sectors.

In the early part of the war, including the months before he became Prime Minister, Churchill pressed for a much more rapid transfer of resources from civil to military use. He resisted vigorously those who were – partly for economic reasons such as the losses involved if we had to sell off our overseas investments too quickly at knock-down prices, shortages of skilled engineering manpower and the dangers of inflation – advocating a slow build-up; this he regarded as a dangerous manifestation of a 'Maginot Line' mentality.

Later, in the spring of 1942, he decided that we had gone far enough and that further transfer of resources to direct military use could be counter-productive. Stafford Cripps had returned earlier that year from being our Ambassador in Moscow and become Lord Privy Seal. Taking the view that our civilians, although their standard of living had already been cut severely, should nevertheless make sacrifices more on the scale of those in Russia, he was in considerable measure responsible for a whole string of 'austerity' measures, and proposals for more – soap rationing; further cuts in the clothes ration, bus services, and retail deliveries; no more private motoring; no more white bread; further cuts in newspapers and dog-racing, and much higher taxes on entertainments; prohibition on manufacture of minor articles like leather suitcases, artificial flowers, manicure sets, cigarette cases. The Prof asked me to work out how much manpower and how much shipping space (the two major bottlenecks) these would save in total. The result was relatively trivial: all the cuts of the previous few months had not saved more than 2 per cent of our imports or given us even 1 per cent of extra manpower. His resultant paper to the Prime Minister made the point that we were in danger of a self-inflicted 'Death of a Thousand Cuts', and that any direct gain to the war effort by such further measures could be swamped by the adverse effects on civilian morale, health, the ability of both men and married women to get to work, and so on; to say nothing of the bureaucratic cost of the regulations involved. This was accepted and for the rest of the war the belligerent Churchill was a great champion of the civilian against the competing demands of the military, many of which he knew to be exaggerated and wasteful – for he had almost incredibly detailed knowledge of what was going on. We prepared many hundreds of charts on the subject which he used to browse over, particularly at Chequers during the weekend; in this way he was often better informed than the military chiefs directly involved when it came to discussions with them.

A final example of a major strategic economic decision also occurred in 1942. The Allies were amassing a large armada in the Atlantic to descend on North Africa from the west, and large military forces and equipment in Egypt to attack from the east. All this was making huge demands on the limited amount of merchant shipping available, leaving less and less available for importing – mainly now across the North Atlantic – to the UK. The forecasts of our imports, already cut to a fraction of the pre-war tonnage, were beginning to look frightening. An index I had constructed of stocks of imported food and materials, measured in tons, was plunging downwards, and looked, on current policies, like going below the minimum safety level within a matter of months. If this had happened, we could have lost the war on the home front, with the people short of food, and factories producing the instruments of war, and the minimum of civilian necessities, without materials to work on, and their workers thrown out of a job. Meanwhile, we knew from our detailed statistical records and calculations that the military equipment in Egypt was in many respects in excess of what could possibly be needed.

After repeated warnings to the Prime Minister, the Prof asked me to work out how much the shipping demanded by the military had to be cut to safeguard the British import situation. We had, by this time in the war, established considerable expertise in these matters and had agreed rules-of-thumb with the relevant departments, often reluctantly on their part. So I was able to work out fairly quickly and confidently that whereas 120 ships had been going out each month round the Cape to Egypt (and other theatres in the so-called 'Indian Ocean' area) in the first half of 1942, this would have to be cut to 60 a month. In reporting to the Prof I said: 'You will never get away with this, so better call it 80.' He said: 'On the contrary, I will call it 40 and it will be argued up by the military to your figure of 60, which I believe.' So in went a recommendation to Churchill for a cut to 40. This, to my amazement, was eventually accepted and a directive went out at the turn of the year 1942/43 to those concerned that it was to be done, with monthly statistical reports to the Prime Minister to prove it. The cut lasted for several months. The military pincer movement in North Africa proved wholly successful; imports into the UK began to recover; and I watched the chart of stocks of imported food and materials levelling off just above the danger level and then beginning to pick up slowly.

I suppose this must have been the most momentous macro-economic decision in which I have ever been involved, although I did not think of it in those terms at the time. It is, incidentally, an example of a matter which the Economic Section of the War Cabinet Secretariat was not equipped to cope with, if only because they had none of the military information (or I think the shipping information and expertise) required; although they were certainly very concerned about the dangers of running out of food and materials in the UK.

COMPARISON WITH PEACETIME

It is hard to draw lessons for peacetime about who should be responsible for the major strategic economic decisions, because conditions were then so very different.

The country was at war and things could be done that would never be tolerated in peacetime. There was one agreed aim – to win the war. There was a coalition Government and a party-political truce. The Prime Minister had huge prestige and power, both within the Government and in the country. Many of the major economic problems were in principle similar to peacetime problems: the allocation of resources and efficiency in their use. But the constraints and bottlenecks and the instruments of control were very different.

At least after Lend/Lease began in the spring of 1941 (when our reserves had fallen virtually to vanishing-point) there was no balance of payments problem and no foreign exchange constraint. There was no serious inflationary problem once the Board of Trade, the Ministries of Food, Supply, Production, Labour and others had been so successful in developing rationing, price control, food subsidies, allocation of materials and so on. In this work economists, not least those in the Economic Section of the War Cabinet Secretariat, made a notable contribution. In the event, taken together with the effects of financial policies influenced by the writings of Keynes, inflation was only half as much as it had been during the First World War. These policies left serious post-war legacies – huge sterling balances, excessive domestic liquidity, a greatly increased national debt – but the relevant point is that the main bottlenecks during most of the war did not include most of the conventional peacetime ones, but were in fact, apart from productive capacity in the earlier part of the war, manpower and shipping space, and bottlenecks derived from these such as shortages of steel, coal and food.

The main instruments of economic policy – at least after direct taxation had been raised to what were regarded as the maximum conceivable levels – were not financial, as in peacetime, but mainly direct controls. Instead of operating through public expenditure, taxation and monetary measures, and the exchange rate, we had rationing, allocation of materials, direction of manpower and man-power budgets, shipping programmes and complete control of the allocation of ships and what went in them. The units in which things were measured and controlled were men and tons, not money.

In the circumstances, it is perhaps not surprising that the Chancellor of the Exchequer was not a member of the War Cabinet for periods totalling some two years – five months in 1940 and nineteen months in 1942 and 1943.

In peacetime, conditions are normally very different. There is continuous party-political warfare. No Prime Minister could, I imagine, have quite the same power and prestige in the country as a whole, or even within government, as Churchill had during the war. There is no single overriding aim but, in contrast, many conflicting ones. All this places a big strain on a Prime Minister, and I doubt very much whether he could possibly acquire the same knowledge and exercise the same detailed control of what was going on as Churchill did.

If, therefore, there is to be some one Minister primarily responsible for general economic policy and strategy it can, in peacetime, hardly be the Prime Minister, except in a much more general supervisory role, as has not infrequently happened. Moreover, as the instruments of economic policy are likely to be mainly financial rather than physical – unless we are driven by misfortune or bad management into a siege economy or, heaven forbid, deliberately choose such a state of affairs – it would seem natural that that Minister should be the Chancellor of Exchequer.

'ROBOT'

My next sortie into Whitehall in 1951–3 made me much more doubtful about the wisdom of giving such a virtual monopoly of general economic knowledge and power to the Chancellor and the Treasury. The 'Robot' crisis and controversy of 1952 have been described in Lord Birkenhead's biography *The Prof in Two Worlds*. The facts and the merits of the case on each side are irrelevant to my present thesis. Suffice it to remind the reader that in late 1951 and early 1952 Britain and the sterling area were in the middle of a sterling crisis largely reflecting the aftermath of the Korean war, which had been accompanied by a rearmament programme in Britain and a violent upswing followed by a violent downswing in world commodity prices which had played havoc with the balances of payments of countries in the Overseas Sterling Area. The Prof and his staff took the view that the fall in reserves could be arrested before they fell to a crisis level by various measures which were in fact taken, including help from the US, both financial and physical, in the form of scarce steel, stricter import controls by sterling area countries, including ourselves, accompanied by tougher fiscal and monetary policies.

This appeared to be the agreed strategy, when suddenly, one Friday morning in February 1952, the Chancellor, supported by the Treasury and Bank of England, very nearly succeeded in persuading the Prime Minister and a small meeting of leading Ministers to accept a complete and drastic change of policy, to be implemented immediately, the merits of which were highly debatable, and which would, they admitted, have had untold consequences for prices and employment at home and, abroad, for our relations with the United States, the Sterling Area, the Commonwealth and Europe. I believe that if the Prof had not been at that meeting, had not insisted on an adjournment over the weekend, and himself written a detailed paper opposing the 'Robot' proposals, they would very probably have gone through then and there. In any case the ensuing week or so during which the main battle raged, and the Robot supporters were eventually defeated, wsa a traumatic period for me and convinced me that – whether or not, as some might claim, I am exaggerating the role played by the Prof – there was a strong case for some offsetting centre of power to ensure that, if major changes of economic policy are proposed by the

Treasury, the opposing arguments can be fully presented and discussed. I was, therefore, rather sad and a little worried when in 1953 the Economic Section of the Cabinet Office – which incidentally had been on our side in the Robot controversy – was formally made part of the Treasury.

NEDDY

Neddy, which I joined at its inception early in 1962, just ten years after the Robot controversy, was in a sense a kind of 'Opposition' to the Treasury, although it had no executive power and no ability to influence Treasury policy directly. The Treasury was, however, somewhat under a cloud in the public eye at the time and the popular view was caricatured one week in a popular TV satirical series then running – 'That Was the Week that Was' – which portrayed Treasury officials as old fuddyduddies compared with the Brave New World of Neddy. Also, the non-Ministerial members of the National Economic Development Council, those representing unions and management and the independents, soon made it clear that they wanted their discussions to be based on papers prepared by their own staff in the National Economic Development Office, rather than on papers by the Treasury. Despite all this I had excellent personal relations throughout with Treasury officials.

A great deal of the distrust of the Treasury was most unfair, but there was something in the view that Neddy and the Treasury had different priorities. Neddy, at that time, emphasised the importance of growth as an objective though it might conflict with short-term objectives, and that its achievement might well require unorthodox action in the external economic field. Most of the possible forms of such action were indeed discussed in an almost daring manner in Chapter D of the so-called 'Orange Book' on *Conditions Favourable to Faster Growth* (published in April 1963), though shortly before the office draft of the document was due to be sent out to members of Council, at the turn of the year 1962/63, the Treasury vetoed a section on exchange rate policy which was in many ways at the crux of the matter.

Neddy also showed the value of a body which would concentrate to a large extent on the *supply* side of the economy as distinguished from demand management – industrial, regional, manpower and other policies that might help to increase the growth of productive potential, i.e. the rate at which the economy could grow at a given pressure of demand. A good deal of action in these fields did in fact follow from Neddy's early discussions. It is also worth recalling that members of the Council were prepared, in the space of just over two months from late

January to early April 1963, to devote six *full* days, including two consecutive ones – a Sunday and Monday – to meetings at which they went through drafts of the 'Green Book' (*Growth of the UK Economy to 1966*, published February 1963) and the 'Orange Book' virtually paragraph by paragraph before authorising them for publication. An average of half a day a month has been the normal ration for Council meetings during most of the time since then.

What is not generally known (or remembered) is that for the following twelve months the Council went through a long process of mutual education on the subject of inflation. The preparation of the Green and Orange Books had brought about a good deal of general mutual understanding around the table between those representing government, unions and management, and in particular on the need to control inflation, and the rate of increase of money incomes, if the economy was to grow faster. The argument was essentially simple. Faster growth required a faster increase in imports of materials and other things from abroad to support it. To pay for these we must speed up the growth of our exports. This depended on price and non-price performance. But at least a necessary condition was that our costs and prices must, at worst, not go up appreciably faster than those of our competitors; and that meant, among other things, that pay increases would have to rise more slowly than in the past. (Devaluation was by mutual consent of the three main parties in the Council ruled out as an acceptable alternative.)

Once these basic propositions had been accepted, and after one meeting at which members of the Council had an opportunity to let off the necessary amount of steam, it became possible to talk about wages, prices, profits, productivity and related matters in a relatively calm, objective manner (a thing that would previously have been quite impossible); and month after month, up until the spring of 1964, the Council discussed increasingly sophisticated papers on such matters as the different nature of profits and wages, the determination of prices, possible forms of control of pay, prices, profits and what the criteria might be, even the machinery for administering prices and incomes policies. The TUC was not prepared to make a deal on these matters with the then Conservative administration, but the mutual understanding resulting from the discussions I have just described was the main reason why, on Labour's return to power in October 1964, George Brown was able to make such rapid progress in agreeing a policy on productivity, prices and incomes with the TUC and with what was soon to become the CBI.

Neddy has never recaptured the enthusiasm of its early days. The interest shown in it by its three main constituents – government, management, unions – has waxed and waned. But it has at least, at the time of writing, survived fifteen years, which is more than can be said of many bodies set up by government during this period to deal with economic and industrial matters, even though some of those that have died have been resurrected in a rather similar form under a different name.

Having been in at the birth in 1962, and having attended four-fifths or more of the Council meetings since then, in various capacities, I have perhaps a bias in favour of Neddy. I have heard a great deal of cynicism, expressions of frustration and general criticism from members. But still it goes on. The main reason is, I think, that the three main parties have recognised the value of regular, scheduled meetings of a Council which has shown that it can discuss, in a way that increases mutual understanding, short-term and long-term problems, in different political situations, and irrespective of changes in the most urgent economic problems, and in fashions about the most appropriate economic policies. It can quite often make contributions on relatively small things, and from time to time it has had, and may in future again have, a very useful role to play in big things. So why give it up? Equally important in their own way are the tripartite meetings of the Little Neddies and Sector Working Parties.

That Neddy has come to be regarded as an established feature of the landscape is, I believe, evidenced by all the current talk about it in relation to the 'Corporate State', and of its possible reform, for example so that it has relations of some kind with the Opposition, and to make it more accountable to Parliament – but I have no space to discuss these problems here.

DEA AND TREASURY

To come back to October 1964 when I joined the newly formed Department of Economic Affairs: its establishment followed on rather naturally from some of the main strands of thought in the early years of Neddy. Three main ideas behind it were (i) that it should be a sort of 'Opposition' to the Treasury, representing the interests of the longer term versus the short term, and of growth versus the balance of payments; (ii) that it should be responsible for initiating and co-ordinating policies on the 'supply' side of the economy; (iii) that it should be responsible for a prices and incomes policy.

With hindsight, the first idea did not really work. The events of July 1966 – when it is well known that George Brown fought in Cabinet (in vain) for a devaluation or depreciation of sterling in the interests of growth – provided a rather macabre justification for the idea of a centre of opposition to the Treasury to ensure that the pros and cons were thoroughly thrashed out when a major economic issue was at stake.

But, in general, 'constructive tension' was not a great success. The Treasury had the real power and I think was bound to win – and probably always would, at least so long as it had control of short-term policies and so long as there was a serious balance of payments problem. (In Germany, for example, Ministries of Finance and Economic Affairs appear to have co-existed, and this may be because of their freedom from balance of payments problems – at least if one does not count an embarrassing surplus as a problem.) In the event, rather a heavy price was paid for any advantages of an 'Opposition' Ministry, in terms of conflict and delay, and duplication of staff.

There was much more justification for a DEA to initiate and co-ordinate policies on the 'supply' side. Indeed it can reasonably be argued that in the conditions of 1964/65 there was too much for one main economic Minister to do, and that another senior co-ordinating one was necessary in addition to the Chancellor of Exchequer. One had a Government that wanted to have a more active industrial policy, a more active regional policy, to prepare within less than a year a comprehensive National Plan with a Programme of Action – and to implement a prices and incomes policy. The Chancellor could not have done all these things in addition to his traditional Treasury responsibilities, especially as there was a serious balance of payments crisis to be coped with. Therefore, one needed another initiating and co-ordinating Economic Minister.

On the other hand, it can, and has been, argued that there was no need for such a Minister and that the functions could have been as well, or better, performed by the executive departments, as was done later under the Labour Government by, for example, the Ministry of Technology, the Ministry of Housing and Local Government, the Department of Employment and Productivity. But it can be argued too that it was sensible to have a DEA in the early days while new policies were being formulated, and equally sensible later on to let the DEA die off and leave it to the executive departments to carry on.

When I moved to the Treasury at the beginning of 1969 I naturally acquired a bias in favour of the idea that the Treasury should be supreme in all economic fields. But under both Labour and Conservative Governments I did from time to time rather wish that there was a department to co-ordinate policy on the 'supply side', e.g. regional policy where the division of responsibility between departments was too diffuse.

I also had an uneasy feeling that the Treasury (with the Prime Minister) had at times too much monopoly of information and power on the major economic decisions, though this could have been remedied by more open discussion with colleagues and without the creation of a new 'DEA'.

Before leaving the Treasury I made a small start in improving its capability on industrial economics. Experience in the CBI has confirmed my view that the Treasury's assessment of the macro-economic situation and outlook, and of the effects of changes in macro-economic policies, quite apart from knowledge about individual sectors, would benefit greatly from more contact with the real world of industry. The Treasury's work on industrial economics has indeed been considerably expanded, particularly in connection with its supervisory and co-ordinating role in the 'Industrial Strategy'. Whether this role will grow to an extent that threatens to overburden the Treasury, especially given its growing burdens in the field of counter-inflation policy, remains to be seen. But what does seem clear is that, were a department similar to the DEA to be considered again at any future time, the division of responsibilities between it and the Treasury should be based not on the short-term versus the long-term (because the long run is a succession of short runs) but rather on financial policy versus policy on the 'real' side, which would include industrial policy.

Where responsibility for any prices and incomes policy should be is an open question. It is very time-consuming for the Minister concerned, and when it was DEA's responsibility it probably overburdened the Secretary of State unduly at the expense of his other functions. On the other hand its transfer to the Department of Employment and Productivity may well have been a mistake since that department and its predecessor the Ministry of Labour have traditionally been concerned with industrial peace rather than the defeat of inflation. The other solution is, as at present, to give the main responsibility to the Chancellor, supported by the other Ministers directly concerned with pay and prices. He too is an extremely busy Minister, but it may well be that future policies on pay and prices will be so related to fiscal, monetary and other economic policies for which he is responsible that he cannot opt out.

The Treasury's growing responsibilities in the fields of prices and incomes and industrial policy, and the need to keep it small – which I regard as most important if it is to function effectively – might be argued in support of those who would separate the taxation and public expenditure functions and take the latter away from the Treasury, possibly combining it with those of the Civil Service Department. This I would not advocate. I believe the argument for restraint in public expenditure most appealing to politicians is that otherwise taxation will have to be increased. There is, therefore, a strong case for arranging ministerial incentives in such a way that the person whose job it is to control his colleagues' expenditure gets political credit for success through his consequent ability to reduce taxes, or avoid raising them, and the corresponding discredit for failure.

SOME GENERAL CONSIDERATIONS

I have mentioned the smallness of the Treasury as a virtue. Its strength, all told, when I was there was about 1000. It covered vast areas, but they were sufficiently related to be brought together in a consistent policy and the professional staff was small enough to permit the personal communication necessary to avoid too many inconsistencies.

There are morals here for other areas of government. When departments and agencies deal directly with large numbers of the general public, scores of thousands of civil servants naturally become necessary. But I am thinking rather of the formulation of policy. Here there is the well-known dilemma of whether it is better to resolve clashes of interest and opinion within departments or between departments. There have been times when there was a craze for the former on the ground that it was more efficient, and super-ministries were created covering huge areas that were to a considerable extent unrelated, and requiring far more civil servants than the Treasury. This, I am sure, was a mistake and involved diseconomies of scale.

But, apart from remembering the merits of smallness, there are no clear rules for the grouping of departmental responsibilities in the economic field (other than those traditionally exercised by the Treasury) such as: sponsoring of manufacturing, distribution and service industries; fuel and power; transport; overseas trade; housing; employment policies; industrial relations; competition policy; regional policy. However these are combined, there will be unsatisfactory features and ragged edges.

Nor are there any absolute rules about how central policy formation should be organised. The best organisation will depend on the situation and will change from time to time; on whether, looking to the past, we were at war or at peace; on what, in peacetime, are the main priorities; and on the type of instruments of policy preferred by the Government of the day or forced on them by circumstances, particularly how far they are financial and non-discriminatory and how far direct and discriminatory.

Finally, since no ideal organisation is obvious, for reasons I have given, it may sometimes not be wholly irrational to allow it to depend, to some extent at least, on the personalities available in the ministerial field.

13 The Politics of Incomes Policy

WILLIAM McCARTHY

By incomes policy I mean the attempt of government to modify the size and pace of pay settlements by seeking to gain acceptance for specified earnings targets or criteria. In this sense no British Government since the war has felt able to do without incomes policy for long. What has varied has been the means used, the degree of success and the extent to which governments have been prepared to own up to their intentions. Since the early fifties policies have become increasingly overt and formal, involving various legal sanctions. From time to time efforts have been made to create a more receptive climate for pay restraint by measures designed to undermine union bargaining power – e.g. allowing the level of unemployment to rise. Yet the relationship between the 'direct' methods of incomes policy and other more 'indirect' techniques have usually remained confused and contradictory. By and large Ministers have been attracted to incomes policy as a way of avoiding the social and electoral consequences of too great a reliance on measures such as unemployment. Conversely, the attractions of demand management have tended to loom largest whenever the problems of applying a given incomes policy appeared to be particularly difficult.

This chapter does not attempt to deal with all aspects of incomes policy. It focuses on the major options available to successive governments in terms of alternative targets and criteria – i.e. 'norms', 'guidelines', and the rules governing 'exceptions' and 'special cases'. There is no consideration of the relationship between incomes policy and price control. Nothing is said about the link between pay policies and policies designed to influence the rate of growth of other types of income. The relationship between 'voluntary' and 'statutory' policy is not considered in any detail. The main reasons for these and other omissions is shortage of space – encouraged by lack of expertise. It is not because I wish to suggest that any of these matters are unimportant.

On the other hand, I do believe that the key to a serious and lasting incomes policy lies in the formulation and application of appropriate targets and criteria. These aspects of policy embody a government's fundamental objectives and they are the iron test of its courage, consistency and political flair. I also feel that there are many obvious lessons to be drawn from the failures of government in the past in this field, once their record is examined and understood.

Therefore the bulk of this paper consists of an analysis of the record of two Labour and one Conservative administrations. These sections are followed by a final one which seeks to draw some lessons from the past. For the purpose of analysis and comparison it is necessary to give successive stages of policy names, letters and numbers. The fourteen phases to be considered in this chapter are set out below:

INCOMES POLICIES SINCE 1965

A   The first Wilson Government (1964–70):
1. 'The Planned Growth of Incomes' – May 1965 to June 1966
2. 'Twelve Month Freeze and Severe Restraint' – July 1966 to June 1967
3. 'Informal Relaxation' (Mark One) – July 1967 to March 1968
4. 'Devaluation and the Hard Slog' – April 1968 to December 1969
5. 'Informal Relaxation' (Mark Two) – January 1970 to June 1970

B   The Heath Government (1970–4):
1. 'Leave it to the parties' – July 1970 to September 1970
2. 'N minus One' – October 1970 to October 1972 (Parts 1 and 2)
3. 'Controlling Inflation: the First Stage' – November 1972 to December 1972
4. 'Controlling Inflation: the Second Stage' – January 1973 to October 1973
5. 'Controlling Inflation: the Third Stage' – November 1973 to February 1974

C   The Wilson–Callaghan Government (1974–):
1. 'Phasing out Stage Three' – February 1974 to September 1974
2. 'Social Contract Mark One' – September 1974 to June 1975
3. 'Social Contract Mark Two' (the £6 Limit) – July 1975 to July 1976
4. 'Social Contract Mark Three' (the 5 per cent Limit) – August 1976 to July 1977

Each phase is named after an appropriate White Paper or Government slogan current at the time. Each administration is given an initial letter, so that successive phases of policy can be linked back to their common political authors.

A   THE FIRST WILSON GOVERNMENT (1964–70)

It is arguable that the Labour Government of 1964–70 developed the most sophisticated and comprehensive policy which has been formulated so far. Yet the general verdict, in 1970, was that it had not been a success. There can be little doubt that its major defect was systematic hypocrisy. Almost nobody expected pretensions to be matched by performance after the first two years. Most of the time there was supposed to be an overall pay movement of about 3 per cent per year, and yet actual movements were usually well above 7 per cent. In June 1970 the policy expired amidst an earnings explosion of more than 12 per cent.

Yet policy in period A was not without a significant impact on inflation. Indeed it has been calculated that in overall terms it was responsible for a degree of pay 'restraint' that was worth between 1 and 2 per cent a year. Unfortunately, this overall impact was very largely the result of the relative success of phases A2 and A4. In A2, the combined effect of a six-month freeze and a modest degree of demand management produced a halving of the inflation rate and a 75 per cent reduction in the rate of increase in average earnings. In A4, similar demand conditions, plus a return to a tougher incomes policy, helped to effect a cut of about 45 per cent in the annual rate of pay increases, despite sharply rising prices. Unfortunately each of these phases was preceded and followed by another – i.e. A1, A3, and A5. In each of these periods the formal targets were largely abandoned by government, unions, and employers. Hypocrisy was the order of the day.

Of course, during A1, it can be argued that the policy was further undermined by the relatively high level of demand in the labour market, but this was much less obviously the case in periods A3 and A5. In these phases the critical factor was undoubtedly a loss of political will. Thus it is fair to term A3, 'Informal Relaxation: Mark One', because, from the beginning, the Minister in charge accepted the inevitability of a 6 per cent pay round, while continuing to pretend that the Government was committed to a target about half that size. A similar combination of factors, plus the desire to engineer a pre-election consumption boom, helped to produce A5, the second period of 'Informal Relaxation', although at this time the Minister in charge was fighting almost alone to save the credibility of her policy.

In retrospect it is easy to see why the Government stumbled into hypocrisy. They had derived their original pay norm from their ill-fated and over-optimistic National Plan. This 'assumed' a link between a 4 per cent growth rate and a $3\frac{1}{2}$ per cent movement in pay. The trouble was that everybody who knew anything about collective bargaining found it impossible to take this target seriously. (Indeed, the General Secretary of the TUC appeared to take a dour delight in pointing out that he had always said it was 'daft'.) Unfortunately, when the National Plan was finally abandoned, it seemed logical to continue to insist on the underlying relationship between the growth rate and pay. Consequently as the wage round rose in size, pay norms were actually revised downwards in periods A3 and A4. Even the A5 target never came to terms with the realities of collective bargaining.

Fortunately for the Government there was a way out. The overall norm had been designed to operate alongside a number of 'exceptions' clauses. These provided for above average increases on four grounds:

1. Where they assisted essential changes in manpower distribution.
2. Where there was widespread recognition that pay was seriously out of line with that paid for similar work, and needed to be improved in the national interest.
3. Where it was generally recognised that pay was too low to maintain reasonable living standards.
4. Where the acceptance of more exacting work or a major change in working practice could be shown to make a direct contribution to increased productivity.

In the light of the subsequent criticism of these criteria it is necessary to stress that they are all inherently reasonable. If incomes policy is to be compatible with the use of the pay structure to induce labour mobility something like criterion 1 is required. If managers are to be allowed to modify the payment system to encourage improvements in performance and consent for change something similar to criterion 4 is essential. Both these criteria can be said to represent an attempt to preserve the essential economic functions of the labour market within the context of a policy for pay restraint.

But it is just as easy to make out a case for criteria 2 and 3. If disturbances in established differentials are to be dealt with within the context of incomes policy there is need for a 'special case' clause which resembles criterion 2. If the claim that incomes policy safeguards a minimum level of real income is to remain credible it can be argued that special provision must be made for the very low-paid. Thus criteria 2 and 3 may be said to represent attempts to leave room for an essential element of flexibility on both political and social grounds.

The problem with such exceptions in period A was they were expected to operate within the context of an unreal overall target, which was also supposed to provide the 'norm' for *non-exceptional* settlements. This meant that the only way that the policy could be made conformable to the realities of collective bargaining was by accepting the legitimacy of an increasing number of nominally 'exceptional cases'.

Now of course officials charged with implementing the policy knew this only too well. They had far fewer illusions than their masters. Their problem was that at the beginning they tended to over-react to the danger of allowing for 'special cases' – especially on the basis of criteria 1 to 3. In effect they were terrified of what might be termed the 'colander syndrome'. They feared that any open acceptance of a special case on these grounds would lead to a situation in which the policy would develop as many exceptions as a colander has holes, and be just about as likely to hold water. Because of this they consistently refused to define what was to count as a labour shortage, or proof of 'similar work' in criterion 2. Nobody was even asked to provide a rough measure of low pay.

Fortunately a rather more relaxed attitude came to be taken towards criterion 4. Largely because the chairman of the Prices and Incomes Board and his chief adviser, Allen Flanders, were enthusiastic advocates of productivity bargaining the board went out of its way to show reluctant employers and unions how to qualify for exceptional treatment on these grounds. It soon became known that a reference to the PIB could provide you with the basis for an above-the-norm settlement. As a result many industries and services, in both the private and public sector, made their first halting steps towards the effective utilisation of labour at this time.

Unfortunately another consequence was that the board soon became overwhelmed with work and its standards began to slip. It was necessary to rename the Ministry of Labour the Department of Employment and Productivity, and establish a special division to provide appropriate clearance. By 1970 these developments had led to a rash of 'phoney claims' and a reaction against the whole idea of productivity bargaining. It became fashionable to imply that nothing had been gained. Yet the facts are that all subsequent studies indicate that most deals helped to raise productivity and efficiency without undue cost. It is even arguable that the general improvement in productivity which was evident at this time owed a great deal to the ideas generated by the PIB under cover of criterion 4.

In any case, Labour's policy suffered from a third major defect which was just as serious as its unrealistic norm and over-concentration on criterion 4. Despite protestations to the contrary the 1964–70 policy exercised a disproportionate degree of influence over the public sector. This over-concentration was reflected in the balance of PIB references. The board spent over half its time on the public sector and virtually every important group was investigated at least once. By contrast many groups in the private sector were never studied by the PIB at all – e.g.

those in port transport and shipbuilding. Nothing was done about the car industry and even Fleet Street was ignored after the first phase of the policy. There were very few company-wide references, even where it was known that certain large companies were the source of much of the wage drift in areas like the Midlands. The obsession with the public sector was also reflected in the use made of the Government's statutory powers. Despite the fact that the public sector employs about a fifth of all workers it attracted about half the standstill orders. (Over three-quarters of all workers affected by standstill orders were municipal busmen.)

I have never heard anybody try to justify this pursuit of public sector workers on grounds of settlement levels. What evidence we have indicates that pay movements were generally substantially higher in the private sector.

By 1968 these three defects had undermined trade union belief in the general credibility and 'fairness' of the Wilson Government's policy. At the same time parliamentary pressure had ensured the 'phasing out' of all forms of statutory support. In these circumstances the Government was forced to turn to its only remaining weapon – half-hearted pressure on management in the public sector. By the time it left office, Labour's incomes policy was intellectually bankrupt and largely cosmetic.

B   THE HEATH GOVERNMENT (1970–4)

Meanwhile, in opposition, the Conservatives had directed growing criticism at all forms of incomes policy. Thus while they began by supporting the notion of productivity bargaining, they were soon suggesting that the reports of the PIB represented an 'unnecessary interference' with the working of a free labour market. When the statutory freeze was introduced in 1966 Edward Heath denounced all forms of legally regulated wage containment.

Increasingly, in the late sixties, the Conservatives came to convince themselves that the problem of wage-induced inflation was inextricably bound up with what they took to be the defective legal basis of industrial relations. The real need, as they saw it, was to make unions 'responsible' for the acts of their members at law. If this could be done, and if collective agreements could be made legal contracts, the problem of wage-induced inflation would recede.

By 1970 the Conservatives were committed to the measures that formed the basis of the 1971 Industrial Relations Act. These entailed an all-out conflict with the TUC and no hope of formal co-operation in the field of incomes policy. Partly for reasons of this kind the Heath

Government decided to make a virtue of necessity. They emphasised how far they had moved away from any desire to regulate wages by the formulation of targets and criteria. This is why it is fair to term period B1 'Leave it to the parties'. This was the declared policy at the Department of Employment during the short, hot summer of 1970. During this period the Government actually restored the balance of a 30 per cent increase awarded to doctors by their independent review body. (Labour had frozen about half of this in the interests of their norm of 4 per cent.)

However, by September the Conservatives were worried about the effect of leaving it entirely to the parties – most immediately in local government. Here a 15 per cent claim by manual workers led to the adoption of a new and novel form of policy, which was soon christened 'N minus One'. This entailed an attempt to lower the 'going rate' of settlements by progressive amounts – e.g. from 15 per cent to 14 per cent, from 14 per cent to 13 per cent and so on. The process was supposed to continue throughout a given wage round until the level of wage inflation was reduced to an acceptable level. (No precise figure was ever published concerning the level that would be needed.) The nearest the Government came to defining targets and criteria was when they gave evidence to the Wilberforce Committee during the electricity pay dispute in early 1971. At that inquiry a representative of the Treasury said that the policy was based on the assumption that:

> the process of wage negotiation goes on more or less continuously with no clearly defined 'rounds'. What is deemed equitable as between one settlement and another often plays an important part. The size of one settlement influences the next: only too frequently the special arguments used in the attempt to justify a large settlement for one group are discounted and dismissed as irrelevant when other groups claim the same amount or more. This is a process which generates its own acceleration and to stop it, it is necessary to break into the circle somewhere. To accept the argument that each group must have as large an increase as the last one or that one group cannot accept a smaller increase until someone else has done so would mean that the slowing down of inflation could never start.

It should be clear that this type of incomes policy is based on a sort of 'domino theory' of the bargaining process. Just as Labour had been terrified of the colander syndrome, so the Conservatives were afraid of a similarly catastrophic 'domino effect'. Once a settlement was made that was higher than previous settlements a process of escalation would inevitably take place – irrespective of the merit or relative significance of the settlement in question. Contrariwise, if only a settlement could be negotiated that was lower than the rest, de-escalation should set in. All that mattered was the trend. It followed that there was no case for trying to estimate and publicise a target for settlements in general. Above all, perhaps, one could not afford to admit the possibility of exceptions.

Of course, as a theory of the actual bargaining process the assumptions of 'N minus One' are at best crude and at worst illiterate. More importantly perhaps, they fly in the face of deeply-held trade union notions of 'equity' and 'fair play'. Nevertheless, it is necessary to stress that during the two years in which it operated even this policy had some impact – especially in the public sector. After a record number of large strikes, for the most part in the public sector, de-escalation began. Thus during a period when the terms of trade were deteriorating, but against a background of rising unemployment and a tighter money policy, the annual rate of increase in earnings fell from the high point of 14 per cent in November 1970 to just under 9 per cent in January 1972. Indeed, by February it was widely said that you could negotiate a settlement with most outstanding groups by offering about 8 per cent. The settlement level had been almost halved in under two years.

Then came the miners' claim. Their relative wage level had been declining for more than ten years, and with a rise in the demand for coal they sought to re-establish their position at the head of the manual workers' earnings league. This involved a claim for more than double the 'going rate'. In the name of 'N minus One' the Government had to refuse to allow the NCB to advance beyond 9 per cent. The inevitable result was one of the most effective and bitter strikes of modern times, which the miners won after new forms of militant picketing had threatened to cut off the nation's fuel supply. Another Wilberforce Committee was established to provide the basis for a settlement. They accepted that the miners were a 'special case' – on grounds that were virtually identical to those set out in period A's criterion 3.

The granting of the miners' claim, and a settlement of similar size in the construction industry later that year, are generally said to have produced the much feared domino effect – although disciples of 'indirect' ways of tackling cost-inflation point to concomitant increases in the money supply and a slight rise in the level of employment. By the spring of 1972 the annual earnings movement was back to 12 per cent. By the autumn it had climbed to around 16 per cent. The Government decided it needed a new incomes policy.

This time Mr Heath thought he would try co-operation with the TUC. He offered an 'index-linked' norm and protection for the lower paid. The TUC liked the formula and did not oppose the idea of an agreement. They demanded higher increases, statutory control of prices and the 'non-operation' of the Industrial Relations Act. By November there was deadlock and the Government had no alternative but to complete its 'U-turn'. It announced a temporary freeze on prices and wages and took time off to think. Conservative policy entered period B3, which lasted till January 1973.

There followed two closely-related and remarkably successful periods of statutorily enforced incomes policy. B4 lasted nine months and was not unlike Heath's offer to the TUC – i.e. a flat-rate increase of £1 plus 4 per cent of the paybill with a personal limit of £250 a year. B5 began in November 1973 and was due to last another twelve months. It provided a basic increase of £2.25 a week or 7 per cent of the paybill. This time the personal limit was £350. The main difference between B4 and B5 was that the latter was supposed to be more 'flexible'. Flexibility took two main forms: first, a '1 per cent flexibility margin', which could be used to improve pay structures or labour utilisation; second, an extra payment for working 'unsocial hours'. Provision was also made for 'flat-rate' threshold payments if the cost of living rose by more than 7 per cent over the year.

The most notable feature of B4 and B5 was the extent to which they were accepted by a trade union movement which never stopped denouncing them. B4 settlements were virtually all within guidelines set out in the new Pay Code. By February virtually all important unions had signed agreements which were within the targets and criteria of B5 and the wage round was almost completed. Of course, one reason for compliance was that, in comparison to targets set in period A, the aims of period B were modest and realistic. There was no attempt to halve the size of the wage round and earnings were still rising by just under 14 per cent when the Government lost office. Nevertheless, it is impossible to deny the impact of all three stages of statutory policy. They played an essential part in averting a major pay explosion at a very difficult time. They might well have been followed by an equally effective B6 and B7, if only B5 had provided for a bit more flexibility in dealing with the miners' claim.

Yet the Government had accepted well in advance that the miners had to be given 'a little more than the rest'. The small flexibilities of the B5 Pay Code – most notably the unsocial hours payments – were specifically designed to provide this and the Government had reason to believe that they would satisfy the NUM. Moreover, the miners were also to be offered the prospect of a 'Relativities Board' in time for B6. The NCB negotiators told the NUM that this should result in the full restoration of the value of the Wilberforce award, within the context of incomes policy.

Unfortunately, the NUM, spurred on by the militants on its executive, refused to wait for B6. They demanded the full value of

Wilberforce as a B5 settlement. In the event, and after prolonged deliberation, the Government were still too afraid of the domino effect to 'bend' their Pay Code to provide for this – even after the TUC offered not to quote the results in what was left of the B5 wage round. In the circumstances there was nothing left but a trial of strength. Partly to strengthen their hand the Conservatives called an election, which they lost. Another Wilson Government conceded the miners' claim in full in March 1974.

C   THE WILSON-CALLAGHAN GOVERNMENT (1974–)

Labour began with few options. While in opposition they had told the TUC that they also would never impose a statutory policy. They were also pledged to abolish the Pay Board. If it had not been for the balance of payments they might well have decided to begin with another period of 'informal relaxation'. As it was they announced a temporary policy (C1) designed to last until the September Congress of the TUC. This was said to involve 'phasing out' the remainder of the B5 wage round. In practice it meant that the Government would not use the Pay Board's statutory powers, but would expect the norms of B5 to be observed on a 'voluntary' basis. Once this was known a rash of 'supplementary' settlements were rushed through in the public and the private sector. Nurses, civil servants, railwaymen and private managers all sought to restore differentials eroded by the low pay targets during B4 and B5. At the same time the continued rise in retail prices activated the B5 threshold clauses and by September most workers received another £4.40 a week. The result was an annual earnings movement of 21 per cent by the end of C1.

C2, or 'Social Contract Mark One', was based on Government acceptance of a General Council resolution moved at the 1974 TUC. This stated that during the next twelve months 'the scope for real increases in consumption is limited'. It suggested that during the next round settlements should be based on 'past *or* prospective movements in prices over a twelve-month period'. The implication was that this would lead to a gradually de-escalating norm, as the retail price index came down during late 1974 and 1975.

It is worth stressing that a policy of this kind, if it could have been made to work, would have made a significant contribution to the problem of inflation. The trouble was that its price assumptions were overoptimistic. More important still, from the viewpoint of criteria, the TUC's resolution was qualified by two fatal 'priority' clauses. The first committed the TUC to aim at a 'low-pay target' of £30 a week. The second said that 'priority' must be given to any agreement that had 'beneficial effects' on 'unit costs and efficiency' or 'reforming pay structures and improving job security'.

It is easy to see why so many commentators have denounced C2 as a cynical exercise in cosmetics. The trouble with this verdict is that it suggests that those who agreed to it actually expected the pay explosion that followed and only pretended not to notice it. I do not think that this is a fair judgement. I believe that those in charge failed to appreciate the damage that would be done by the £30 target. They did not realise that it would spark off compensatory demands further up the pay structure. I also believe that the cost of consolidating the B5 thresholds, and their effect on pay structures, was little understood. On the other hand, I cannot deny that there was a wilful refusal to face facts as the round proceeded.

By May it was calculated that in the private sector settlements were running at about 13 per cent above the relevant price movement. In the public sector the figure was 11 per cent. By this time the annual movement in earnings was up to 28·4 per cent and the movement in basic rates even higher – i.e. 33·5 per cent. In other words, there had been an escalation in the pace of wage inflation of just under 40 per cent in eight months. And all the signs were that the level of settlements was still rising.

The Government decided that it could not ignore what was happening any longer. A new initiative was launched against the background of another sterling crisis in June and July. Once they were convinced of the results of the crisis the TUC responded with an unprecedented offer designed to cut the inflation rate in half during the next twelve months. This involved a 'flat rate' increase of £6 per week. Those earning more than £8500 a year were to receive no increase at all. No exceptions or special cases were to be allowed.

C3 represented a 10 per cent movement in the national paybill. As such it contained one of the toughest overall targets of the post-war period. This involved a two-thirds reduction in the current settlement rate and a significant cut in real incomes. Moreover, since the policy was once again designed to protect the position of the lower-paid, the impact on the higher reaches of the pay structure was especially severe. The nearest equivalent, in terms of overall severity, was also Labour's second phase of policy in period A. But it must be remembered that this was reinforced by a statutory freeze of six months and enforced by an active PIB.

Nevertheless, C3 must count as our most effective period of incomes policy since the war. Virtually all settlements were for £6 or less. As a result, by July 1976, when it was replaced by C4, the annual earnings movement had been cut to 13·8 per cent. Over the same period the annual increase in prices had also been cut more or less in half. Most unusual of all, in comparison to previous periods of 'tough policy', such as A2 and A4, C3 was not followed by a period of relaxation – either formal or informal. On the contrary, C4 was designed to produce a further reduction in the level of prices by a lowering of the rate of pay settlements by about 50 per cent. The aim was a pay movement of about 5 per cent to be secured by a mixture of flat rate and percentage payments with an upper limit of £4 a week.

And at the moment of writing (May 1977), C4 is virtually completed. Once again, almost all groups have settled within its limits. However, for reasons that are not yet clear, its impact on total earnings growth has been less than it should have been – although there has been some de-escalation over the wage round as a whole. More seriously, in relation to the prospects for C5, the declining value of the pound during C4 has meant that retail prices have not fallen as they were expected to do. Thus most observers consider that there will be price increases of at least 15 per cent during the course of 1977/78.

LESSONS FROM THE PAST

What lessons can we learn from this brief résumé of the aims and achievements of fourteen different policies over more than twelve years? Here I only have room for some of the more obvious and I must present them in a dogmatic and summary way.

The first two concern the interrelationship between incomes policy and other aspects of economic management. In the first place the record suggests that commitment to published norms and criteria in the field of pay does not allow politicians to avoid the need for realistic action in other fields – e.g. in respect of fiscal, monetary and exchange-rate policies, or control over the rate of growth of public expenditure. On the contrary, the effectiveness and acceptability of incomes policies in periods A1, B3, B4, C1 and C2 were all blunted and occasionally ruined by overoptimism and inaction in one or another of these areas. One way of putting this point is to admit that the strongest card in the hand of opponents of incomes policy is the fact that over and over again it has been seen by government as a way of avoiding the need to take necessary action in relation to other aspects of economic management.

On the other hand, and this would be my second lesson, the record also indicates that whatever politicians may say when they are out of office, they tend to find they cannot avoid trying to do something positive to reduce the size of particular wage rounds whenever they are actually responsible for running the country. And there are many good reasons for this. It is not merely that once governments appear to countenance a 'free-for-all', or lose faith in incomes policies, or turn their back on events, they help to precipitate a wage explosion – e.g. in periods A3, A5, B1, C1 and C2. It is also that the only periods in which a sharp and significant impact has been made on the forces of wage-induced inflation have been those when appropriate supplementary policies have been reinforced by serious incomes policies – i.e. in periods A2, A4, B4, C3 and C4. It is surely self-evident to anybody but the most perverse of monetarists that the reversals of A2, or B1, or C3 could not have been achieved in any other way. It should also be clear that if the draconian targets of C3 had not been followed by an equally effective C4 there would have been no chance whatever of achieving a further reduction of 50 per cent in the level of pay settlements. The fact is that the case for doing without serious attempts at incomes policy is at its most persuasive when stated in abstract and general terms; it tends not to survive the problems inherent in dealing with an actual wage round. No doubt the difficulties of gaining consent for further restraint, in the absence of an explosion, sometimes induce politicians to believe, for a while at least, that they can afford almost total 'relaxation' – but the evidence of the past seems to suggest that this mood does not last for long. Soon there is talk of a new initiative – albeit in a different form, perhaps by another government. In this sense it is now very difficult to believe in a sustainable 'free-for-all'.

The third lesson I would draw relates to what is meant by 'serious' incomes policy and the role of the Government itself in setting an example. To my mind the first Wilson Government only took incomes policy seriously in periods A2 and A4. The rest of the time their targets and criteria were something of a joke, even in the public sector. Then again the Conservatives only gave incomes policy real priority towards the latter end of B2 and in periods B3, B4, and B5. Throughout B1 they tried to look unconcerned, and throughout the whole of the first part of B2 they expected conventional techniques of demand management to produce the decisive impact, especially in the private sector. In C1 it was known from the start that the Government would do nothing to prevent any settlement, however high it was. It was not until C3 that the stated norms came to be regarded as a crucial element in the Government's economic strategy.

Taking incomes policy seriously is partly a matter of how far senior members of the Government involve themselves in the task of gaining and sustaining support for stated targets and criteria. It is also partly a matter of being willing to create and staff the institutions needed to apply and monitor a given policy. It is very closely connected with the responses permitted by the Government in the public sector – both directly and indirectly. One way of putting this point is to say that once government lets it be known that they cannot countenance the risk of a strike in any important part of the public sector, they have, in effect, decided not to operate a serious incomes policy. And if the record shows nothing else it indicates that unless governments are prepared to take their own incomes policy seriously they have no chance of influencing the behaviour of anybody else.

But it may be said that it is no use taking an unrealistic policy seriously, which brings me to the fourth lesson. It is easy to state in general terms but difficult to apply to particular cases. The record suggests that overall targets must be realistic in terms of trade union expectations and aspirations for the coming wage round – i.e. in the twelve months or so following the annual settlement for manual workers in local government which begins a new round. The difficulty lies in deciding what is 'realistic' in given circumstances. Until C3 it looked as if period A indicated that it was fatal to try to reduce the 'going rate' or settlements by 50 per cent or more in any one round. This seemed to involve too sharp a reduction in expectations and aspirations, which was likely to generate a subsequent pay explosion. In contrast to this the more modest aims of periods B4 and B5 appeared to be more sustainable, despite the final defection of the miners.

I confess to arguing at this time that the long-run limits of incomes policy appeared to be set by three main variables – the level of the previous round and past and future price trends. A policy was 'realistic' if its authors were content with a modest and gradual reduction in the level of the previous round (say no more than 25 per cent) and then only if this did not involve too sharp a reduction in the level of real income. It may appear as if the double success of C3 and C4 indicates that this figure was far too modest, given sufficient commitment and support from the trade unions. But it is possible to take a different view. All the signs are that C4 will need to be followed by a much more 'relaxed' policy, and there are strong demands on the union side for something like a 'free-for-all'. It is difficult not to conclude that the decision to cut pay targets by a further 50 per cent helped to create many of these pressures. In retrospect, it might appear to have been wiser to aim for a more modest reduction during C4 – e.g. around 25 per cent.

The problem is that in practice what is found to be 'realistic' depends as much on the selection of appropriate criteria as it does on the size of the overall target. But this brings me to my fifth lesson, which lies at the heart of a successful long-run policy. I think the record also indicates that in incomes policy it is essential to try to navigate the narrow channel that lies between the colander and the domino. In other words we must try to provide for an element of flexibility and the odd 'special case'. I believe the record shows that this is difficult, but not impossible. The problem with all A periods was that the general settlement level was too low to give the exceptions criteria a chance.

If it had been high enough to protect living standards I doubt if there would have been nearly as many 'phoney' productivity deals.

The problem with all B periods was that the Government never really accepted that there were legitimate special cases. Even in B5 the so-called 'flexibilities' were mechanistic and predetermined. There was no room for real negotiation and the men in the Pay Board could not afford to respond to a justifiable case. Of course it may be said that on this argument it is difficult to see why C2 was such a disaster. It had a realistic settlement level plus a number of exceptions criteria. My answer is that exceptions criteria are only operable if they are clearly defined and backed by an adequate institutional framework to apply them to special cases. It also helps if the Government is taking the policy seriously itself and is interested in whether or not it is working. I accept that the contrast between C2 and C3 and C4 appears to strengthen the case for a policy without exceptions. But I think these policies worked because there was the will to work them – rather than because their criteria were simple and easy to apply.

In any case I remain unconvinced that we can develop and operate a policy for more than a year or so that makes no allowance for three of the exceptions specified in period A. I do not see how you can expect employers to observe a policy indefinitely that does not allow them to use their pay structure to deal with severe labour shortages or improve performance. I am convinced that future policies will be blown off course unless they provide for cases like the miners in 1972. There must be a way for some groups to justify a lasting change in their relative position. Both miners' strikes had this simple and essentially reasonable objective at their centre. It was the fault of the incomes policy at the time that it failed to provide for a peaceful solution in either case.

In other words, the trick, as I see it, is to combine exceptions criteria on these grounds with a realistic settlement level and adequate institutions; and to specify the upper limit allowed under each one of the criteria in any given year. I appreciate that sceptics will reply that this kind of policy has never been tried: I can only say that on the record of the past I think we shall come to it in the end.

This brings me to my sixth and penultimate lesson. I am increasingly sceptical of the long-run viability of policies that contain special provisions in favour of the lower-paid. The low-pay priorities of B4 and B5 contributed to the revolt of the miners in 1974 because they eroded the value of the Wilberforce award. Almost all supplementary settlements, which helped to produce the high rate of increase in earnings at the end of C1, were justified by reference to the effect of the low-pay targets on established differentials during the same two periods. It is also clear that the £30 low-pay limit in period C3 contributed very significantly to its breakdown. From the very start of the round it produced settlement rates of 30 per cent or more and these were widely quoted. It is equally obvious that the flat-rate threshold payments of periods B5 and C1 helped to fire the inflation process during C2.

In other words, it seems to me, since 1973 a long succession of different devices were used to give priority to low-paid workers in five successive phases of incomes policy, and they all had inflationary consequences. Taken together they contributed to the collapse of every incomes policy we have experienced in that time.

Of course, it may be said that since 1975 we have experienced two periods of unprecedentedly effective and severe policies which gave even greater priority to low pay – i.e. C3 and C4. My answer is that I do not see how we can expect to avoid the long-run consequences of either of them. Somehow the pay structures they squeezed and distorted will have to be dealt with. One only hopes that this can be done in a way that is not completely self-defeating.

I also think it is time we paid some heed to the mounting evidence that low-pay priorities are an extremely inefficient way of dealing with the problem of low incomes, not to mention the related problem of family poverty. I mention this because I would not want to be thought to be arguing from the standpoint of one who is content with the present distribution of income.

My seventh lesson is in some ways the most obvious. The best guarantee of any policy's success is that trade union leaders are prepared to 'go along with it'. This is not the same thing as campaigning enthusiastically to make it work. At its lowest it means no more than reluctant acquiescence: a refusal to commit themselves or their organisation to a determined attempt to 'break the policy'. It is tempting to conclude that the existence of legal sanctions is an important contributory factor in producing this frame of mind. This seems to have been the case during the whole of A2, B3, and B4. The continued existence of sanctions also affected the great bulk of the trade union movement during B5 until the miners' dispute was settled in defiance of the Pay Code.

But it is important not to overstress the role of sanctions. During A2 there was general acceptance of the need for a six-month freeze. Most observers thought it would have been observed without legal sanctions. B3 lasted less than two months and the increases allowable under B4 and B5 were accepted relatively easily. Then there is the riddle of C3 and C4. If legal sanctions are important to secure general acceptance how have they been made to work so well?

The short answer is that union attitudes towards incomes policy are much more complex. In my opinion when sanctions assist it is because they appear to guarantee an element of equity: they make it credible to believe that a given policy stands a chance of being observed by all groups. The moment this is not thought to be the case, as in periods A3, B5 or C1, legal sanctions become counter-productive. It follows from this that non-legally-based policies *can* result in a much higher level of commitment and observance if they are genuinely regarded as equitable in themselves. This is part of the answer to the riddle of C3 and C4. The problem is that just because a policy is thought to be equitable at the time it does not follow that it will not create major difficulties in the future. This is part of the riddle posed by C5.

In any case notions of equity and fairness are almost certainly mixed up with related ideas about what is reasonable and possible in particular circumstances. I doubt if we can appreciate why both C3 and C4 worked unless we are prepared to accept that they were accompanied by a general reduction in expectations, touched off by a genuine fear of the consequences of runaway inflation. It may well be that in the future the chances for viable and effective incomes policies will be influenced more than anything else by government's ability to mobilise and channel feelings of this kind amongst rank-and-file trade unionists.

Looking back at the period since 1964 the overwhelming impression one has is of lost opportunities – if only the overall targets of the first Wilson Government had been more modest; if only the PIB had been allowed to define and apply the other exceptions criteria as well as productivity; if only they had been given half-a-dozen strategic references from the private sector; if only the Government had not abandoned serious incomes policy in periods A3 and A5. And how much better it would have been if the Heath Government had not felt that it had to begin by pretending to abandon all forms of incomes policy; what a pity they felt they must abolish the PIB; how stupid to allow the irrelevance of the 1971 Act to push them into a position where they had to try to cobble together the targets and criteria of 'N minus One'. And even if this was bound to happen, what a tragedy it was that they failed to act after the first miners' strike until its effects had been felt in the private sector. Why could not they escape their terror of the domino effect during the more realistic policies of B3, B4 and B5? Why was the offer of the TUC so summarily rejected?

But the record of 1974–7 bristles with similar queries. Why did the second Wilson Government do nothing about formulating the outlines of a new policy until the autumn of 1974? Why was the drift from the norm during period C2 denied for so long? Is it really the case that there was nothing to do but wait for the crisis that produced the deceptive simplicities of the £6 limit? And would it not have been more sensible to seek to move away from the constrictions and compressions of C3 during C4, under cover of a somewhat higher norm? And why was it not appreciated that the double rigidities of C3 and C4 were bound to generate demands for a much more relaxed C5, if not a 'free-for-all'? Most important of all, when are politicians going to understand that low-pay targets are time-bombs, ticking away at the centre of any incomes policy?

On reflection there would seem to be an eighth lesson to be learnt. The most important long-run limiting factor of the survival of any incomes policy appears to be the extent to which those in charge understand what they are trying to do and have the courage to see it through. For although incomes policy, in one form or another, has become an important and permanent aspect of economic management, the formulation and application of its norms and criteria are essentially a matter of political judgement. It requires nerve, sensitivity, and a detailed knowledge of the day-to-day pressures on unions and management. One can only hope that in the future those who undertake initiatives in the vital area will learn something from the mistakes of their predecessors. One can only hope.

Interim Bibliography: the Writings of Norman Chester

Compiled by CHRISTINE KENNEDY

1932
'Local rates and industry', in *An industrial survey of the Lancashire area (excluding Merseyside)*, made for the Board of Trade by the University of Manchester (HMSO, 1932) ch. 14, pp. 278–92.

1933
Contributor, *An industrial survey of Cumberland and Furness: a study of the social implications of economic dislocation*, by J. Jewkes and A. Winterbottom (Manchester University Press, 1933) xii, 175 pages.

1935
'The optimum size of a local authority', *Manchester Statistical Society Group Meetings* 1934–35, pp. 46–50 [summary only].

1936
'Local authorities and industrial activity', in *Re-adjustment in Lancashire*, by members of the Economics Research Section, University of Manchester (Manchester University Press, 1936) ch. 8, pp. 103–21.
Public control of road passenger transport: a study in administration and economics (Manchester University Press, 1936) xi, 226 pages.

1937
'Problems of a local authority in an industrially distressed area (Lancashire)', *Public Administration* 15, 3 (July 1937) pp. 269–77.

1938
'The city manager', *Guild Journal* 24, 17 (Nov 1938) pp. 379–81.

1940
'The war and local finance. What will happen to the rates – an inevitable rise?', *Manchester Guardian*, 3 Jan 1940, p. 6.

1942
Secretary of Committee, *Social insurance and allied services: report by Sir William Beveridge*, Cmd 6404 (HMSO, 1942) 299 pages.

1943

'Organisation and control of the Civil Service', *Public Administration* 21, 1 (Apr 1943) pp. 43–6.

1943–66

Editor, *Public Administration*: the journal of the [Royal] Institute of Public Administration.

1946

'Britain broadens franchise', *National Municipal Review* 35 (Dec 1946) pp. 593–7.

'Research in public administration', *Public Administration* 24, 2 (summer 1946) pp. 92–101.

'Social insurance legislation: some issues raised by the National Insurance Bill', *Social Welfare* 6, 7 (July 1946) pp. 191–6.

'What coal will cost', *Spectator* 176, 6143 (22 Mar 1946) pp. 291–2.

1947

'How planning will work', *Spectator* 178, 6190 (14 Feb 1947) pp. 200–1.

'Miners and concentration', *Spectator* 178, 6194 (14 Mar 1947) pp. 262–3.

'A policy for local finance', *Local Government Finance* 51, 5 (May 1947) pp. 115–18.

1948

British public utility services (Longmans, Green, for the British Council, 1948) 32 pages.

'Central government and the social services', mimeographed notes for a speech at the Fabian Society 'Machinery of Government' Conference, Buscot Park, Jan 1948, 1 page.

'The efficiency of the central government', *Public Administration* 26, 1 (spring 1948) pp. 10–15.

The nationalised industries: a statutory analysis (Institute of Public Administration, 1948) 48 pages [revised 1951].

'Post-mortem on the Local Government Bill', *Local Government Finance* 52, 2 (Feb 1948) pp. 31–2.

'Problems of the large public concern', *Listener* 39, 989 (8 Jan 1948) pp. 44, 69–70.

Contributor, 'Sir Gwilym Gibbon' [obituary], *Public Administration* 26, 2 (summer 1948) pp. 124–5.

1948–56

Committee member, *Report[s] of the Interdepartmental Committee on Social and Economic Research*, 3 vols (HMSO: Cmd 7537, 1948; Cmd 8091, 1950; 1956).

1949

'British central government', mimeographed response to a questionnaire issued for the Lisbon Conference of the Institut International des Sciences Administratives [n.d.], 15 pages.

'Nuffield College at Oxford and the social studies', *Social Studies* 40, 8 (Dec 1949) pp. 353–4.

'Nuffield College, Oxford', *Nature* 163, 4153 (4 June 1949) pp. 862–3.

Committee member, *Report of the [Masterman] Committee on the Political Activities of Civil Servants*, Cmd 7718 (HMSO, 1949) 42 pages.

'The work of the Local Government Examinations Board', in *Establishment work in local authorities* (Institute of Public Administration conference papers and reports, 1949) pp. 123–37, followed by discussion, pp. 139–57.

1950

'Development of the Cabinet 1914–1949', in *British government since 1918*, by Sir Gilbert Campion and others (Allen & Unwin, 1950) ch. 2, pp. 31–55.

'Enterprise, public and private', in *Chambers's Encyclopaedia* (new ed., Newnes, 1950) vol. 5, pp. 354–6.

'Note on the price policy indicated by the nationalization Acts', *Oxford Economic Papers* n.s. 2, 1 (Jan 1950) pp. 69–74.

'Organisation of the nationalised industries', *Political Quarterly* 21, 2 (Apr–June 1950) pp. 122–34.

'Progress in political studies', mimeographed paper for the Social Sciences Conference, Balliol College, Oxford, Apr 1950, 7 pages.

'Robert Morant and Michael Sadler', *Public Administration* 28, 2 (summer 1950) pp. 109–16.

'War: adaptation of the machinery of government', in *Chambers's Encyclopaedia* (new ed , Newnes, 1950) vol. 14, pp. 422–7.

1951

'The British constitution', lecture delivered to the London Society of the Institute of Municipal Treasurers and Accountants, Feb 1951, 11 pages.

'Cabinet and Cabinet policy', mimeographed notes of an address to the West Midlands Branch of the Institute of Public Administration, Birmingham, Oct 1951, 6 pages.

Central and local government: financial and administrative relations (Macmillan, 1951) ix, 421 pages.

'The central machinery for economic policy', in *Lessons of the British war economy*, edited by D. N. Chester, ch. 2, pp. 5–33.

Contributor, 'Economists urge: "Tell the people the truth" ', *Picture Post* 53, 9 (1 Dec 1951) pp. 40, 41, 44, 47.

'The future of local revenues', in *Report of the Proceedings at the 69th Annual Meeting and Conference* (Incorporated Association of Rating and

Valuation Officers, 1951) pp. 84–95, followed by discussion, pp. 96–102.

Editor, *Lessons of the British war economy* (Cambridge University Press, 1951) xii, 260 pages.

'Local finance', *Lloyds Bank Review* n.s. 21 (July 1951) pp. 33–47.

The nationalised industries: an analysis of the statutory provisions (rev. 2nd ed., Allen & Unwin for the Institute of Public Administration, 1951), 93 pages.

1952

'The consumer', mimeographed address to the Advertising Association Conference, Brighton, May 1952, 13 pages.

'Differences between business and public administration', *District Bank Review* 102 (June 1952) pp. 1–13.

'The English borough council', mimeographed paper for the International Political Science Association Congress, The Hague, Sep 1952, 10 pages.

'Machinery of government and planning', in *The British economy 1945–50*, edited by G. D. N. Worswick and P. H. Ady (Oxford: Clarendon Press, 1952) ch. 15, pp. 336–64.

'Management and accountability in the nationalised industries', *Manchester Statistical Society Transactions* 1951–52, 34 pages [reprinted in *Public Administration* 30, 1 (spring 1952) pp. 27–47].

'The nationalised industries', *Three Banks Review* 16 (Dec 1952) pp. 23–46.

1953

'The Exchequer equalization grant', *Local Government Finance* 57, 4 (Apr 1953) pp. 78–81.

Chairman of Sub-Committee, *Local government statistics*, Guides to official sources (sponsored by the Interdepartmental Committee on Social and Economic Research) 3 (HMSO, 1953) v, 34 pages.

'100 years of local finance', *Manchester Guardian*, 27 Mar 1953, p. 18 [reprinted as 'Survey of a century of U.K. local government finance', *Economic Digest* 6, 5 (May 1953) pp. 227–30].

'Morant and Sadler – further evidence', *Public Administration* 31, 1 (spring 1953) pp. 49–54.

'Participation by the citizen in the bureaucratic process', paper for Session 3 of the International Political Science Association Round Table, Paris, June 1953.

'Public corporations and the classification of administrative bodies', *Political Studies* 1, 1 (Feb 1953) pp. 34–52.

'Select Committee on Nationalised Industries: second report', *Public Administration* 31, 3 (autumn 1953) pp. 269–75.

1954

'Analysis of rateable value of England and Wales, 1st April, 1952', *Local Government Finance* 58, 1 (Jan 1954) pp. 14–15.

'The Crichel Down case', *Public Administration* 32, 4 (winter 1954) pp. 389–401.

'Local government and its critics', paper given at the Annual Conference of the Association of Municipal Corporations, Mar 1954, 20 pages.

'Time to end "derating"?', *The Times*, 27 July 1954, p. 9; 28 July 1954, p. 9.

1955

'The development of the Cabinet', *Parliamentary Affairs* 9, 1 (winter 1955) pp. 43–7.

1956

'The formation of economic and financial policy [a symposium]: introduction', *International Social Science Bulletin* 8, 2 (1956) pp. 217–28.

'The future of ministerial responsibility', mimeographed paper for the 6th Annual Conference of the Political Studies Association of the United Kingdom, Oxford, Mar 1956, 6 pages.

Contributor, *New sources of local revenue: Report of a Study Group of the Royal Institute of Public Administration* (Allen & Unwin, 1956), 260 pages.

'Recent changes in British central government', *Administration* (Dublin) 4, 1 (spring 1956) pp. 13–33.

'The Select Committee on the Nationalised Industries', *Public Administration* 34, 1 (spring 1956) pp. 93–5.

'Tendencias recientes en el Gobierno central británico', *Revista de estudios políticos* 58, 90 (Nov–Dec 1956) pp. 57–84.

1957

The organization of British central government 1914–1956: a survey by a Study Group of the Royal Institute of Public Administration, edited by D. N. Chester, written by F. M. G. Willson (Allen & Unwin, 1957), 457 pages [second edition by F. M. G. Willson, 1968].

'The Treasury, 1956', *Public Administration* 35, 1 (spring 1957) pp. 15–23.

1958

'Boards and Parliament', *Public Administration* 36, 1 (spring 1958) pp. 87–92.

Contributor, *Interest groups on four continents* [results of a Round Table held by the International Political Science Association at Pittsburgh, Sep 1957], edited by H. W. Ehrmann (Pittsburgh University Press, 1958) xiv, 316 pages.

'The Local Government Bill – some general thoughts', paper for the

Conference of the Institute of Municipal Treasurers and Accountants, Eastbourne, June 1958, 22 pages.

'Local government under attack', *Municipal Affairs* 24, 278 (Oct 1958) pp. 9, 11, 57–8.

'The Select Committee and the National Coal Board', *Public Administration* 36, 3 (autumn 1958) pp. 285–7.

'Sources of local revenue', *Municipal Affairs* 24, 279 (Nov 1958) pp. 11, 13; 24, 280 (Dec 1958) pp. 11, 13, 45.

Speech of reply to HRH Prince Philip, Duke of Edinburgh, at the luncheon on 6 June 1958, in *Nuffield College annual report* 1957–58, pp. 23–7.

1959

'Nuffield College', *American Oxonian* 46, 2 (Apr 1959) pp. 49–53.

'Political science in the United Kingdom', mimeographed communication to the International Political Science Association Round Table, Opatija, Sep 1959, 15 pages.

Chairman, 'Steel' [Report of the *Spectator* Commission of Inquiry into the Steel Industry], *Spectator* 202, 6820 (13 Mar 1959) pp. 359–70.

1960

'Great Britain', in *Konferenz über den Stand der politischen Wissenschaft in Europa* [proceedings] (Universität Heidelberg, Institut für Politische Wissenschaft, July 1960, mimeographed) pp. 1–6, followed by discussion, pp. 11–25.

'The independence of Chief Constables. II – Some questions', *Public Administration* 38, 1 (spring 1960) pp. 11–15.

'Neue Entwicklungen in der britischen Kabinettsregierung', *Politische Vierteljahresschrift* 1, 1 (Oct 1960) pp. 37–46.

1961

Chairman, Board of Editors, *Administrators in action: British case studies.* vol. 1, by F. M. G. Willson, 350 pages; vol. 2, by G. Rhodes, 117 pages (Allen & Unwin for the Royal Institute of Public Administration, 1961, 1965).

1962

Questions in Parliament, written with N. Bowring (Oxford: Clarendon Press, 1962) [8], 335 pages.

'Research as an aid in public administration', *Public Administration* 40, 1 (spring 1962) pp. 53–64.

'The Treasury, 1962', *Public Administration* 40, 4 (winter 1962) pp. 419–26.

'Who governs Britain?', *Parliamentary Affairs* 15, 4 (autumn 1962) pp. 519–27.

1963

'British government observed', *Public Administration* 41, 4 (autumn 1963) pp. 375–84.

Committee member, *Democracy, decentralisation and development*, by H. Maddick, sponsored by the International Political Science Association (Asia Publishing House, 1963) xii, 305 pages.

'Lord Beveridge, 1879–1963' [obituary], *Journal of the Royal Statistical Society* (series A) 126, 4 (1963) pp. 618–20.

Contributor, 'Managerial and industrial education symposium', *The Manager*, Mar 1963, pp. 21–30, 35.

The Parliamentary control of nationalised industries in Great Britain (Ankara: Public Administration Institute for Turkey and the Middle East, 1963), 12 pages.

'The Plowden Report: 1. Nature and significance', *Public Administration* 41, 1 (spring 1963) pp. 3–15.

1964

'An administrator in politics', *Political Studies* 12, 1 (Feb 1964) pp. 93–6.

'The British Treasury and economic planning', *Indian Journal of Public Administration* 10, 2 (Apr–June 1964) pp. 159–71.

'Double-banking and deputy ministers', *New Society* 89 (11 June 1964) pp. 10–11.

'The finances of Oxford, 1950–1963', *Local Government Finance* 68, 6 (June 1964) pp. 203–7.

'The finances of the City of Oxford, 1946–63', mimeographed, Oxford, Feb 1964, 14 pages.

'IPSA', *Political Studies* 12, 1 (Feb 1964) pp. 97–8.

Contributor, 'The organisation of graduate studies and the training of graduates' [a Symposium], *Universities Quarterly* 18, 3 (June 1964) pp. 241–60.

Committee member, *Report of the Committee on Postgraduate Studies*, reprinted, *Oxford University Gazette* 94, 3185, Supplement* 2 (Feb 1964) pp. 12–34.

'Rola premiera w brytyjskim systemie politycznym', *Państwo i Prawo* 19, 12 (Dec 1964) pp. 860–7.

Committee member, *University appointments boards: a report by the Rt. Hon. the Lord Heyworth* (HMSO, 1964) xii, 127 pages.

1965

'Graduate studies in Oxford', in *Evidence* of the University of Oxford [Franks] Commission of Inquiry (Oxford University Press, 1964–5) Part XIV, pp. 26–34.

'Management in local government: a paper submitted to the Maud and Mallaby Committees', *Local Government Finance* 69, 9 (Sep 1965) pp. 347–54.

'Memorandum to the Robbins Committee' in *Evidence* of the University of Oxford: [Franks] Commission of Inquiry, Part VII, pp. 183–8. [An abbreviated version of the *Memorandum* originally submitted to the Committee on Higher Education, 1961–3, and 'available for public inspection in . . . the Public Record Office'.]

'Recruitment to the Civil Service', Memorandum to Sub-Committee E of the Estimates Committee, HCP 308, Session 1964–65 (HMSO, 1965) pp. 230–4, followed by Examination of the Witness, pp. 234–40.

Foreword, *Tariff-making and industrial reconstruction: an account of the work of the Import Duties Advisory Committee 1932–39*, by Sir Herbert Hutchinson (Harrap, 1965) pp. 5–6.

1966

'The British Parliament 1939–1966', *Parliamentary Affairs* 19, 4 (autumn 1966) pp. 417–45.

Member of Advisory Committee, *Central departments and local authorities*, by J. A. G. Griffith (Allen & Unwin for the Royal Institute of Public Administration, 1966), 574 pages.

'The Editor looks back', *Public Administration* 44, 4 (winter 1966) pp. 387–9.

'Local finance', *Political Quarterly* 37, 2 (Apr–June 1966) pp. 180–91.

Contributor, *Management education: report of a conference at Ditchley Park, Nov 1966* (Enstone: The Ditchley Foundation, n.d.) 30 pages.

'Their cup runneth over', *Spectator* 217, 7206 (5 Aug 1966) p. 170.

'World cup countdown', *Spectator* 217, 7202 (8 July 1966) p. 38.

1967

'Oxford', in *Voting in cities: the 1964 borough elections*, edited by L. J. Sharpe (Macmillan, 1967) pp. 165–90.

1968

'Committees in the House of Commons', in *Sprache und Politik: Festgabe für Dolf Sternberger . . .*, edited by C. J. Friedrich and B. Reifenberg (Heidelberg: Lambert Schneider, 1968) pp. 445–58.

'Local democracy and the internal organization of local authorities', *Public Administration* 46, 3 (autumn 1968) pp. 287–98.

'The nationalised industries – external organisation', memorandum to Sub-Committee A of the Select Committee on Nationalised Industries, HCP 371–II, Session 1967–68: *Ministerial control of the nationalised industries* (HMSO, 1968) pp. 522–6, followed by Examination of the Witness, pp. 544–65.

Chairman, *Report of the Committee on Football* (HMSO, 1968) vii, 135 pages.

'The report of the Fulton Committee on the Civil Service', *Public Administration* (Sydney) 27, 4 (Dec 1968) pp. 295–310.

Committee member, *Research in political science* [an SSRC review of current research, introduced by W. J. M. Mackenzie] (Heinemann, 1968) viii, 64 pages.

1970

'Questions in Parliament', in *The Commons in transition*, by Members of the Study of Parliament Group, edited by A. H. Hanson and B. Crick (Fontana/Collins, 1970) ch. 5, pp. 93–113.

Consultant, *Review Body on Local Government in Northern Ireland 1970* [*Macrory*] *report*, Cmd 546 (Belfast: HMSO, 1970) vii, 68 pages.

1971

'Nuffield College', *Oxford* 24, 1 (May 1971) pp. 77–87.

1972

'Memorandum', in *Report from the Select Committee on Parliamentary Questions* . . ., HCP 393, Session 1971–72 (HMSO, 1972) pp. 87–91, followed by Examination of the Witness, pp. 91–8.

'Restoring power to the people', *The Times*, 16 February 1972, p. 14.

1975

'Memorandum of evidence to the [Layfield] Committee of Inquiry into Local Government Finance', mimeographed, Apr 1975, 12 pages. [The Committee's Report states that: 'All the main evidence is available for inspection at the Public Record Office.']

The nationalisation of British industry 1945–51 (HMSO, 1975) xv, 1075 pages.

'Political studies in Britain: recollections and comments', *Political Studies* 23, 2–3 (June–Sep 1975) [1950–1975 Anniversary Issue, edited by F. F. Ridley] pp. 151–64. [This issue was reprinted as *Studies in politics* (Oxford University Press, 1975).]

'Review article: *English local government reformed* by Lord Redcliffe-Maud and Bruce Wood, Oxford University Press, 1974', *Local Government Studies* n.s. 1, 1 (Jan 1975) pp. 81–5.

1976

'The Layfield Report: constitutional implications', *Local Government Studies* n.s. 2, 4 (Oct 1976) pp. 65–9.

1977

'Questions in the House', in *The Commons in the Seventies*, edited by S. A. Walkland and M. Ryle for the Study of Parliament Group (Martin Robertson and Fontana/Collins, 1977) ch. 8, pp. 149–74.

Index